FCE

Gold

PLUS

Exam Maximiser
with key

Sally Burgess

with Jacky Newbrook and Judith Wilson

PEARSON
Longman

Contents

Introduction to the *FCE Gold Plus exam maximiser*

The *FCE Gold Plus exam maximiser* is specially designed to maximise your chances of success in the First Certificate in English examination.

The *exam maximiser* will help you prepare for the First Certificate exam by offering you:

- **further practice and revision** of all the important vocabulary, grammar and skills (reading, writing, listening and speaking) that you study in the *FCE Gold Plus coursebook*.

- **more information** about the kinds of questions you will have to answer in the First Certificate exam.

- **guidance** with the strategies and techniques you should use to tackle exam tasks.

- **exam-style exercises** so that you can practise using the techniques

- **a complete sample exam** which you can use for practice just before you sit for the exam. This means that you will know exactly what to expect in each paper and that there are no unpleasant surprises.

How can I use the *FCE Gold Plus exam maximiser*?

The *exam maximiser* is very flexible and can be used by students in a variety of situations and in a variety of ways. Here are some typical situations:

1
> You are doing a First Certificate course with other students probably over an academic year. You are all planning to take the exam at the same time.

You are using the *FCE Gold Plus coursebook* in class. Sometimes you will also do the related exercises or even a whole unit from the *exam maximiser* in class, though your teacher will ask you to do exercises from it at home as well. You will use the entire *exam maximiser* or you will use it selectively, depending on your needs and the time available.

2
> You have already done a First Certificate course and you are now doing an intensive course to prepare for the exam.

Since you have already worked through the *FCE Gold Plus coursebook* or perhaps another First Certificate coursebook, you will use the *exam maximiser* in class. This, together with the *First Certificate Practice Tests Plus* New Edition (2008) will give you a concentrated and highly focused short exam course.

3
> You have a very short period in which to take the First Certificate exam.

Your level of English is already nearing First Certificate exam standard, though you have not been following a First Certificate coursebook. You now need exam skills. You will use the *exam maximiser* independently, without a coursebook, because you need practice in the exam tasks and how to approach them.

4

> You are re-taking the First Certificate exam as unfortunately you were not successful in your first attempt.

You may be having to re-take the exam because you were not sufficiently familiar with the exam requirements. You will not need to follow a coursebook, but you will use the **exam maximiser** to develop your exam techniques and build up your confidence.

5

> You are preparing for the exam on your own.

Maybe you are not attending a First Certificate class, but wish to take the exam and prepare for it independently. You will get the practice and preparation by using the **exam maximiser** by itself. You can give yourself additional practice by using the **First Certificate Practice Tests Plus** New Edition (2008) just before taking the exam.

What is in each unit?

Each unit in the **exam maximiser** contains **Vocabulary** sections. These practise the words and expressions which you studied in the **FCE Gold Plus coursebook** and introduce you to some new words and expressions as well. There are plenty of exercises to do, including exam-style tasks from Paper 3 (Use of English) and crosswords and wordsearch grids for a bit of fun.

You will find several **Grammar** sections in each unit. By doing the exercises in these sections, you can practise and revise the grammar points you have studied in the **FCE Gold Plus coursebook**. Once again, there are always exam-style tasks from Paper 3 (Use of English) as well as opportunities to practise the grammar points through Paper 5 (Speaking) tasks. In these tasks, you write your answers in the **exam maximiser** and then check them by listening to the

recordings of good First Certificate candidates performing the speaking tasks.

Every unit has a **Listening** section. These sections help you train for each of the four parts in Paper 4 (Listening). First, you read some information **about the exam** and then you are given some advice on the **strategy** you should use in that particular part. You do an exercise to help you practise the strategy and then an exam-style listening task. The tasks get more difficult as you move through the units in the **exam maximiser**, so that by the end of the book they are at the same level as the exam.

There is also a **Reading** section in each unit. Like the Listening sections, these provide you with information **about the exam** and **strategies** to use in each of the four parts of Paper 1 (Reading). You do some exercises to help you with the strategy and then you do an exam-style task. There is a vocabulary activity at the end of most reading sections as well, so that you can practise dealing with unfamiliar words and phrases. Like the listening sections, the reading sections are easier at the beginning of the book but at the level of the exam at the end.

At the end of each unit you will find a **Writing** section. Once again, you are given information **about the exam** and the kinds of writing tasks you have to do in Parts 1 and 2 of Paper 2 (Writing). You are also given a **strategy** to follow and then have an opportunity to put it into practice by doing some exercises, often using sample answers. You write your answers to these exercises in the **exam maximiser**. Finally, you look at an exam task and write your own answer to this task.

Once you have worked through all the units, you will be ready to try the **Practice exam** at the back of the book.

Then you'll be really well prepared for the First Certificate Exam.

Good luck!

Exam overview

There are five papers in the First Certificate in English exam. The papers are:

Paper 1 Reading (1 hour)
Paper 2 Writing (1 hour 20 minutes)
Paper 3 Use of English (45 minutes)
Paper 4 Listening (approximately 40 minutes)
Paper 5 Speaking (14 minutes)

Each paper receives an equal weighting of one fifth of the marks. Your overall grade is based on the total score for all five papers. There are three passing grades, A, B and C. To pass with a grade C, you need about 60% of the total marks.

For Papers 1, 3 and 4, you have to write your answers on a separate answer sheet.

Paper	Formats	Task focus
Reading three texts, 30 reading comprehension questions	**Part 1:** answering multiple-choice questions **Part 2:** choosing which sentences fit into gaps in a text **Part 3:** deciding which of 4–6 short texts contains given information or ideas	**Part 1:** reading for detailed understanding of the text **Part 2:** reading to understand text structure **Part 3:** reading for specific information
Writing **Part 1**: one compulsory task **Part 2**: one task from a choice of four	**Part 1:** using given information to write a letter or email of 120–150 words **Part 2:** producing one piece of writing of 120–180 words, from a choice of four: informal letter or email, review story, report, article or essay. Question 4 is on the set book.	**Part 1:** selecting from and comparing given information to produce a transactional letter or email **Part 2:** writing for a specific reader, using appropriate layout and register
Use of English four texts, 42 questions	**Part 1:** multiple-choice cloze: choosing which word from a choice of four fits in each of 12 gaps in the text **Part 2:** open cloze: writing the missing word in each of 12 gaps in a text **Part 3:** word formation: changing the form of the word given so that it fits into the gaps in a text **Part 4:** key word transformations: completing a new sentence with two to five words so that it means the same as the sentence given	**Part 1:** vocabulary **Part 2:** grammar and vocabulary **Part 3:** grammatical accuracy and vocabulary **Part 4:** vocabulary and grammar
Listening four parts, 30 questions	**Part 1:** eight short texts each with one multiple-choice question **Part 2:** long text with ten sentence completion questions **Part 3:** five short texts to match to one of six prompts **Part 4:** long text with seven multiple-choice questions	**Part 1:** understanding gist meaning **Part 2:** understanding specific information **Part 3:** understanding gist meaning **Part 4:** understanding attitude and opinion as well as both specific information and gist meaning
Speaking four parts	**Part 1:** interview: the examiner asks each student questions on basic personal information **Part 2:** comparing and contrasting two pictures: each student has to speak for one minute **Part 3:** interactive task: students discuss a task together using a visual prompt **Part 4:** discussion: the examiner asks questions related to the theme of Part 3	**Part 1:** giving personal information. **Part 2:** giving information and expressing opinions. **Part 3:** exchanging ideas and opinions and reacting to them. **Part 4:** expressing and justifying opinions and ideas.

UNIT 1 What's on?

Vocabulary 1: recording vocabulary ▶ CB page 8

1 Complete the following welcome message with words from the box. Change the form where necessary. You do not need to use all the words.

star	characters	script	costumes	released
lighting	lines	role	performance	
preview	acting	star	set	

★★ *COMING SOON!* ★★

First Certificate Gold Plus: The Movie!

You may be surprised to find out that preparing for First Certificate is a little bit like (0) *starring* in a movie! I'll explain how.

To prepare for an important (1) .... an actor has to become familiar with the complete (2) .... and you, as a First Certificate student, have to become familiar with the grammar, vocabulary and skills you need for the exam. An actor has to learn all his or her (3) .... perfectly and know when to say them. In the same way, you have to make sure that you have learnt the language you need to use in the exam and that you know when to use it. The film director tells the actors about the (4) .... they are playing in the film, and explains what they need to practise more or change in their (5) .... The *First Certificate Gold Plus Exam Maximiser* is a bit like the director because it tells you about the exam and what you have to do in each paper. It gives you lots of strategies so that you know exactly how to use what you know to get good marks. It also gives you lots of practice with the grammar and vocabulary you need so that when you get to the exam itself you will do well. There is one more similarity. The actors and directors usually see a (6) .... of the movie before it is (7) .... to the general public. At the end of the *First Certificate Gold Plus Exam Maximiser* there is a complete practice exam so that you can use all that you have learnt before you do the exam itself.

So now you're the (8) .... of the film! Welcome to the *First Certificate Gold Plus Exam Maximiser!*

2 Look at the mind map from *First Certificate Gold Plus* Coursebook and decide where to put the following words.

screenwriter	dialogue	aerial view	cut	cast
aisle	character	make-up	premiere	

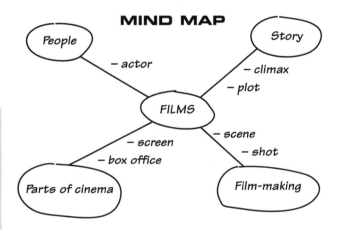

3 Read these sentences from cinema-goers about a new film. Use the words from Exercise 2 to complete the sentences. There is one word you do not need to use.

1 'I like to sit in a middle row when I go to the cinema – preferably next to the .... But it was so crowded, we had to sit right at the front.'

2 'Did you know the film was originally much longer? The director was told to .... about six scenes at the last minute.'

3 'It was based on a novel wasn't it?'
'Yes, a .... adapted it for the film.'

4 'It got its world .... at the Cannes Film Festival, you know. The critics loved it.'

5 'The film begins with an .... of Paris. It's fantastic – you can see the whole city.'

6 'I thought some of the .... was a bit artificial. People don't talk like that in real life, do they?'

7 'Not all the members of the .... were professional actors. Some of them had never acted before.'

8 'The .... was really good – the heroine really looked like an old woman by the end of the film, even though she's only in her 30s.'

4 Use of English: multiple-choice cloze (Part 1)

About the exam: In Paper 3, Part 1, you read a text with gaps and choose the best word from four options to fit each gap. The correct word may be:
• the only one that makes sense in the sentence.
• a word that goes with the word before or after the gap.
• part of a fixed phrase.
• part of a phrasal verb.

Strategy
1 Read the title and the whole of the text for general understanding.
2 Always look at the words before and after the gap. This will help you choose the correct alternative.

Read the text below about a popular film and decide which answer (A, B or C) best fits each gap. There is an example at the beginning (0).

Note: In this task there are only three options to choose from.

THE CENTURY'S BEST FILM

Many film **(0)** ...B..... think that *The Matrix* is one of the best films of the 21st century so far. In my opinion, the main reason for this is that the **(1)** .... is both original and extremely mysterious. Of course the special **(2)** .... are amazing as well, especially all the fight **(3)** .... when the actors do incredible *kung fu* **(4)** ....

For me, the most memorable **(5)** .... in the film is the one where Keanu Reeves, who **(6)** .... the part of Neo, and Morpheus meet for the first time. The tension reaches a **(7)** .... when we learn the truth about the Matrix.

I first saw this film in the front **(8)** .... of my local cinema but like many people I have watched it many times since then on DVD, on the small **(9)** .... of my lap-top computer. Although the **(10)** .... didn't quite live up to my expectations, I still think the first film is great.

---

0 **A** surveyors   **B** critics   **C** judges
B *is the correct answer because* critics *is the only word that goes with* film.

1 **A** plot   **B** scene   **C** role

CLUE: Which word makes sense in the sentence?

2	**A** efforts	**B** effects	**C** actions
3	**A** areas	**B** places	**C** sequences
4	**A** acts	**B** games	**C** stunts
5	**A** scene	**B** situation	**C** location
6	**A** does	**B** plays	**C** makes
7	**A** summit	**B** top	**C** climax
8	**A** line	**B** queue	**C** row
9	**A** screen	**B** board	**C** top
10	**A** sequels	**B** remakes	**C** developments

Grammar 1: revision of simple tenses
▶ *CB page 8*

1 Underline the correct form of the verb in the following questions. Then match the questions to the answers below.

1 The actor, Cate Blanchett, became famous about five years ago. Where *has she started / did she start* acting?
2 How long *did Antonio Banderas know / has Antonio Banderas known* his wife, American actress Melanie Griffith?
3 The British actress, Kate Winslett, is best-known for her role in *Titanic*. Which town *did she grow up / has she grown up* in?
4 How many different film versions of the *Titanic* story *have there been / were there* up to now?
5 In which 2002 film *does David Beckham appear / has David Beckham appeared*?
6 How often *has the average British person been / does the average British person go* to the cinema in the last six months?
7 Where *is the worst place / has been the worst place* to sit in a cinema?
8 How long is it since *you last / you have last* bought a DVD?

☐ a) *Bend it like Beckham.*
☐ b) Somewhere near the middle.
☐ c) Three called *Titanic* and another called *A Night to Remember.*
☐ d) In Australia.
☐ e) Since 1994 when they acted together in *Too Much.*
☐ f) In Reading, a town near London.
☐ g) About once every three weeks.
☐ h) I bought ten at Gatwick airport last week.

2 Use of English: key word transformations (Part 4)

About the exam: In Paper 3, Part 4, you read eight unconnected sentences and, for each sentence, complete a new one so that it has a similar meaning, using a 'key' word given in bold. This part tests a range of grammatical structures and vocabulary.

Strategy
1 Try to work out what the sentence is testing.
2 DON'T change the key word. You must use the same form of verbs and nouns.
3 Write two to five words. (Contractions, e.g. *don't,* count as two words.)

CLUE: What grammatical structure are all the following sentences testing?

Complete the second sentence so that it has a similar meaning to the first sentence, using the word given and no more than four other words. Do not change the word given.

0 I met Peter ten years ago.
known
I *have known Peter for*........ ten years.

1 I haven't seen a film since July.
last
I .... in July.

2 It's been months since I have seen a good movie on TV.
time
The last .... a good movie on TV was months ago.

3 We bought a DVD player when Nicholas got his new job.
until
We didn't .... Nicholas got his new job.

4 This is the first time I have been to the cinema on my own.
never
I .... the cinema on my own before.

5 I've worn my hair like this for as long as I can remember.
started
I can't remember .... wearing my hair like this.

6 I haven't been to Rome before.
first
This is .... been to Rome.

3 Use of English: open cloze (Part 2)

About the exam: In Paper 3, Part 2, you read a text with 12 gaps. You have to complete each gap with one word. The words can be grammar words such as prepositions (*in, on,* etc.), pronouns (*which, her,* etc.), articles (*a, an, the*) and auxiliary verbs (*has, been,* etc.).

Strategy
1 Read the title and the whole text to make sure you understand what it's about.
2 Look at the words on either side of each gap.
3 Try to decide what part of speech is missing.

Read the text below and think of the word which best fits each gap. Use only one word in each gap. There is an example at the beginning (0).

MOVIE MONSTERS

Two films that came out **(0)** *in*...... in 1931, *Dracula* and *Frankenstein*, have changed cinema history. There have **(1)**.......... hundreds of remakes of these stories.

Frankenstein's monster and Count Dracula **(2)**.......... both originally characters in novels. It is a strange coincidence that **(3)**.......... first written versions of these stories were probably created in the same place and **(4)**.......... the same time. Nearly 200 years **(5)**.........., in the summer of 1816, the English writer, Mary Shelley, spent a holiday in Italy **(6)**.......... a group of friends including a man called Doctor Pollidori. One night, **(7)**.......... all played a party game in which everyone **(8)**.......... to think of a horror story. The story Mary told was about Frankenstein and Pollidori's was called *Vampyre*.

(9).......... the last 200 years, these stories have been told over and over again and the characters themselves **(10)**.......... changed a lot. Two recent film versions **(11)**........... the stories were *Interview with a Vampire*, starring Tom Cruise, and *Mary Shelley's Frankenstein*, starring Kenneth Branagh. I wonder **(12)**.......... Mary Shelley and Doctor Pollidori would think of these movies if they could come back and see them.

Reading: multiple matching (Part 3)

About the exam: In Paper 1, Part 3, you match questions or statements to several short texts.

Strategy
1 Read the text through quickly to get an idea of what it's about.
2 <u>Underline</u> key words and phrases in the questions.
3 Find expressions in the text that have a similar meaning to the key words.

1 You are going to read four descriptions of the most successful programmes in the history of television. Read the texts very quickly and decide if these statements are true (T) or false (F).

a) Not all of the programmes are American. ☐
b) All these programmes are still on television. ☐

2

1 Now look at the questions. The key words and expressions have been <u>underlined</u> for you.

2 For each of the questions, choose from the programmes A–D.

Which television series:

gained <u>a faithful group of admirers</u> almost as soon as it started? **1** ☐

is about <u>someone's brave acts</u>? **2** ☐

was suddenly <u>taken off the air</u>? **3** ☐

is set <u>outside a big city</u>? **4** ☐

has continued for <u>longer than</u> originally <u>planned</u>? **5** ☐

was interrupted because of a <u>quarrel about wages and conditions</u>? **6** ☐

continued for <u>longer than most of its imitators</u>? **7** ☐

has <u>not made the same mistakes</u> as other similar programmes? **8** ☐

is called <u>something different</u> by people who are fond of it? **9** ☐

<u>can adapt easily</u> if an actor wants to leave? **10** ☐

<u>didn't</u> begin as a <u>complete programme</u>? **11** ☐

demands <u>great skill from actors</u>? **12** ☐

is very popular both <u>at home and abroad</u>? **13** ☐

originally had <u>shorter episodes</u>? **14** ☐

IN THE LONG RUN

A Gunsmoke
Gunsmoke, the longest running dramatic series in the history of television, was shown for the first time in September 1955 and for the last time in September 1975. Two of the stars, James Arness and Milburn Stone, were in the series for all twenty seasons. The series started out as a half-hour show and expanded to an hour in its seventh year on TV. Before *Gunsmoke*, westerns were generally about fantasy characters, but *Gunsmoke* was one of the earliest 'adult westerns' with more realistic content. It centred around the [1]*exploits* of Marshal Matt Dillon in the frontier town of Dodge City, Kansas, in 1873. *Gunsmoke* started a long-term trend for TV westerns. At one point, there were as many as thirty Westerns on TV at the same time. *Gunsmoke* [2]*outlasted* almost all of them. When the television network decided not to show it any more, there was only one other western still on the air.

B Neighbours
Neighbours is Australia's longest running soap opera and one of its most successful television exports. After more than 2000 episodes, it still attracts worldwide audiences of over 50 million viewers, many of them British. It was the first programme in Britain to be shown twice daily, five days a week by the BBC. The action revolves around the lives of the people living and working in Ramsay Street, Erinsborough, a [3]*fictitious* suburb of Melbourne. It was initially based around three families, but there was always plenty of [4]*scope* for other characters to come and go, often as far away as the UK, where the same characters would sometimes even appear in one of the British soaps. The show was in fact [5]*axed* by Channel Seven in late 1985, but was then bought by a rival network who added more glamorous and exciting characters, one of whom was played by pop star Kylie Minogue. *Neighbours* remains one of the most popular domestic soap operas of all time.

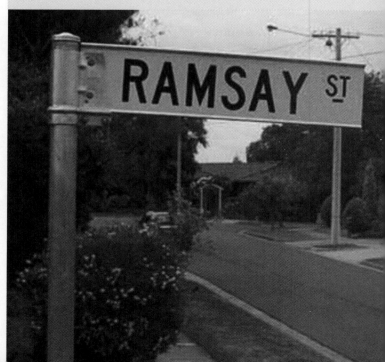

C The Simpsons

10-year-old Bart, his dad Homer and the rest of the Simpson family are about to go into TV history as stars of the longest running sitcom ever. The animated characters were introduced in a series of short sequences on *The Tracey Ullman Show* in 1987. *The Simpsons* premiered as a series on December 17th 1989. While following the lives of a mythical family, *The Simpsons* has always included lots of humour about the real world and avoids the **6**pitfalls of many comedies that seem trapped in the time period when they started. Recently there was even an episode in which the family took part in a reality show. As cartoon characters, Homer, Marge, Bart and Lisa never grow old and, unlike live actors, can't demand more money. However, there was a **7**dispute about contracts with the people who provide the characters' voices a few years ago. This held up production for a couple of weeks.

D Coronation Street

Coronation Street, the longest-running and most successful British soap opera, was first broadcast on Friday 9 December 1960. *The Street*, as it is **8**affectionately known, has been at the top of the UK ratings for over thirty years. Set in the homes, pubs and shops of a fictional town in the North of England, the series began with a limited number of thirteen episodes but this was extended as its cast of strong characters, its northern roots and sense of community immediately created **9**a loyal following. These factors, combined with well written and often amusing scripts, have ensured its continuing success. Early episodes were recorded live without **10**editing and required a very high standard of performance from actors, something that has been maintained throughout the series' long history.

3 Match the numbered words or phrases in the texts with their meanings below.

a) put an end to suddenly and
   without warning ....
b) a group of admirers ....
c) mistakes that can easily be made ....
d) something brave or interesting
   that someone has done ....
e) fondly ....
f) preparing for broadcast by
   cutting out mistakes ....
g) continued for longer than ....
h) an argument or quarrel between
   one group or organization and another ....
i) something invented or made up ....
j) chance for action or thought ....

Grammar 2: present perfect simple and continuous

1 Put the verbs in brackets into the present perfect simple or continuous tense.

FILM EXTRAS

We (0) .._have all seen_... (*all/see*) movies in which the set is crowded with hundreds of people, but
(1) .... (*ever/wonder*) who these people are and how they got the parts? In fact, many hopeful Hollywood actors (2) .... (*be able*) to make a living from working as 'extras' while they wait for their movie careers to take off.

Eleanor Walton is just one example. She
(3) .... (*live*) and working in Hollywood for a year, but so far she (4) .... (*not manage*) to get any major speaking roles. She
(5) .... (*recently/register*) with an agent, and for the last couple of weeks she
(6) .... (*appear*) as an extra in a new film due to be released later in the year. Her agent
(7) .... (*promise*) to try and find her more work.

One problem for people like Eleanor is that film directors (8) .... (*begin*) to use 'virtual extras' more and more often when they need to shoot crowd scenes. 'Virtual extras' are computer-generated images of people, which can be copied many times and made to move naturally. The increased use of virtual extras instead of real people (9) ....
(*make*) film production much cheaper, but perhaps it
(10) .... (*also/spoil*) Eleanor's dreams of becoming a star.

2 Speaking: giving personal information (Part 1).

About the exam: In Paper 5, Part 1, the examiner encourages you to give information about yourself. Some of your marks in Paper 5 depend on grammatical accuracy.

Strategy

1 Make sure you know how to give information about where you are from, your family, free time activities etc.
2 Make sure you can use tenses accurately.

Read the following extract from a Part 1 interview. Find and correct six more mistakes with verb tenses.

Examiner: Do you live near here?

Student: Yes, I ~~am~~ **have been** living here since I was six years old.

Examiner: Where did you live before that?

Student: My parents are from the north and they have lived there when they first got married.

Examiner: Is this a nice place to live?

Student: Yes, I think so. There are a lot of things for young people to do like skiing and other kinds of winter sports.

Examiner: Is yours a large or a small family?

Student: Quite large actually. I am having two brothers and a sister.

Examiner: Are they older or younger than you?

Student: They are all older.

Examiner: What do they do?

Student: They are all studying at university for several years now. The eldest, Carlo, is studying Law and both Alessandro and Rafaella are studying engineering.

Examiner: Tell me what subjects you enjoy most at school.

Student: I've always been liking all my school subjects but my favourite is art. I want to be a graphic designer.

Examiner: What do you do during a typical weekend?

Student: On Friday night, I am going out with friends. On Saturdays I am normally playing football with a local team but lately I have been having some trouble with a knee injury so I haven't played so much.

Vocabulary 2: word formation ▶ *CB page 13*

1 Complete this table. The words are all from Vocabulary 2, Exercise 2 on page 13 of the Coursebook.

Noun	Noun (person)	Verb	Adjective	Adverb
1	–	enjoy	2	–
3	–	disappoint	disappointing	4 ....
5	–	prepare	(well-) prepared	–
6	–	explain	explainable	–
survival	7	8	–	–
9	donor	donate	–	–
finance	financier	finance	10	11 ....

2 Complete these sentences with words from the table. You have been given the first letter of each word to help you. Be careful! You need to make one word plural.

1 You could see the audience's e.......... on their faces as they watched the show.
2 The actor Jeff Bridges played the part of a s.......... of a plane crash.
3 She is one of the few stars who makes regular d.......... to charity.
4 As part of the p..........for her latest role she had to gain almost five kilos in weight.
5 I found his last film a bit d.........., actually – I expected it to be better.
6 The ending of the film was a bit confusing and my friend had to e.......... it to me afterwards.
7 The show was a f.......... disaster even though the critics loved it.

3 **Use of English:** word formation (Part 3)

About the exam: In Paper 3, Part 3, you read a text with ten gaps. You have to fill each gap by changing the form of a word given in CAPITALS so that it fits in the sentence.

Strategy
1 Read the title and the whole of the text to make sure you understand what it is about.
2 Before you fill in the gaps, decide what part of speech the missing word is.

Read the text on the next page. Use the word given in capitals at the end of each line to form a word that fits in the gap in the same line. There is an example at the beginning (0).

AN ACTOR'S LIFE IS NOT A HAPPY ONE

Many people who think they have a **(0)** ..*professional*.. future in
films go to Hollywood only to find **(1)** .... instead of success.
They often have to give up the more **(2)** .... aspects of their
chosen career to play parts in **(3)** .... because these provide
(4) .... security – but they are not satisfying. For many actors,
even basic **(5)** .... can be difficult. Some do not earn enough to
pay their rent or **(6)** .... bills, and the time and money they
invest in the **(7)** .... of a portfolio for interviews is often wasted.
Of course there is a possible **(8)** .... why only 1% of actors
are really **(9)** .... There are just too many people who believe
that their next **(10)** .... will be the one that makes them a star!

0	**PROFESSION**
1	**DISAPPOINT**
2	**ENJOY**
3	**ADVERTISE**
4	**FINANCE**
5	**SURVIVE**
6	**ELECTRIC**
7	**PREPARE**
8	**EXPLAIN**
9	**SUCCEED**
10	**PERFORM**

Listening: sentence completion (Part 2)

About the exam: In Paper 4, Part 2, you hear one or
two people speaking. You complete ten sentences.

Strategy
1 Always read the questions carefully before you
   listen.
2 Decide what kind of information you need to
   listen for, e.g. a number, a date or a place.

1   You are going to hear a radio interview about a
survey of the kind of entertainment students prefer.
First look at the sentences and decide which two of
the following questions students were <u>not</u> asked:

1 How often do you go out each week? ☐
2 How much money do you spend on
   entertainment? ☐
3 What do you think of the entertainment
   facilities on campus? ☐
4 What do you like doing most/least in
   your spare time? ☐

2   Now listen and complete the sentences.
Then listen a second time to check and
complete your answers.

1 The students were interviewed .... on
   Thursday, 25th of March.
2 The interviewers managed to find ....
   who were willing to take part in the survey.
3 The most popular activity was ....
4 Students also spend at least fifteen hours a
   week ....
5 Going to the cinema, ... and shopping
   were also popular kinds of entertainment.
6 The least popular activity was ....
7 For a lot of students, money can be ....
8 Students spend about £20 to £35 a week
   ....
9 Students don't go to the theatre in town
   because ....
10 Most students spend at least .... each
   week in the games room.

Writing: informal letters and emails (Part 1) ▶ CB page 16

About the exam: In Paper 2, Part 1, you have to write a letter or email in which you include information that you are given. The letter or email may be semi-formal or informal.

Strategy
Read the task carefully, paying attention to:
1 who you are writing to (another student, a potential employer etc.)
2 what your relationship is to that person. (Do you know their name? Have you met them or not?)
This will help you decide whether you should write a semi-formal or an informal letter or email.

1 Look at these extracts from Part 1 writing tasks and decide what style you should write in:
a) semi-formal   b) informal

The relevant parts of the tasks have been underlined.
1 Your friend has sent you an email …   ....
2 The principal of the college where you are studying has asked you to write …   ....
3 A student at a college in another country has written asking …   ....
4 You have decided to apply for the job advertised below …   ....
5 You have agreed to write to the mayor of your town complaining about …   ....
6 You have had a letter from a boy you met …   ....

2 Now look at these phrases and sentences from letters and email messages. Decide if they are:
a) formal   b) informal

1 To whom it may concern, ...
2 Hi Gloria, ...
3 Dear Dr Barnes, ...
4 Dear Nicolas, ...
5 I am writing to express my concern about the closure of the Westgarth Cinema.   ....
6 Thank you for letting me know about the grants for young filmmakers.   ....
7 I got your message about next Friday. Let's meet outside the entrance at 6 p.m.   ....
8 It was a lovely surprise to hear from you after all this time.   ....
9 I am really glad that you and your family are planning to come to my country.   ....
10 I am sure some other solution can be found and I look forward to receiving your response.   ....
11 Love, Ana   ....
12 With kind regards, Ana González   ....
13 Yours faithfully, Ana González   ....
14 Best wishes, Ana   ....

3 Each of the phrases and sentences in Exercise 2 matches one of the following tasks. Match the sentences to the tasks.

A

Your friend has sent you an email asking you about arrangements to attend a music festival next week. Reply to her email.

Sentences: ..*2*.., ..*7*.., ...

B

The mother of one of your school friends has sent you some information about financial support for young filmmakers. Reply to her letter thanking her and asking if she will act as a referee.

Sentences: ...., ..., ...

C

A boy you met last summer on an English course has written to say that he will be visiting your country on holiday next month. He has asked for advice on what places he and his family should visit. Reply to his letter.

Sentences: ...., ..., ..., ...

D

You have seen the following announcement in the paper: 'Closure of Westgarth Cinema: The cinema is to be closed to make way for the new shopping mall. The Board of Directors'. Write a letter of complaint.

Sentences: ...., ..., ..., ...

4 Choose one of the letters or emails in Exercise 3. Finish it, using the phrases and sentences from Exercise 2 and your own words and ideas.

UNIT 2 Worth the risk?

Listening: multiple matching (Part 3)

About the exam: In Paper 4, Part 3, you hear five short extracts. You listen to people speaking about the same theme. You match the extracts to statements or questions. There is an extra statement or question that does not go with any of the extracts.

Strategy

1 Read the instructions and the alternatives carefully.
2 Underline the key words in the statements before you listen. Then listen out for these key words when you hear the extracts the first time.
3 When you hear the extracts the second time, decide on the correct alternative.

> **TIP!** If you change your mind the second time you listen and match an extract with another statement, don't forget to change the other answer as well.

1 You will hear five people talking about rescues. Look at the questions (A–F) below and try to decide in which extracts the person was the rescuer and in which extracts the person was rescued by someone else. Mark the questions RR (rescuer) or RD (rescued). Underline the words that tell you (the key words).

Which speaker (1–5):

A nearly drowned? ......
B had given up hope? ......
C had the right equipment? ......
D called someone for help? ......
E acted without thinking? ......
F heard what sounded like an animal? ......

Speaker 1 [1]
Speaker 2 [2]
Speaker 3 [3]
Speaker 4 [4]
Speaker 5 [5]

2 Now listen to the extracts. Listen out for the key words you have underlined and check your answers to Exercise 1. Try to match the speakers to the questions.

3 Listen again and check your answers. Remember, there is one extra question you do not need to use.

Vocabulary 1: adjectives of feeling ▶ CB page 19

1 Look at these pairs of adjectives of feeling. Mark them + if they are positive in meaning and – if they are negative.

0	flattered	flattering	**+**
1	depressed	depressing	......
2	confused	confusing	......
3	encouraged	encouraging	......
4	annoyed	annoying	......
5	frustrated	frustrating	......
6	frightened	frightening	......
7	interested	interesting	......
8	irritated	irritating	......

2 Complete the following sentences with a suitable adjective from Exercise 1. The first letter of each adjective has been given to help you.

0 I find this cold, grey weather really d*epressing* . We haven't seen the sun for months.
1 She hit her head when she fell and woke up feeling very c............... .
2 I think she was a bit i............... because you kept interrupting her.
3 I found learning to rollerblade really f............... . I just kept falling over.
4 She was extremely f............... when someone mistook her for Anna Kournikova.
5 He kept losing matches and ended up getting very d............... .
6 I wish you would stop doing that. It's really a............... .
7 Would you be i............... in helping me train for my next match?

15

8 Some people are f............... of hurting themselves and don't enjoy dangerous sports.

9 I found what my coach said about my last match very e............... .

10 She felt f............... because, despite all her hard work, her serve was still not strong enough.

11 Would you find it f............... if a sports clothing company offered you a modelling contract?

12 I read a really i............... article about personal sports trainers the other day.

13 She got very a............... about the umpire's bad decisions and stormed off the court.

3 Form adjectives from the verbs in the box to complete the following sentences.

embarrass	soothe	relieve	insult
concern	humiliate		

1 I am a bit .... about Daniela. She seems to have lost a lot of weight.

2 If you have a sore throat, a cup of hot lemon drink with honey can be very ....

3 He was so .... when she rushed up and kissed him that he went very red in the face.

4 The local people found the rude behaviour of the visitors really ....

5 Her parents were very .... when they heard she had been found safe and sound.

6 I wish you wouldn't criticise me in public like that. I find it really ....

4 **Use of English:** key word transformations (Part 4)

About the exam: Paper 3, Part 4 tests vocabulary as well as grammar. You may have to change a verb to an adjective.

Complete the second sentence so that it has a similar meaning to the first sentence, using the word given. Do not change the word given. You must use between two and five words, including the word given. There is an example at the beginning (0).

0 I get very embarrassed when people find out that I used to be on television.

it

I think _it is very embarrassing_.. when people find out that I used to be on television.

1 Nothing irritates me more than email advertising.

more

There is nothing .... than email advertising.

2 She thinks it's insulting when people won't take her advice.

feels

She .... by people not taking her advice.

3 The match was so thrilling that the crowd wouldn't stop cheering.

were

The crowd .... the match that they wouldn't stop cheering.

4 Her nerves were soothed by the gentle music.

was

The gentle music .... for her nerves.

5 The idea of flying can be frightening for some people.

are

A lot of people .... the idea of flying.

Reading: multiple-choice (Part 1)

About the exam: In Paper 1, Part 1, you read a text and choose between four alternatives to answer questions. Only one of the alternatives is correct.

Strategy

1 Read the title, any subheadings and the text through quickly to get a general idea.

2 Look at the questions and try to answer them without looking at the alternatives.

3 Find support for your answers in the text.

4 For each question, choose the alternative that is closest to your answer.

5 Make sure you have reasons, such as the following, for rejecting the other alternatives:

• This might be true but the text doesn't say it.

• The text says the opposite.

• The text says this, but it is not relevant to the question.

1 You are going to read an article about the young woman in the photograph. Read the article once quickly and say whether this statement is true or false.

Ellen MacArthur won the famous yacht race she entered.

SEA CHANGES

The sea has been the most important thing in Ellen MacArthur's life since she spent a summer on her Aunt Thea's boat on the English coast when she was eight years old. Her bedtime reading at that time was a [1]*biography* of a famous yachtsman who had sailed round the world three times and her dream was to do the same thing. Her parents, who are both teachers, understood that cross-country running and hockey were not going to provide enough adventure for their daughter, and that they could do nothing to alter her decision. Ellen had already started to save up her pocket money to buy a boat.

But as Ellen knew, it is easy to dream of doing a round-the-world voyage, but finding the money and learning how to go about it is more difficult. At the age of eighteen she was only 163 cm tall and weighed a little over 50 kilos, but she made her first solo trip around the coast of Great Britain. For her this was a test to see if she could cope with the [2]*hardships* of a lone voyage. In 1994 she started talking about entering the Vendee Globe, the famous French [3]*single-handed*, non-stop, round-the-world race. By 1996, she knew she had to do it.

Then the real [4]*struggle* began. Ellen lived in a caravan to save money for the race and even slept under her boat for a few nights during a Northern English winter while she got it ready for the heavy seas. She wrote two thousand letters asking for sponsorship from companies and got two replies.

One of these was from the Kingfisher brewery, and an alliance was born. She named her boat after them, and they are still her [5]*sponsors* today. 'My strongest quality is that I just don't give up,' she says.

By the time the boats lined up for the start of the 2000 Vendee Globe race, Ellen MacArthur had sailed 120,000 kilometres in eight months in her beloved *Kingfisher*, more than anyone else in the race had sailed in the previous two years. By now she was also a very experienced racer and was considered to be one of the favourites. Nevertheless, the sight of this tiny figure at the [6]*helm* of the enormous ocean racing yacht made almost everyone in France feel protective towards her. For the next three months, the news bulletins on French television contained not only race reports but also medical [7]*updates* on Ellen.

Ellen believes that everyone who finishes the Vendee Globe is a winner, but she still must have been disappointed to come second. She had overtaken Michel Desjoyeaux, who eventually won, days before the finish but ultimately he snatched back the lead. In the spirit of the race, Ellen went back to the finish line to [8]*greet* most of the other sailors on their return, including the 60-year-old Frenchman who finished last after nearly five months at sea. 'For me, it's part of the tradition of the event,' says Ellen. 'You're there at the start, you should be there at the finish.'

2 Now read the text again and choose the answer (A, B, C or D) which you think fits best according to the text.

1 How did Ellen MacArthur's parents feel about her ambition?
A They wanted her to take up other sports.
B They thought she would change her mind.
C They realised it was inevitable.
D They thought it would cost too much money.

2 What made Ellen decide to enter the Vendee Globe race?
A She had proved to herself she could do it.
B She wanted to learn more about sailing.
C She was tired of sailing around Britain.
D She wanted to become famous.

3 Once Ellen had decided to enter the Vendee Globe race, the most difficult thing for her was
A finding somewhere to live.
B adapting to the cold weather.
C getting financial support.
D feeling she wanted to give up.

4 Why did the French public like Ellen?
A She had already won a lot of races.
B She looked very small and vulnerable.
C She overcame medical problems.
D She appeared on French television a lot.

5 How does Ellen feel about yacht racing?
A She finds losing very disappointing.
B She thinks winning is the most important thing.
C She thinks competing is the real achievement.
D She thinks some of the traditions are pointless.

3 Match the numbered words in the text to these dictionary definitions.

a) welcome someone when you meet them ....
b) without help from other people ....
c) difficult situations which cause suffering ....
d) reports with the latest information ....
e) a great effort to do something difficult ....
f) the wheel which guides a boat ....
g) an account of a person's life written by someone else ....
h) people or businesses who provide money for a sports event ....

Grammar 1: making comparisons
▶ *CB page 22*

1 Complete these quiz questions with the comparative or superlative form of the adjectives in brackets.

0 Which county has produced ..*the largest*... number of Olympic medal-winning swimmers? (*large*)
1 Which of these two sports involves ....
risks: snowboarding or surfing? (*high*)
2 Which of these sports is ....: rowing, swimming or golf? (*physically demanding*)
3 Which of these two skills is .... to learn: ice-skating or roller-blading? (*easy*)
4 In which sports do people suffer from ....
injuries: downhill ski racing, cycling or windsurfing? (*bad*)
5 Which of these sports is ....: cricket, swimming or football? (*international*)

2 Here are the answers to the questions in Exercise 1 but there are mistakes with comparative and superlative forms in each of them. Correct the mistakes and match the answers to the questions.

☐ a) Surfing because there are ~~most~~ *more* potential risks in the ocean than there are on a mountain.

☐0 b) The United States has won the more gold medals in men's swimming events, closely followed by Australia.

☐ c) They are all demanding in different ways but rowing is the most tough because you push and pull with the lower and upper part of the body.

☐ d) The level of difficulty is about the same but you don't usually get as colder and as wet roller-blading.

☐ e) Everyone knows that cricket is least international. Swimming is next but football is played in every nation on Earth.

☐ f) Cyclists are more likely to suffer seriouser injuries than either downhill ski racers or windsurfers.

3 Underline the correct alternatives in these conversations.

1

A: What subjects did you enjoy studying
(0) *more* / *most* at school?

B: I really liked languages and science subjects. The other subjects were not (1) *nearly* / *near* as challenging or interesting for me.

A: Would you prefer (2) *to study* / *study* languages or science at university?

B: I'd rather (3) *to do* / *do* medicine (4) *that* / *than* anything else. I really want to be a doctor.

2

A: Tennis is (5) *more* / *far* less expensive than surfing. I mean, you only have to buy a racket and some trainers. Surfing is (6) *very* / *much* more expensive than a lot of other sports. A board can cost £400 and if you want to buy a wetsuit it will cost (7) *a lot* / *a few* more.

B: So, you think it would be a (8) *better* / *worse* idea to choose the tennis course, do you?

A: Yes, tennis is (9) *no* / *not* worse than any of the other sports on the list, as far as I'm concerned anyway.

Vocabulary 2: word formation (negative prefixes) ▶ *CB page 23*

1 Complete this chart using the prefixes in the box to make the opposites of the adjectives and verbs given.

in- im- un- mis- dis-

Adjective/Verb	Opposite
active	0 ...*inactive*...
secure	1 ....
capable	2 ....
experienced	3 ....
possible	4 ....
fortunate	5 ....
conscious	6 ....
healthy	7 ....
understand	8 ....
calculate	9 ....
approve	10 ....
obey	11 ....

2 In most of these sentences there are mistakes with the part of speech or the form (positive or negative) of the word in italics. Correct the mistakes.

0 Simon is really ~~healthy~~. He smokes a packet of cigarettes every day and he never does any exercise.
  unhealthy

1 It's very difficult to get a job without *experienced* and if you've just left school you probably don't have any.

2 He had the very good *fortunate* to meet someone who warned him about the current as he was going into the water.

3 He was *able* to finish the match because of an ankle injury.

4 During the summer the local government organise sporting *activities* on the beach.

5 My flatmate and I had a serious *understanding* about the housework and didn't speak to each other for a couple of days.

6 Our seats for the match were so far back that it was *possible* to see what was happening on the court.

7 Her feelings of *insecure* stopped her taking part in competitive sport.

8 I was *unconscious* of someone watching me but when I looked around, I couldn't see anybody.

9 We *calculated* how long it would take us to get to the airport and we missed our plane.

3 Use of English: word formation (Part 3)

Strategy
Look at the meaning of each sentence. Check if you need to add a negative prefix (e.g. *un-*) or a negative suffix (e.g. *-less*).

Read the text below. Use the word given in capitals below the text to form a word that fits in each gap. There is an example at the beginning (0).

CHILDREN WITHOUT FEAR

Research has shown that when they were children, many (0) *successful* sportspeople were more
(1) .... than their friends. Why is this? It seems that some children have very little (2) .... of the potential risks of doing (3) .... like climbing trees or jumping from heights. They have such faith in their own (4) .... that even when they do make some kind of (5) .... which results in a fall or an injury, they do not change their behaviour. Such children continue to ignore or
(6) .... adults who tell them not to do dangerous things and their parents' (7) ....
does not seem to make any difference to them. While some (8) .... children may panic when faced with the (9) .... of danger, others seem to ignore it and appear to be (10) .... These may be the ones who go on to be the sportspeople of tomorrow!

---

0 SUCCESS
1 ADVENTURE
2 UNDERSTAND
3 ACTIVITY
4 ABLE
5 CALCULATE
6 OBEY
7 APPROVE
8 SECURE
9 POSSIBLE
10 FEAR

Grammar 2: articles ▶ *CB page 26*

1 Complete the text with *a*, *an*, *the* or (–) when no article is needed.

COURAGEOUS YOUNG ATHLETES

Nearly 400 children and young people with (1) ..... physical disabilities from all over (2) ..... Australia, (3) ..... United States, (4) ..... New Zealand and (5) ..... South Africa have been competing in (6) ..... National Junior Games for the Disabled. They have taken part in (7) ..... swimming, (8) ..... basketball, (9) ..... archery and (10) ..... tennis. (11) ..... Games were opened by (12) ..... Prime Minister, who is (13) ..... Olympic sprint champion herself.

TRAINING FOR SUCCESS

(14) ..... recent report in (15) ..... *Sport and Science* magazine explains how (16) ..... sports training programmes need to be designed to fit (17) ..... needs of (18) ..... individual athletes. (19) ..... factors such as (20) ..... age, (21) ..... lifestyle and even (22) ..... language background are all important. (23) ..... most successful training programmes are planned specifically for each individual athlete. (24) ..... decisions about (25) ..... diet and even how much sleep they need can really affect their chances of success.

SURF CONTEST CANCELLED

(26) ..... Fifth International Women's Surf Championships scheduled to take place on (27) ..... island of Mauritius, in (28) ..... Indian Ocean, have been cancelled due to (29) ..... bad weather. There were (30) ..... waves as high as (31) ..... three metres yesterday afternoon, and (32) ..... strong winds are making (33) ..... conditions even more dangerous. (34) ..... Organising Committee hopes (35) ..... Championships can be held in (36) ..... week's time once (37) ..... weather has improved.

2   Use of English: open cloze (Part 2)

About the exam: In Paper 3, Part 2, there are two kinds of gaps: gaps for 'grammatical' words and gaps for phrasal verbs (*get **through** to, **catch up** with*) or fixed expressions (*in **order** to, **spend** time, **do your** homework*).

Strategy
1 Read the title and the whole text to make sure you understand what it is about.
2 Look at the words on either side of each gap.
3 Try to decide whether the missing word is a grammatical word, or a word from a phrasal verb or fixed expression.

1 **Complete the following sentences with a phrasal verb or fixed expression.**

1 Some people enjoy taking .... in dangerous or life-threatening activities.
2 Women probably .... twice about taking risks because they are more sensible than men.
3 I think you've got a good .... of winning the match.
4 Make .... you get enough sleep before the exam.
5 When Diana Rios took the job, she had no .... getting to work would be so dangerous.
6 In which month does the Boston Marathon .... place?
7 I'm so busy. I don't know how I'm going to get .... the next seven days.

2 **Read the title and the text, and think of the word which best fits each gap. Use only one word in each gap. There is an example at the beginning (0).**

ICE SKATING

Many girls dream of a career **(0)** ..*as*..... an ice skater. The costumes and graceful movements make **(1)**.......... seem a very romantic thing to **(2)**.......... . What's more, young skaters **(3)**.......... Carolina Kostner attract huge numbers of fans whenever they compete. Nevertheless, ice skating, like most sports, is very demanding and Carolina **(4)**.......... to work hard. She **(5)**.......... hours practising complicated routines and follows a fitness programme at the gym. Carolina is naturally slim, but she still has to watch her diet and make **(6)**.......... she eats the right food to get her **(7)**.......... such a busy schedule. She **(8)**.......... needs plenty of sleep. Even **(9)**.......... all the celebrations when she wins a competition, Carolina is usually in bed by 9 p.m. She travels with her family so she doesn't usually feel lonely, though she says she sometimes misses **(10)**.......... at home with her own things. For Carolina, ice skating is lots of **(11)**.......... and she enjoys competing **(12)**.......... other young skaters like herself.

Writing: letter or email (semi-formal) (Part 1) ▶ *CB page 28*

Strategy

An appropriate style for a semi-formal letter or email means using polite forms for requests and questions.

1 Look at these requests and questions and make them more polite by using the introductory phrases given. Remember to make any necessary punctuation changes as well.

0   Explain how to get from the station to your house.
     Could you *explain how to get from the station to your house?*

00 When does the course start?
     Could you *tell me when the course starts?*

1   I want to stay with a family.
     I would like ....

2   Learning to play a musical instrument sounds interesting.
     I would be interested ....

3   Can I spend an extra week in Australia?
     Would it be possible ....

4   Tell me what clothes I need to bring.
     Could you ....

5   What will the weather be like in October?
     I would like to know ....

6   I'd rather do the grammar and vocabulary course.
     I would prefer ....

7   Save me a place with the group making a class website.
     I would be grateful ....

2 Now look at a letter a student wrote to Sue Riley, the director of a sports and study programme. The student's teacher has underlined parts of the letter that are too informal. Rewrite these parts in an appropriate style in your notebook.

Dear Sue,
Thank you for the letter and brochure you sent about the sport and study programme. *I think that taking part in the programme sounds pretty interesting but there are a few things I want to know.* First of all, *what nationalities are the other students?* I am Argentinian and *I'd rather not be with a lot of other Spanish speakers. Tell me more about the English courses.* I need to improve my English so *reserve a place for me on one of your courses. Can I study more than one sport* in the afternoons? I like tennis and football and it will be hard to choose between them. *Who are the trainers for tennis and football?* This might help me to decide.
Write back soon.
All the best

Guillermo Torres

3 Divide the letter into paragraphs.

4 Look at the following task and say whether the following statements are true (T) or false (F).

1 You do not know the name of the person you are writing to.   .....
2 You have all the information you need about the job.   .....
3 You should write your letter in a semi-formal style.   .....
4 You should provide some information in your letter.   .....

Task

You have seen this advertisement in the newspaper. Read the advertisement on which you have made some notes. Then, using the information in your notes, write a letter of inquiry.

> **WE ARE LOOKING FOR FIT, ADVENTUROUS YOUNG PEOPLE INTERESTED IN ACTING AS GUIDES ON OUR WALKING TOURS IN EUROPE.**
>
> *You will need to have a knowledge of English as most of our clients are British. Free food, accommodation and all your expenses covered.*
>
> **Write and tell us where in Europe you would like to work, what your English is like and the dates you would be available.**
> **Alba Dupont**
> **Director**
>
> **Walk** Europe

guide??
work alone or with others?
exactly what level?
salary?

5 Write your answer to the task in your notebook in about 120 words.

UNIT 3 Fact or fiction?

Vocabulary 1: phrasal verbs with *look, see* and *hear*

1 Match the sentence halves.

1 When I read, I try not to look up
2 The government are looking into
3 My cousin Claudia is really looking forward
4 Like most children, Christopher had always looked up
5 In the past very rich families often looked down

- [ ] a) on people who had less money than they had.
- [ ] b) to his older brother.
- [ ] c) ways of saving energy.
- [ ] d) every unfamiliar word in the dictionary.
- [ ] e) to starting university.

2 Complete the following sentences using words from the box.

over	from	through	round
back	out	about	

1 I look .... on the summer of 2000 as one the happiest times in my entire life.
2 Look ....! There's a car coming.
3 We looked .... the historic centre of the town and then went to have lunch in a restaurant in the harbour.
4 Would you mind looking .... my composition to see if I've made any mistakes?
5 I used to think Lisa was a wonderful person but then I saw .... her.
6 Have you heard .... Tania since she went to live in Manchester?
7 Where did you hear .... the concert? I didn't see it advertised anywhere.

3 Use of English: key word transformations (Part 4)

Complete the second sentence so that it has a similar meaning to the first sentence, using the word given. Do not change the word given. You must use between two and five words, including the word given. There is an example at the beginning (0).

CLUE: All the sentences require a phrasal verb.

0 I haven't received any news from Pedro since the end of July.
heard
I *haven't heard from* .... Pedro since the end of July.

1 We decided to spend the afternoon exploring the shops.
looking
We decided to spend the afternoon .... the shops.

2 I haven't had a chance to examine the documents for the meeting yet.
look
I haven't had a chance .... the documents for the meeting yet.

3 I got the information about the scholarship through a friend of mine.
heard
I .... the scholarship from a friend of mine.

4 I will always remember that year as a very happy one.
look
I will always .... that year as a very happy one.

5 I don't understand why he couldn't recognize the truth about her.
see
I don't understand why he couldn't .... her.

6 I shouted at him to be careful but he still ran across the road without looking.
out
I shouted at him to .... but he still ran across the road without looking.

Reading: gapped text (Part 2)

About the exam: In Paper 1, Part 2, you read a text with missing sentences. After the text you find the sentences in jumbled order. You decide where they go in the text. There is always one extra sentence that does not fit anywhere.

Strategy
Look at words like pronouns (e.g. *it*, *she*), demonstratives (e.g. *this*, *that*) and possessive adjectives (*her*, *their*) in the sentences that have been removed from the text and decide what they refer to.

1 Read these sentences from the *Reality TV* text on pages 10–11 of the Coursebook and decide what the underlined words refer to.

Ron Copsey was one of a group of contestants who agreed to live for a year on a desert island, with cameras following <u>their</u> attempts to survive together. (1) ....
But there is nothing ordinary about Denise. <u>She</u> is a blind woman of amazing determination who has succeeded against all the odds. (2) ....
She had always dreamed of a musical career, but <u>this</u> was prevented by the births of her children. (3) ....
His first single *Evergreen* became the fastest-selling single of all time. It sold over a million copies in <u>its</u> first week. (4) ....

2 You are going to read an article about an unusual photograph. Six sentences have been removed from the article. Choose from the sentences A–G the one which fits each gap (1–6). There is one extra sentence which you do not need to use. The key words in the sentences have been <u>underlined</u> to help you.

THE MAN IN THE DOORWAY

A couple of years ago my friend Jack gave me a poster as a birthday present. It's an aerial photograph of a huge wave breaking around a lighthouse during a terrible storm. Standing in the doorway of the lighthouse is a man. This person must be the lighthouse keeper, and the whole picture is very dramatic.

I put the poster on my bathroom wall and I have looked at it almost every day since Jack gave it to me. I've seen postcards with the same picture, and a couple of my friends have the same poster. **1** One of my friends claimed that the man had been killed by the wave a few seconds after the photograph was taken. She said that this was common knowledge and that that was why the photograph was so popular.

I was horrified. It seemed terrible that someone would make money out of a photograph taken just before someone had died. Worse still, since it had been taken from the air, the photographer must have been safe in a helicopter. **2** The more I thought about it, the less comfortable I felt about the poster. Eventually, I took it down and put it in a cupboard.

Even though it wasn't on the wall any more I couldn't get it out of my mind. The photographer's name, Jean Guichard, was in small print just below the image and I decided to try to contact him. **3** Guichard himself seemed to have disappeared without trace and there was no way of getting in touch with him.

I did, however, find some information on a website about urban myths. **4** This site described the same story my friend had told me about the photographer capturing the last few seconds of the lighthouse keeper's life. A lot of people believed this story, and they had complained to the poster company about the publication of such a macabre image. I then followed the link to the poster company's webpage and it was there that I discovered the real story, which the company had published to stop the complaints.

Apparently the storm had lasted for days and the lighthouse keeper, Theodore Malgorne, was holding on, hoping the lighthouse would survive the strong waves. Malgorne had heard the noise of the helicopter, and was intrigued. In spite of the danger, he opened the door of the lighthouse to see who was flying by on such a terrible night. **5**

The poster company obviously thought that some people might not simply take their word for it. **6** There are two images: the one in the poster and a second one showing Malgorne stepping inside and closing the door. So that's one mystery solved. The really strange thing is that there's no information about Guichard, the photographer. Now I wonder what happened to him!

3 Find words or phrases in the texts and sentences (A–G) that mean the following.

1 from the air (section 0)

....

2 something known by most people (section 1)

....

3 not leaving any evidence (section 3)

....

4 strange, frightening and often connected with death (section 4)

....

5 very interested (section 5)

....

6 not hurt (section 5)

....

7 believe them (section 6)

....

Grammar 1: *like, as, as if/though*
▶ *CB page 33*

1 There are mistakes in most of these sentences. Find the mistakes and correct them.

0 Do you look ~~as~~ *like* either of your grandparents did when they were your age?

1 You seem like familiar. Have I met you somewhere before?

2 Do like I say. Don't stop to talk to strangers under any circumstances.

3 She works like a press officer for one of the biggest charities.

4 It looks as though it will be a nice day tomorrow. Shall we go to the beach?

5 Like I told you, Simon and Natalie aren't going out together anymore.

6 I like to do relaxing things at the weekend as going for walks in the mountains.

7 I have always thought of Santa Cruz like my home.

8 How's the weather like in September?

9 Do you feel as going out for a pizza tonight or would you rather get a take-away?

A These are stories that many people believe but which often have no basis in fact.

B I was talking to them about it one day and we were discussing what had happened to the lighthouse keeper.

C To avoid this, they provided extra photographs to back up their explanation.

D Then, after satisfying his curiosity, he simply closed the door again and was completely unharmed.

E Although I searched the Internet for ages I was unable to find an address for him, though there were hundreds of sites where I could buy the poster.

F I wondered why he hadn't tried to rescue the lighthouse keeper, instead of just taking photographs of him from the aircraft.

G The wind is very strong, and it is surprising that the man looks unafraid.

2 **Speaking:** interview and long turn
(Parts 1 and 2)

About the exam: In Paper 5, Part 2, you
have to compare and contrast two photos
and say something about them, according
to the examiner's instructions.

Strategy
Make sure you can use the language of
comparison accurately.

 Underline the correct alternatives in these
extracts from Speaking tests, then listen to
see if you were right.

Part 1 (interview)

Examiner: How long have you lived here?
Candidate: Nearly two years.
Examiner: (1) *What's / How's* it like living here?
Candidate: It's great. I think of it
(2) *like / as* my home now.
Examiner: It certainly sounds as
(3) *though / always* you enjoy it. What would
you (4) *think / like* to do when you finish
university?
Candidate: I want to work (5) *as / like* an
interpreter. (6) *Like / As* I explained before, I
am going to do a course at a university in
Australia. I've always wanted to do
something involving foreign languages
(7) *such / like* translating or interpreting.

Part 2 (long turn)

❛ These photographs are (8) *like / similar*
because they both show people reading but
they are very different in other ways. In the first
photograph there are two women reading on a
crowded train. It looks (9) *as / like* a London
underground train but I'm not really sure if it is
or not. It (10) *seems / looks* to be winter
because most of the people are wearing coats
and the blonde woman looks (11) *as / like*
though she is very interested in the book. The
man in the second photograph is probably
somewhere (12) *as / like* Jamaica or Barbados.
It's a very beautiful beach and he is obviously
very relaxed. ❜

3 **Use of English:** open cloze (Part 2)

Read the text below and think of the word which best fits each gap. Use only one word in each gap. There is an example at the beginning (0).

CLUE: In this text most of the missing words are *like*, *as*, *seem*, *if* or *though*.

STRANGER THAN FICTION

Stephen King is a very famous author today **(0)** ..*but*........ it was not always that way. He had to work hard to become successful, **(1)** .... most writers. Until he began to make money from his writing, he worked in a laundry and then later **(2)** .... a teacher. Although his stories are full of strange characters and terrifying events, at the same time they **(3)** .... to be very realistic to most readers.

A few years ago, King himself was involved **(4)** .... a terrible accident. He was walking along a country road **(5)** .... he saw a car coming towards him. It was moving dangerously from one side of the road to the other almost **(6)** .... if there was no one driving it. In fact, there was a driver but he was drunk. Although King tried **(7)** .... hard as he could to get out of the way, the car hit him. The driver was not hurt but behaved as **(8)** .... he didn't care at all.

King said later that he felt just **(9)** .... a victim in one of his novels. The man even looked **(10)** .... someone King had once written about. It took Stephen King **(11)** .... than a year to recover from the accident and even things he had always loved doing, **(12)** .... writing, were almost impossible for him.

Listening: multiple-choice (Part 4)

About the exam: In Paper 4, Part 4, you hear a person speaking alone or with other people. You will be asked to answer multiple-choice questions.

Strategy:
1 Read the questions and the three options.
2 The first time you listen, underline any key words you hear and mark the possible answer.
3 The second time you listen, check your idea.

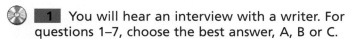

1 **You will hear an interview with a writer. For questions 1–7, choose the best answer, A, B or C.**

1 Alice became a writer because
   A she was always writing stories as a child.
   B she wanted to do what her aunt did.
   C she was keen to do any job that did not involve routine.

2 What does Alice say about learning to be a writer?
   A The writing courses she did were a waste of time.
   B She learnt to write by doing it.
   C She found it harder than she expected.

3 What does she say has been a problem for her?
   A learning to use a computer
   B finding a reliable editor
   C promoting her books

4 What does Alice like most about being a writer?
   A the fact that she has become quite famous
   B the unpredictable nature of the work
   C the freedom to choose when she works

5 What does she say about the money that she earns?
   A She makes sure that she saves some of it.
   B She dislikes the system of payment.
   C She finds it difficult to live on.

6 What does she say about travel?
   A She wishes she had more time for it.
   B She can't afford to do it very often.
   C She feels it interferes with her work.

7 Which of the following best describes Alice's attitude to her job?
   A She thinks she isn't capable of doing another job.
   B She regards it as more difficult than just a job.
   C She thinks that her income from it should be higher.

Grammar 2: adverbs ▶ *CB page 35*

1 Underline the correct alternatives in the following sentences.

> Our team didn't do too (1) *bad / badly* in the championships – we came fourth. Of course we had hoped to do (2) *best / better* but we certainly could have done a lot (3) *worst / worse*. If we try a bit (4) *harder / more hardly* next year, we might even get to the final!

> She behaved (5) *very unfriendlily / in a very unfriendly way* when I saw her at Stephen's party. She just stood (6) *still / in a still way* and stared (7) *straight / straightly* ahead when I spoke to her. I thought she hadn't heard me so I said, 'Hello' again a bit (8) *loudlier / louder* but she still didn't answer. I think I've offended her somehow!

> The University told me that I would be registered for the course (9) *automatic / automatically* as soon as they received my money, but unfortunately my letter with the cheque arrived (10) *late / lately*. Now they say they'll put me on a waiting list but it's (11) *high / highly* unlikely that I'll get a place on the course now.

> I've been so busy (12) *late / lately* that I've (13) *hard / hardly* had time to send any emails to anyone – but it was great to hear from you. I haven't got much news really except that the other night Tina and I managed to get into a Maná concert (14) *free / freely!* Tina knew someone who was working in the theatre. It was a great concert!

2 **Use of English:** key word transformations (Part 4)

Complete the second sentence so that it has a similar meaning to the first sentence, using the word given. Do not change the word given. You must use between two and five words, including the word given. There is an example at the beginning (0).

0 The doctor told me the injection would not hurt very much at all. **hardly**
The doctor told me the injection *would hardly hurt* at all.

1 I think the concert will probably not take place. **highly**
I think it's .... the concert will take place.

2 Make sure you wear clothes that don't restrict your movements. **allow**
Make sure you wear clothes that .... freely.

3 You don't have to pay to go into that museum. **get**
You can .... free.

4 People who make more effort usually do better than others. **try**
People who .... usually do better than others

5 I thought his behaviour was very silly. **behaved**
I thought he .... way.

6 He didn't stop on the way home. **straight**
He .... home.

3 **Speaking:** asking for and reacting to opinions (Part 4)

About the exam: In Paper 5, Part 4, you have a discussion with the other candidate and the examiner.

Strategy
Make sure you know how to:
- express your opinion
- ask someone for their opinion
- agree/disagree politely.

Read what two students said while they were answering a question in Part 4. Put the adverbs in brackets in the best place.

Examiner: What kinds of things do people like to read nowadays?

Student A: Well, I think that young people enjoy reading magazines more than books (*usually*). What do you think?

Student B: Sure, but we read books too. My parents are buying books (*always*) and my brother and I borrow them and read them (*sometimes*).

Student A: I don't mean (*certainly*) that young people read books (*never*), just that magazines are probably more popular. Don't you agree?

Student B: I suppose so but I think it's important to remember that books are important too (*still*). It seems to me that a new bookshop opens somewhere in town (*almost every day*).

Student A: Yes, and as well as that it's very easy to order books on the Internet (*nowadays*).

Vocabulary 2: modifiers/ intensifiers ▶ *CB page 38*

About the language: Extreme adjectives cannot be used with adverbs like *very*. For example, you cannot say *I am very exhausted*. Adjectives like these are called 'ungradable' adjectives. They are used with adverbs like *absolutely* and *totally*. 'Gradable' adjectives like *tired* cannot be used with adverbs like *absolutely* and *totally*.

1 Mark the <u>underlined</u> adjectives in these sentences G (gradable) or U (ungradable).

1 He told us an absolutely <u>amazing</u> story about a trip he went on in Venezuela. ....

2 Apparently it is quite <u>dangerous</u> to camp in the open there. ....

3 It's really <u>hard</u> to learn a foreign language when you are older. ....

4 It was totally <u>impossible</u> to get tickets for the concert. ....

5 My friend went and she said his latest book was actually a bit <u>boring</u>. ....

6 We went to Adam's party and had an incredibly <u>good</u> time. ....

7 Alejandra hasn't been feeling well but she looked absolutely <u>fantastic</u>. ....

8 There was an extremely <u>narrow</u> opening in the rock that we managed to climb through. ....

2 <u>Underline</u> the correct alternatives in the following sentences.

A: My cousin is travelling around South East Asia on her own.

B: Isn't that (1) *terribly / absolutely* dangerous?

A: No, she says it's actually (2) *quite / utterly* safe.

A: I think it would be (3) *really / fairly* amazing to fly all the way from Europe to New Zealand.

B: Do you? I think it would be (4) *extremely / totally* uncomfortable and boring being on a plane for so long.

A: Daniel is (5) *incredibly / absolutely* good at rollerblading. He can do lots of (6) *really / fairly* fantastic tricks.

B: Let's face it. As far as you're concerned Daniel is (7) *very / just* fantastic in every possible way!

A: You were (8) *quite / totally* right about Stephen King having written *Friday 13th*.

B: Yes, but I was (9) *a bit / totally* wrong about him having directed the film.

Grammar 3: narrative tenses ▶ *CB page 38*

1 Complete the story by putting the verbs in brackets into the correct form: past simple, past continuous or past perfect.

NOT DROWNING BUT WAVING

I (1) .... (*walk*) along the beach talking to my friend when suddenly I (2) .... (*see*) a man in the water who (3) .... (*wave*) frantically. I (4) .... (*not hesitate*) for a moment, but (5) .... (*run*) straight into the water to try and save him. Earlier that summer I (6) .... (*do*) a special course to learn how to rescue people and I (7) .... (*be*) keen on using my new skills.

I (8) .... (*swim*) as fast as I could to where I (9) .... (*see*) the man waving but when I (10) .... (*get*) there, he (11) .... (*disappear*) completely. I (12) .... (*look*) around desperately but he (13) .... (*be*) nowhere to be seen.

I (14) .... (*feel*) very upset when I (15) .... (*get*) out of the water. Then I (16) .... (*see*) the man again. He (17) .... (*stand*) with my friend and they (18) .... (*laugh*). It (19) .... (*turn*) out that he (20) .... (*be*) an old family friend but they (21).................... (*lose*) contact and (22) .... (*not see*) each other for years. He was just waving to try and attract her attention!

2 Use of English: word formation (Part 3)

Strategy
1 Remember to read the title and the whole text before you start.
2 Decide what part of speech goes in each gap.

Read the following text. Use the word given in capitals below the text to form a word that fits in each gap. There is an example at the beginning (0).

A GOOD SHORT STORY

Reading has always been an enormous source of **(0)** .enjoyment. for me. I particularly like short stories, especially those with surprising **(1)**.......... .

One of the most **(2)**.......... stories I've ever read is called *Exit*. It was in a **(3)**.......... of short stories we read when I was at school. It is not exactly a ghost story, but it is very **(4)**.......... .

In the story, a group of people at a country hotel are playing party games. A man called Desmond says he can make one of the other guests vanish without a trace. At the beginning of the story, there is a brief **(5)**.......... of each of the people so the reader knows that two of the guests are on their honeymoon.

The lights are turned out so that the room is in total **(6)**.......... . The game starts, but none of the guests is taking it very **(7)**.......... . Desmond describes the physical sensations that the person who is going to vanish will feel. When the game ends, the lights are switched back on and everyone laughs and says how **(8)**.......... it was. They all get ready to go to bed. It is only then that the reader realises that the girl who was on her honeymoon is now single. Neither she nor any of the other guests is aware of the **(9)**.......... of her husband. In fact, they don't have any recollection of his **(10)**.......... . He has, as Desmond promised, vanished without trace.

0	ENJOY
1	END
2	USUAL
3	COLLECT
4	MYSTERY
5	DESCRIBE
6	DARK
7	SERIOUS
8	AMUSE
9	APPEAR
10	EXIST

Writing: story (Part 2)
▶ *CB page 40*

About the exam: In Paper 2, Part 2, you choose one question to answer out of four. One of the questions may ask you to write a story.

Strategy
1 Use time linkers to show the sequence of events.
2 Use narrative tenses correctly.

1 Read the following story and choose which time expression (A, B or C) fits each space.

A TERRIBLE MISTAKE

We got to the little hotel in the village square very early in the morning. **(1)** .... we thought there was no one there because although we rang the bell again and again there was no answer. We were just going to give up **(2)** .... suddenly the door opened and an elderly porter let us in. We did our best to explain in our very bad French that we were sorry to disturb him, and **(3)** .... he seemed to understand.

(4) .... Susan was filling in the register, I took our cases up to the room. **(5)** .... I opened the curtains and looked out into the square, I knew we had made a terrible mistake coming here again. There, sitting at a table in the outdoor café, was Charles.

(6) .... I had had a chance to move away from the window, he looked up and saw me. It had taken him six years but he had **(7)** .... found us.

	A	B	C
1	Firstly	First	At first
2	when	then	while
3	at the end	eventually	later
4	When	Then	While
5	Soon	As soon as	No sooner
6	Before	When	As soon as
7	then	soon	finally

2 Read this story. <u>Underline</u> the time expressions and decide if the verbs (1–21) are in the correct tense form. If not, correct them.

At first, I could hardly believe it when my father (1) *had told* us that we (2) *were going* to visit my aunt in Miami. I always (3) *wanted* to go there and now my dream (4) *was* about to come true. The night before, Dad (5) *was ordering* a taxi to take us to the airport so we (6) *hadn't needed* to take our car. In the taxi we were all so excited about our holiday that nobody (7) *was noticing* that it (8) *seemed* to be taking much longer than usual to get to the airport. My father (9) *had asked* the driver why it (10) *was taking* so long and he (11) *said* that this (12) *was* his first day as a taxi driver and he (13) *wasn't* really sure how to get there. It was only then that my father (14) *realised* how far away from the airport we (15) *had been* at that moment. It was at least an hour away, and our plane (16) *was leaving* in an hour and a half. Finally my father (17) *persuaded* the taxi driver to let him drive and eventually we (18) *had arrived* at the international terminal. We all (19) *rushed* to the check in with our suitcases, but as soon as we got there we discovered that the flight (20) *was being cancelled* due to bad weather. Our frantic rush (21) *had been* for nothing.

3 Look at these stages of a story. Which order should they come in?

- [ ] a) first events and/or a problem
- [ ] b) background information
- [ ] c) final outcome
- [ ] d) later actions or results

4 Look back at the story in Exercise 2. Does it follow the same order? Divide it into four paragraphs.

5 Look at the sentences below. Decide which stage of a story (A, B, C or D) each one comes from.

1 At last he managed to reach the shore, and he knew he was safe. □
2 It was a warm, summer's evening and a light breeze was blowing across the bay. □
3 She never forgot the old man's kindness. □
4 When we finally got there, most of the other guests had already left. □
5 I knew it was going to be a bad day as soon as I heard the phone ringing at 6 a.m. □
6 Delia didn't recognise Matthieu at first, but as soon as he spoke she knew who he was. □
7 He knew that she never remembered their wedding anniversary. □
8 Suddenly he looked around and realised that he was alone – the ordeal was over. □

6 Choose one of the 'background information' lines from Exercise 5 to begin your own story. Plan the other stages of your story. Then write it in four paragraphs in your notebook. Remember to use sequencing words, and to check the form of the verbs you use.

4 Food for thought

Vocabulary 1: food ▶ CB page 42

1 Match the words in the box to the pictures.

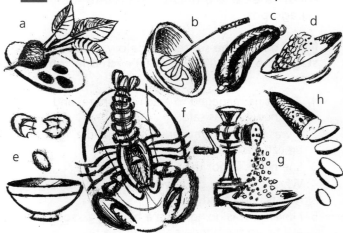

batter	seafood	beans	beetroot	mince
aubergine	yolk	cucumber		

a .... b .... c .... d ....
e .... f .... g .... h ....

2 Complete the following sentences using the words from Exercise 1.

1 Mayonnaise, which is made with egg ....,
olive oil and a little vinegar, is a French invention.

2 The bright pink colour of the Russian soup called
borscht comes from ....

3 The Japanese speciality sushi is made with rice
soaked in vinegar, raw ...., vegetables and
dried seaweed.

4 Chilli con carne, which originated in Mexico, can be
adapted for vegetarians by using more ....
instead of meat.

5 The fish fillets in traditional fish and chips are
coated in .... and deep fried.

6 The Greek dish moussaka is made with sliced
................, meat, tomatoes and a béchamel sauce.

7 Gazpacho, the traditional Spanish chilled soup, is
often served with diced .... and red and
green peppers.

8 Spaghetti Bolognese, with a sauce made from
................, garlic, onions and tomatoes, was well
known outside Italy long before pizza.

3 **Use of English:** multiple-choice cloze (Part 1)

Read the text below and decide which answer (A,
B, C or D) best fits each gap. There is an example
at the beginning (0).

Note: In this task there are only 10 gaps. In the
exam there will be 12.

> **CLUE:** The missing words in this task are all words
> that go with other words in fixed phrases
> connected with food and eating. For example,
> *concerned* is the right answer to 0 because none
> of the other adjectives go with *about*.

EATING WELL

People today are probably more **(0)** *concerned* about
food than ever before. We worry about eating foods
that **(1)** .... too much fat or carbohydrates and
so we cut **(2)** .... on things like meat, bread,
potatoes and dairy **(3)** .... The problem with
making dramatic changes to our eating **(4)** ....
like these is that we may also be cutting out good
(5) .... of iron or other vitamins and minerals.
Suddenly we start feeling tired and irritable.

The secret of a **(6)** .... diet is to reduce foods
that are **(7)** .... in cholesterol while, at the same
time, eating those that are **(8)** .... in calcium
and iron like soy protein, sesame seeds, spinach and
broccoli. Eating well does not mean that you should
cut out all your **(9)** .... foods; it just means
eating sensibly and trying to avoid too much
(10) .... food!

0	**A** interested	**B** concerned	**C** keen	**D** fed up
1	**A** hold	**B** contain	**C** enclose	**D** carry
2	**A** out	**B** off	**C** down	**D** up
3	**A** products	**B** specimens	**C** examples	**D** samples
4	**A** customs	**B** rules	**C** norms	**D** habits
5	**A** bases	**B** origins	**C** sources	**D** causes
6	**A** balanced	**B** neutral	**C** steady	**D** solid
7	**A** large	**B** tall	**C** high	**D** big
8	**A** strong	**B** rich	**C** full	**D** wealthy
9	**A** preferred	**B** lovely	**C** favourite	**D** admired
10	**A** rubbish	**B** junk	**C** trash	**D** garbage

Listening: sentence completion (Part 2)

About the exam: In Paper 4, Part 2, you complete sentences. The sentences always come in the same order on the recording. You only need to write between one and four words. You use the same words as the words you hear.

Strategy

1 Read the instructions and the sentences carefully and try to guess what kinds of things are missing e.g. a job or profession, a time of year, a number, a nationality.
2 Listen and complete the sentences. If you miss an answer, go on to the next sentence.
3 Complete any missed sentences when you listen the second time.
4 Check to make sure your answers are grammatically correct and that there are no spelling mistakes.

1 Look at the task below. A student has tried to predict the answers, but he has made some grammar and spelling mistakes. Correct the mistakes.

You will hear part of a radio interview with a personal trainer. For questions 1–10, complete the sentences.

John King used to work as a **(1)** _teacher_ .

He opened his first gym **(2)** _on 1999_ .

He studied **(3)** _sychology_ at the University of Florida.

In his gyms he gives clients training programmes and also **(4)** _advices about nutrition_ .

The thing he likes best about the job is **(5)** _get to know_ his clients.

He suggests that people begin by working with a trainer **(6)** _three time_ a week.

A **(7)** _three-month_ course with a trainer can cost up to €2000.

John says that the success of a personal training programme depends on **(8)** _the equipments_ .

Many personal trainers have **(9)** _carreers in sport_ as well as their work.

John is hoping to compete in the London Marathon **(10)** _the next week_ .

 2 Now listen to the recording to check the student's answers. Change any incorrect answers.

 3 Listen again to check and complete your answers.

Vocabulary 2: prepositions
▶ *CB page 43*

Use of English: open cloze (Part 2)

Read the text below and think of the word which best fits each space. Use only one word in each space. There is an example at the beginning (0).

> **CLUE:** All the missing words are prepositions.

RECIPE FOR SUCCESS

There are very few women who have succeeded **(0)** _in_ the competitive world of French cooking, but one of them is Helene Darroze. Although Helene had always been keen **(1)** .... cookery, she did not decide to become a chef until she was **(2)** .... her twenties.

She graduated **(3)** .... business studies and then made **(4)** .... her mind to spend a year working in a restaurant kitchen. A famous chef took Helene **(5)** .... as an apprentice and she was put **(6)** .... charge of managing the other staff. She also helped to choose the menus that were cooked every day. Thanks **(7)** .... this first class training, Helene Darroze decided to become a chef.

She worked **(8)** .... the hotel and restaurant her family owned in southwest France for a few years and then set **(9)** .... her own restaurant in Paris. She was a success, and after only four months her restaurant won its first Michelin star – a sign of great achievement. In 2003, her restaurant won another star, which made Helene the first woman **(10)** .... thousands of male chefs to win two stars.

Reading: multiple-choice questions (Part 1)

1 Read this article about the Japanese speciality *sushi* and choose the best title.

a) Speeding things up at Sushi University ☐

b) Training to be a sushi chef: a short history ☐

When engineer Tsutomu Takada lost his job, he decided to make a complete change in his life. He took off his business suit and put on an apron – and started a course to became a chef. 'I had always dreamed of doing this, even when I was an engineer,' says Takada. 'And now, here I am,' he says with a laugh.

He is a student at Tokyo's Sushi University. This is the only university in Japan which is [1]*devoted* entirely to teaching the art of sushi. What is sushi? It is Japan's famous dish of raw fish, dried seaweed and rice soaked in vinegar. Traditionally it takes decades of training to become a sushi chef, but Sushi University trains chefs in one year.

As well as providing quick retraining, the university's approach reflects a growing change in Japanese society – a move away from the traditional ways of doing things. 'Society has changed,' sighs university principal Katsuji Konakai, who started as a sushi [2]*apprentice* more than sixty years ago. 'People today wouldn't put up with the tough training I had. When I made mistakes, my teacher hit me on the head with his knife handle!'

Sushi hasn't always been a matter of studying hard and being hit on the head. It started in ancient China, where people preserved fish by packing it in rice and salt. They did not eat the rice. It is said that this process probably came to Japan between 300 BC and AD 300. Adventurous Japanese cooks began to serve the pickled fish together with vinegared rice. This combination of rice and fish was called sushi.

The most important thing about sushi is that it has to look attractive. In fact, the most carefully prepared sushi meals can cost hundreds of dollars! There are 45,000 sushi businesses in Japan today, including take-away, as some people like to eat it for lunch in their offices. There are also cheap self-service restaurants, where customers sit at a counter which has different coloured plates with different types of

sushi on them. These plates move around the counter on a conveyor belt, and customers choose the sushi they want to eat. When they have finished eating, the waitress counts the coloured plates and works out the bill.

Mr Konakai has made sushi for Japan's emperor. He says sushi preparation is an art, but he also believes that Sushi University's intensive course is necessary. 'Of course people complain this is not the way to do it,' he says, 'but we tried to make it easier for those who wanted to learn about sushi, and for those who want to take it overseas.' Many of the students already have jobs [3]*lined up* in places like Australia, Italy and Singapore.

But the course is really just the beginning for the new chefs. According to Mr Konakai it takes five, ten or even twenty years to become a [4]*top-notch* sushi chef. 'To make good sushi, you have to have skill but you also need a warm heart,' he says.

2 Look at the questions and read the text again. The parts of the text which give the answers to the first three questions have been underlined. Look at the last three questions and underline the parts of the text that will help you answer them.

1 What made Tsutomu Takada start training as a sushi chef?
2 Why is Sushi University so revolutionary?
3 What does Katsuji Konakai say about the old training methods?
4 Who was responsible for the invention of sushi?
5 What is the main feature of contemporary sushi?
6 What does Mr Konakai think about Sushi University?

3 Look at the questions and choose the answer (A, B, C or D) which you think fits best according to the text.

1 What made Tsutomu Takada start training as a sushi chef?
   A He wanted to fulfil an ambition.
   B He didn't want to work in an office.
   C He didn't know what else to do.
   D He thought he would make a lot of money.

2 Why is Sushi University so revolutionary?
   A It has unusual teaching methods.
   B You have to wait a long time to get into a course.
   C It only offers courses in sushi preparation.
   D You can only study there for a short time.

3 What does Katsuji Konakai say about the old training methods?
   A They are no longer acceptable.
   B They were too violent.
   C They were too traditional.
   D They were too quick.

4 Who was responsible for the invention of sushi?
   A People who caught the fish.
   B The Chinese people.
   C Japanese chefs who used the rice.
   D People who wrote about the history of cooking.

5 What is the main feature of contemporary sushi?
   A It is always expensive.
   B It is very popular.
   C It must look nice.
   D It is sold as a take-away.

6 What does Mr Konakai think about Sushi University?
   A It provides courses that are needed.
   B The training is too intensive.
   C It stops students having to study abroad.
   D The methods used in teaching are not right.

4 Look at the numbered words in the text and tick (✓) the best meaning in the context.

1 a) given completely to ☐
  b) loving someone very much ☐

2 a) someone who has agreed to work with an employer for low wages in order to learn a skill ☐
  b) a student at a college or university ☐

3 a) arranged ☐
  b) in a queue ☐

4 a) of highest rank or quality ☐
  b) a bunch of hair on top of the head ☐

Grammar 1: countable and uncountable nouns ▶ CB page 46

1 Underline the correct alternatives in the following sentences.

1 She found a / some very cheap accommodation not far from the college.
2 She spent a lot of money on a new clothing / new clothes.
3 Maths has / have never been my best subject.
4 There is / are always a lot of traffic at this time of day.
5 My grandmother only has one trouser / pair of trousers.
6 Can you pass me the scissor / scissors? They're / It's hanging on that hook.
7 Could you give me some / an information about cookery courses?
8 She was only going away for a week but she had a lot of luggage / luggages.
9 When did you take up aerobic / aerobics?
10 Have you had any / a news from Guillermo lately?

2 Complete the sentences using *few, a few, little* or *a little*.

1 I knew very .... people at the party so I decided to leave early.
2 .... of us are planning to get together next weekend. Would you like to come along?
3 Could I have .... more milk in this coffee? It's too strong for me.
4 There was only .... information about Thai food in the library, so I looked on the Internet.
5 I've got very .... spare time this week. Can we put off our meeting for a few days?
6 There are .... chocolates left in the box. Would you like one?
7 Let me give you .... advice. Take up a sport like tennis if you want to meet people.
8 .... plants provide such a rich source of protein as the soy bean.

3 **Use of English:** word formation (Part 3)

Read the following text. Use the word given in capitals below the text to form a word that fits in each gap. There is an example at the beginning (0).

UNDERSTANDING FOOD ALLERGIES

Allergies can **(0)**.*dramatically*. affect the lives of millions of people. Flowers, pets and even house dust can make people itch, sneeze, scratch and feel generally **(1)**.......... . There are also a lot of foods that cause allergic **(2)**.......... . Some of these are so extreme that they can be really dangerous. That's why a **(3)**.......... of which foods potentially pose a threat can save someone's life. Only a small number of foods cause the **(4)**.......... of allergies. These include milk, eggs, nuts, wheat, fish and shellfish. The most common symptoms are **(5)**.......... breathing, skin rashes and **(6)**.......... . Sometimes the symptoms appear **(7)**.......... after the person has eaten a meal including one of these ingredients. If the throat swells and the person cannot breathe properly, expert **(8)**.......... advice from a hospital or health centre should be sought. This may sound **(9)**.........., but in fact only a few people who believe they have food allergies really do have them. Most are actually only suffering from some form of 'food **(10)**..........' and as unpleasant as this may be, it certainly won't kill you.

0	DRAMA	6	SICK
1	MISERY	7	IMMEDIATE
2	REACT	8	PROFESSION
3	KNOW	9	ALARM
4	MAJOR	10	TOLERATE
5	DIFFICULT		

Grammar 2: future forms ▶ *CB page 49*

1 Some of these sentences have missing words. Insert the words in the correct place.

0 This time next month, I'll ⌄*be* lying on a beach gazing at the sea.

1 That coffee spill if you're not careful.
2 I going to apply for a job as a chef.
3 Fires are burning in many parts of the Mediterranean.
4 A coffee for me and my friend have an orange juice.
5 By the time you get back, I have finished cleaning the flat.
6 I leave for London next Wednesday morning at 10 a.m.
7 I can't come to class next week. I be in New York.

2 Underline the correct alternatives in these conversations.

1
A: What do you hope to be doing this time next year?
B: I know what (1) *I'll be doing / I'm doing*! (2) *I'll be studying / study* food science. I've already been accepted on the course.
A: (3) *Will you / Are you going to* be able to study that here?
B: No. (4) *I'm going to live / I'm living* in Madrid, actually, but (5) *I'll come / I come* back here for the summer holidays each year.

2

A: What can we do to reduce the amount of water we use?

B: It's a very difficult question, but if we (6) *don't / won't* do something soon, there (7) *is / 'll be* a real crisis.

C: Yes, apparently by the year 2050, half the world's population (8) *will live / will be living* without access to clean water. In my house (9) *we are going to / we will* start being much more careful about how much water we use.

B: Next month in my town we (10) *'ll have / 're having* a day when we are not supposed to use any water apart from bottled water. It's so that we can all see what it would be like to have to carry all the water we use.

Vocabulary 3: body and health
▶ *CB page 50*

1 Find words for parts of the body in the wordsearch grid below and use the words to complete the idioms.

m	o	n	u	f	o	o	t
s	h	o	u	l	d	e	r
t	t	s	h	e	w	y	r
o	i	e	s	g	t	e	e
m	l	b	o	w	t	s	o
a	e	h	a	n	d	s	h
c	f	i	n	g	e	r	i
h	n	n	e	p	b	t	e

1 Ela is always sticking her .... into other people's business – no one has any secrets from her!

2 His new car must have cost him an arm and a .... It's a beautiful red sports car.

3 Could you give me a .... with this suitcase? It's a bit too heavy for me to carry.

4 Tony is so lazy – he won't lift a .... to help me with the housework.

5 I don't have the .... for violent films. I spend the whole time with my hands over my eyes.

6 She always knows the right thing to say – in fact, she never puts a .... wrong.

7 Sara used to have lots of boyfriends but now she only has .... for Adam.

8 If you need a .... to cry on, I'll be there.

2 Complete the following sentences using words from the box.

weak   nimble   strong   flat   chubby   broken
swollen   sore

1 He had a fever and a very .... throat so he went straight to bed.

2 The doctor said her wrist was probably not .... but that he would bandage it anyway.

3 The baby had lovely .... cheeks and curly black hair.

4 Most young people want to have .... stomachs so that they can wear the latest fashions.

5 People who ski usually have very .... thighs.

6 Climbing lots of stairs is not good if you have .... knees.

7 Your ankle looks a bit .... Do you think you might have sprained it?

8 You need .... fingers to fix small machines.

3 **Use of English:** key word transformations (Part 4)

Complete the second sentence so that it has a similar meaning to the first sentence, using the word given. Do not change the word given. You must use between two and five words, including the word given. There is an example at the beginning (0).

0 The meal in the restaurant may have been extremely expensive but it was really delicious.   **leg**
The meal in the restaurant may have cost *an arm and a leg*.... but it was really delicious.

1 Would you mind helping me move this sofa?   **hand**
Would you mind .... this sofa?

2 I'm involved in a lot of projects at the moment. **finger**
I've .... a lot of pies at the moment.

3 When I needed someone to talk to about my problems, Bill was always there.   **shoulder**
When I needed .... , Bill was always there.

4 Since I met Mark, I haven't looked at other boys. **eyes**
Since I met him, I .... Mark.

5 He was playing so well it seemed as if he couldn't make a mistake.   **foot**
He was playing so well it seemed he couldn't .... wrong.

Writing: article (Part 2) ▶ *CB page 52*

Strategy
Make sure each of your paragraphs:
- has a sentence that introduces the main idea in a **general** way (topic sentence)
- develops the topic using **specific** examples
- uses expressions to link the ideas together (e.g. *Firstly, in addition*, etc.).

1 Underline the correct alternatives in the text below.

People today are very conscious of their physical appearance. (1) *For example / However*, women around the world spend millions of dollars on cosmetics. Increasingly, male consumers are being targetted by the cosmetics companies (2) *as well / though*. This usually involves trying to persuade them to use face creams and lotions. (3) *Furthermore / Unfortunately*, many of these products are over-priced and not particularly effective.

2 Look at the sentences below and decide if they are general (G) or specific (S).

1 Many people claim that young people are addicted to junk food. ......
2 More and more people around the world suffer from allergies. ......
3 In some cases, this involves giving up red meat only. ......
4 Many tennis players, for example, suffer from shoulder, knee and ankle injuries. ......
5 The food we eat has probably never been as international as it is today. ......
6 Furthermore, even walking can be good exercise. ......

3 Put these sentences into the correct order. Remember to start with the general idea and then provide specific examples.

☐ a) Many sweets, for example, contain artificial colouring to make them more attractive.
☐ b) Many food companies deliberately target child consumers.
☐ c) As well as this, the companies increasingly use additives of various kinds.
☐ d) This can involve packaging and advertising aimed at children.

Strategy
Make sure the topic sentence in your first paragraph does not copy the words in the writing task.

4 Look at this task and the first paragraph a student wrote. Underline the topic sentence in the paragraph.

Young people today are addicted to junk food. Do you agree? Write us an article telling us what you think. The best article will be published next month. Write your article in **120–180** words.

Hamburgers, crisps, soft drinks and sweets: most of us enjoy these things and we eat them from time to time. But have young people exchanged healthier foods for mass-produced rubbish? Many people think that they have.

5 Think of a title and then write the rest of the article in your notebook.

Vocabulary 1:
consumer society
▶ *CB page 56*

1 There are spelling mistakes in some of these sentences. Find the mistakes and correct them.

0 If you buy more than two products in this range, you get a 25% d*i*scount.

1 The logo for the sporting goods company Nike is a tick.

2 Sports Clubwear lounched their spring collection at a huge street party in London.

3 Coca-Cola has always been famous for its expensive advertising campains.

4 Our teacher sent a letter of complaint to the Consummer Protection Authority.

5 My cousin Michael used to work for an advertising agency.

6 Film director, Ridley Scott, has also directed over 2000 advertisments.

7 Have you seen the latest Sony commercial? It's really good.

2 **Use of English:** multiple-choice cloze (Part 1)

Read the text below and decide which answer (A, B, C or D) best fits each gap. There is an example at the beginning (0).

Note: In the exam, there will be 12 gaps.

THE HARD SELL

Most companies spend a large **(0)** *proportion* of their budgets persuading us to buy their products, and it is their **(1)** .... executives who have to decide how to make consumers aware of new products. To do this, they usually set up an advertising **(2)** .... of some kind. Generally, **(3)** .... a new product involves TV and radio commercials, and there may also be large advertisements on **(4)** .... along motorways and major roads.

In the past, companies employed people to sell the product **(5)** .... but nowadays there is a far more popular technique which uses the telephone. Staff in large call-centres telephone potential **(6)** ...., tell them about the product and try to convince them that it is worth buying. Another technique is to **(7)** .... the new product by post. The company sends colourful **(8)** .... to every house even though people haven't asked for them. They are so unpopular that people call them **(9)** .... mail – and even though they may contain free **(10)** .... or discount vouchers, many people just put them straight into the rubbish bin!

	A	B	C	D
0	section	**proportion**	division	fraction
1	selling	publicity	marketing	propaganda
2	programme	campaign	approach	operation
3	starting	commencing	launching	beginning
4	hoardings	boards	displays	screens
5	in person	to face	at hand	on show
6	shoppers	investors	buyers	customers
7	promote	sponsor	support	demonstrate
8	catalogues	prospectuses	reviews	journals
9	rubbish	garbage	junk	waste
10	samples	tests	pieces	bits

Reading: multiple matching (Part 3)

About the exam: The questions in Paper 1, Part 3, are not in the same order as the information in the texts.

Strategy
You don't need to read the text in detail. Look for words or expressions that mean the same as the key words in the questions.

1 You are going to read four descriptions of products and how they were marketed. Read the texts very quickly and decide if these statements are true (T) or false (F).

a) None of the inventors of these products marketed them successfully. ☐

b) All these products are still used today. ☐

2 For each of the statements choose from the products A–D.

> **CLUE:** The underlined words and phrases in the text are parallel expressions that go with the key words and phrases in questions 1 to 11.

This product

is no longer the most popular brand. **1** ☐

followed another important development. **2** ☐

had the support of famous people. **3** ☐

was made by someone who we know very little about. **4** ☐

made very little money for its inventor. **5** ☐

was developed by two people working together. **6** ☐

was demonstrated by people who knew how to use it. **7** ☐

was copied and improved. **8** ☐

was originally sold to customers by its inventors. **9** ☐

outsold its competitors for two decades. **10** ☐

was invented because people were not satisfied with another product. **11** ☐

THE BEST THINGS SINCE SLICED BREAD?

A   THE BREAD SLICER

Two American towns claim to be the home of sliced bread: Chillicothe in Missouri and Battle Creek, Michigan. Journalist, Kathy Stortz Ripley, is in favour of Chillicothe. When she was researching the town's history, she came across a news item dated 7th July 1928 announcing that the Chillicothe Baking Company had started marketing wrapped loaves of sliced bread. There was an advertisement on the same page that read 'The greatest forward step in the baking industry since bread was wrapped: Sliced Kleen Maid Bread'. Ripley did some more research and found that the inventor of the slicing machine, Otto Rohwedder, had almost vanished from the history books. Rohwedder, a jeweller by trade, spent thirteen years working on his invention before persuading bakers to give it a try. He sold his patent in 1930 before sliced bread had really caught on. It was the Wonder Bread company that made sliced bread truly famous with an advertising campaign showing smiling families packing sandwiches for picnics.

B   THE SKATEBOARD

It is impossible to say who was responsible for the invention of the skateboard. In the 1950s, many Californian surfing enthusiasts, frustrated that weather and waves were not always suitable for surfing, began nailing the bases of roller skates to the front and back ends of wooden planks. Although these boards were very unstable, they allowed for 'sidewalk surfing' along streets and down hills. It was not long before the fad spread through the major cities of the United States and beyond. The first commercially-produced boards were made by Makaha Skateboards and designed by surfer Larry Stevenson. Makaha chose a team of top riders to showcase their boards. Soon bicycle manufacturers and toy companies were following suit and producing stable, unbreakable boards with more speedy and reliable plastic wheels. At the moment, skateboarding is the sixth most popular sporting activity in the United States.

C   TRAINERS

In 1958, Phil Knight, a student at the University of Oregon and an athlete, <u>complained</u> to his coach, Bill Bowerman <u>about the clumsy American running shoes of the time</u>. <u>They formed a company</u> in 1964 to market a lighter and more comfortable shoe designed by Bowerman. In 1968, this company became Nike, named after the Greek goddess of Victory. <u>At first ,Knight and Bowerman sold their shoes in person</u> at athletics meetings but soon this wasn't necessary. Knight's first great marketing ploy was announcing that 'four of the top seven finishers' in the marathon at the 1972 Olympic Trials had worn Nikes. <u>Through the 80s and 90s, Nike's advertisements helped make it the foremost retailer of athletic shoes worldwide,</u> thanks to <u>endorsements from superstars</u> like Michael Jordan, and catchy slogans like 'Just do it'.

D   LIP BALM

Chap Stick was the brainchild of a Lynchburg, Virginia doctor named C.D. Fleet. His product, which was distributed locally, was not very successful however. <u>In 1912 he sold the rights</u> to John Morton, another Lynchburg resident, <u>for only $5</u>. Morton marketed the product so well that today it makes its manufacturer $63 million a year. Both the way the lip balm is presented and its ingredients have changed a lot since the 1880s, when it was first produced. Now apart from sticks there are tubes and jars and the balm itself comes in many different flavours such as cherry and chocolate. Although Chap Stick has long been a leader in the lip balm market <u>it was overtaken in 1996 by another company</u>, Blistex.

3 Read the text again and find words or phrases that mean the following. The words and phrases are in the same order in the texts.

0	found by chance	*came across*
1	right to sell or make something	....
2	became popular	....
3	a temporary popular trend	....
4	demonstrate the good qualities of something	....
5	tactic	....
6	easy to remember	....
7	good idea	....
8	passed	....

Vocabulary 2: describing objects
▶ *CB page 58*

1 Complete these advertisements using words from the box.

> compact   offer   selection   discounts   control
> sample   prices   appearance   handy

Elroy's Electronics

(1) .... slashed on DVD players!

Come in and see our wide (2) .... of home cinema systems.

Big (3) .... on all your favourite videos too.

UKAN FIXIT

Our small, (4) .... toolkit fits easily into your briefcase or handbag and the (5) .... carrying case means that you take it with you wherever you go.

Confidence International

Be in total (6) .... of even the most challenging situations.

Improve your (7) .... and dress sense

Speak in public without ever feeling nervous again.

COURSES START EVERY TUESDAY.

Bronzed and beautiful

Special (8) ....! This week with your copy of *Beautiful*, a free (9) .... of Rimlon's fabulous new self-tanning gel!

2 There are mistakes with prepositions and particles in some of these sentences. Find the mistakes and correct them.

1 This electronic dictionary is just what you need for help you when you travel abroad.

2 This torch key ring really comes in handy when you are trying to open your door in the dark.

3 Microwave ovens are very useful to people who don't have much time to cook.

4 This is the perfect gift to the woman who has everything.

5 That sofa would be ideal for a spare bed when guests come to stay.

6 A dishwasher is very convenient for large families with plenty of plates and cutlery.

7 This hairdryer is designed for convert itself into a travel iron.

Grammar 1: indirect speech
▶ *CB page 59*

1 Look at these questions from a market research survey and put them into indirect speech. Begin: *She asked her … .*

0 Do you enjoy shopping?
She asked her if she enjoyed shopping.
....

1 How often do you go shopping?
....

2 When did you last go shopping?
....

3 Did you go alone or with someone else?
....

4 Is there a shopping centre near where you live?
....

5 Do you prefer to shop there or in the town centre?
....

6 Have you ever bought anything on the Internet?
....

7 Can you access the Internet from home?
....

8 Are you confident that Internet shopping is safe?
....

9 Will you be making your next important purchase in a shop or online?
....

2 Match these answers to the questions in Exercise 1.

☐ a) I'm going to buy a new laptop and I'll probably get it from a shop.

☐ b) Yes. I've bought a lot of books and CDs as well as some clothes.

☐ c) At least once a week.

☐ d) Yes, it's one of my favourite activities.

☐ e) Two days ago.

☐ f) I went with my best friend.

☐ g) I prefer to shop in the town centre.

☐ h) No, I can't, but there's a cyber café round the corner.

☐ i) Yes, I think so.

☐ j) Yes. It's called Botany Bay.

3 Now complete the market researcher's report.

She said that shopping (1) .... one of her favourite activities and that she (2) .... at least once a week. She told me that (3) .... shopping with her best friend two days' earlier. Although she said there (4) .... a shopping centre called Botany Bay near where she (5) ...., she (6) .... to shop in the town centre. She said that she (7) .... books, CDs and clothes online, although she explained that she (8) .... the Internet from home and that she usually (9) .... to a cyber café nearby. She said that she (10) .... a new laptop soon and that she (11) .... probably get it from a shop.

4 Use of English: key word transformations (Part 4)

Complete the second sentence so that it has a similar meaning to the first sentence, using the word given. Do not change the word given. You must use between two and five words, including the word given. There is an example at the beginning (0).

0 'Do you want to come over and watch a movie?' she asked.

if

She asked me .....*if I wanted*..................... to come over and watch a movie.

1 'Where do you buy most of your clothes?' she asked.

know

She wanted to .... most of my clothes.

2 'Can I borrow your leather jacket?' he asked.

if

He asked me .... my leather jacket.

3 'I have to get a new laptop tomorrow,' she said.

that

She said .... a new laptop the next day.

4 'I won't be here next week,' she explained.

there

She explained that she .... the following week.

5 'We're going to paint the living room yellow,' she announced.

that

She announced .... to paint the living room yellow.

6 'I haven't ever been on a plane before,' she said.

never

She explained that .... on a plane before.

7 'Who did you see at the party?' he asked.

know

He wanted to .... at the party.

8 'Were you living in London when you met Celia?' she asked.

if

She asked him .... in London when he met Celia.

Listening: multiple-choice (Part 4)

Strategy
1 Read the instructions.
2 Look at the questions carefully and highlight key words and phrases.
3 Listen to the recording first for words and phrases that are similar in meaning to the key words.
4 Listen to the recording again to check.

1   You will hear an interview with a young man who works for an advertising agency. Look at these questions and <u>underline</u> the key words.

1 Tim started to work in advertising because
   A he couldn't get another job.
   B he had always wanted to.
   C he needed to earn a salary.

2 Tim thinks up his best slogans
   A on his own.
   B when he works with other people.
   C on his way to work.

3 According to Tim a good slogan should
   A make people laugh.
   B sound like natural speech.
   C sound old-fashioned.

4 The thing Tim likes best about his job is
   A the competition.
   B the money.
   C the creativity.

5 Tim watches advertisements on TV
   A when he's in another country.
   B when he gets home from work.
   C during the working day.

6 Tim wants to set up his own company because
   A he wants to be his own boss.
   B he wants to work on his own.
   C he doesn't enjoy the work he's doing.

7 Tim disagrees that
   A people criticise each other a lot.
   B advertising is a young person's profession.
   C doing stimulating work stops you getting old.

 2   Now listen to the recording and choose the best answer, A, B, or C.

Grammar 2: reporting verbs ▶ *CB page 60*

1   There are mistakes in some of these sentences. Find the mistakes and correct them.

0   Helena promised me that she ~~will~~ *would* come to the party.

1   Clara persuaded us staying for dinner.

2   Alexandre accused Tomasso that he had taken the jewels.

3   Marisa offered giving me a lift home.

4   Lidia accepted being wrong.

5   Adam refused to apologise to Guillermo.

6   Susana told that she would be late.

7   We agreed meeting outside the cinema at eight o'clock.

8   Tania suggested us to see the historical museum.

9   Can you remind me to go to the post office tomorrow?

2   **Use of English:** key word transformations (Part 4)

Complete the second sentence so that it has a similar meaning to the first sentence, using the word given. Do not change the word given. You must use between two and five words, including the word given. There is an example at the beginning (0).

0   'You should get more sleep', the doctor told me.   **advised**
The doctor ...*advised me to get*...more sleep.

1   'Eating more fruit is good for you too,' she said.   **recommended**
She .... more fruit.

2   'Why don't you come for a coffee?' Nigel said to me.   **invited**
Nigel .... for a coffee.

3   'I wasn't anywhere near the bank that day', he said.   **denied**
He .... anywhere near the bank that day.

4   'I won't be able to finish the assignment,' she said.   **explained**
She .... be able to finish the assignment.

5   'I am not going to let you in,' she told him.   **refused**
She .... in.

6   'You won the match. Well done!' the coach said to them.
congratulated
The coach .... the match.

7   'If you don't turn that music down, I'll call the police,' said the man downstairs.   **threatened**
The man downstairs .... the police if we didn't turn the music down.

8   'Don't walk around alone after dark. It's dangerous,' the teacher told us.   **warned**
The teacher .... around alone after dark.

3   **Use of English:** open cloze (Part 2)

Read the text below and think of the word which best fits each gap. Use only one word in each gap. There is an example at the beginning (0).

MOMENTS OF PERFECTION

My cousin had a terrible experience
(0) ...*when*.... she was working for a big advertising agency. Her boss had ordered
(1) .... to think up a new slogan for a very important client. After a week, my cousin had not **(2)** .... able to think of any good slogans so she went to her boss and apologised **(3)** .... being so slow. He warned her
(4) .... if she didn't think of something in the next twenty-four hours the company might lose **(5)** .... client and that it would be her fault.

My cousin stayed awake **(6)** .... night trying to think of a catchy slogan. She was about to phone her boss and admit that she **(7)** .... not thought of anything when her flatmate suggested that she should try listening **(8)** .... some of her favourite records for inspiration.

(9) .... first, nothing seemed very inspiring **(10)** .... then she heard a song called *Simply the best*. My cousin rang her boss and told **(11)** .... that she thought that it would make a great slogan. He accused her
(12) .... having copied another very famous advertising campaign in which the same slogan had been used.

Vocabulary 3: shopping and leisure facilities ▶ *CB page 62*

1 Choose the best alternatives in the following sentences.

1 This jacket was a .... bargain. It was reduced from £100 to £25.
   A big   **B** real   **C** important   **D** complete

2 I didn't have much cash so I decided to pay .... cheque.
   A in   **B** on   **C** with   **D** by

3 There was a really .... queue outside the cinema.
   A large   **B** long   **C** wide   **D** broad

4 I always wait to buy my clothes .... the sales.
   A on   **B** with   **C** to   **D** in

5 We try to budget .... all the unexpected expenses that can come up.
   A with   **B** for   **C** to   **D** on

6 I got a big discount .... this table because it had a scratch on it.
   A with   **B** for   **C** to   **D** on

7 I asked them but they wouldn't .... me a refund.
   A give   **B** do   **C** make   **D** have

8 This DVD player doesn't work. We'll have to .... it back to the shop.
   A return   **B** bring   **C** have   **D** take

9 Do you have these trousers .... grey?
   A in   **B** on   **C** for   **D** at

10 The men's clothes are .... the fourth floor.
   A in   **B** on   **C** for   **D** at

2 **Speaking:** long turn (Part 2)

Complete the comments a student made about these two photographs using the words in the box and other words.

borrow	fountains	magazines	library
shelves	librarian	slides	trolley	leisure

❝ Both these photographs show places where people go to spend their (1) .... time. The first one (2) .... to be a (3) .... There are people taking books down from the (4) .... and looking at them. Some of them are sitting down at tables reading the books, (5) .... and newspapers. It's not very (6) .... but I think I can see a (7) .... in the background sitting behind a desk. Perhaps people go up to him if they want to (8) .... a book. There is a (9) .... with lots of books on it. I suppose someone is going to put them back where they belong.

The other photograph is very different. It shows a big swimming pool complex with (10) .... and (11) .... I'm not (12) .... but it might be in Germany or somewhere like that because the name, Sommerland, looks quite German. ❞

Writing: letter of complaint (Part 1) ▶ CB page 64

About the exam: In Paper 2, Part 1, you sometimes have to write a letter of complaint. The notes will tell you what to complain about.

1 Look at this letter of complaint that a student wrote in answer to the task on page 64 of the Coursebook. The sentences are in the wrong order. Put them in the right order.

> **CLUE:** Use the underlined linking expressions to help you.

Dear Sir or Madam,

a) I would be grateful if you would remove the advertisement from the newspaper as soon as possible so that other readers are not misled.

b) _Finally,_ the advertisement stated clearly that all the CDs were up-to-date. The newest one, however, was already six months old.

c) I am writing to complain about a misleading advertisement which was published in your newspaper yesterday.

d) CDs Incorporated _also_ promised that there would be huge discounts on everything whereas in fact there was only a small discount on some products.

e) The advertisement, which was for CDs Incorporated, was misleading in several ways.

f) _To make matters worse,_ they said that they would open the doors at nine o'clock but we did not get there till ten and the doors were still closed.

g) _First of all,_ the advertisement claimed that prices would start at £2 but in fact nothing was less than £5.

Yours faithfully,
Alessandra Duranti

2 Group the sentences into paragraphs under these topics in your notebook.

Why you are writing
The problem
What you want the person to do

3 Now read this task. Use the notes and the points in the advertisement to complete the sentences below.

You recently bought a DVD player because of this advertisement you saw in the local newspaper. You are not at all satisfied with the machine and you have decided to write to the newspaper to complain. Look at the advertisement and the notes you made and write your letter.

DVD Depot

The widest selection of DVD players in town! — only three brands

Show DVDs bought anywhere in the world on our multi-system machines. — wouldn't show DVDs we bought in Australia

SPECIAL OFFER! Choose three free DVDs from our huge range of classics and recent hits to start your library. — had to take what they gave us

Your money back if you're not completely satisfied. — no refunds! – said we had to choose another machine

1 First of all, the advertisement said that .... but in fact ....
2 They also claimed that .... However, ...
3 To make matters worse, they offered .... but ....
4 Finally, in the advertisement they promised .... whereas they refused .... and told us ....

4 Write the first and final paragraphs of your letter in your notebook.

UNIT
6 It's your call

Vocabulary 1: technology
▶ *CB page 68*

1 Find words in this wordsearch grid to complete the sentences.

a	k	e	y	p	a	d	f
m	o	n	i	t	o	r	o
o	c	g	o	m	p	i	c
u	u	a	t	e	r	v	u
s	c	g	f	i	l	e	s
e	a	e	m	a	i	l	n
l	o	d	p	l	u	g	m

1 Tina must be downloading something from the Internet. Her phone has been .... for hours.

2 To move the cursor on a laptop you generally use a small pad or button instead of a ....

3 I'd really like a new flat screen .... for my computer.

4 The .... on my mobile phone is so tiny I can hardly see the numbers.

5 When we uploaded the photos we took at the party, unfortunately they were all out of ....

6 I had to buy a special .... so that I could recharge my mobile phone in the UK.

7 I generally save important .... onto a CD just in case something goes wrong with the hard .... of my computer.

8 Do you check your .... from an Internet café when you're on holiday?

2 Complete this text using the words from the box.

recharge   check   downloads   hard
saves   screen   CD   laptop   flat

My friend Sam loves technology. He always has the latest mobile phones and then he (1) .... ringtones from the Internet so that he knows who's calling him without even looking at the little (2) .... He's got a (3) .... computer and a special card so that he can (4) .... his email in airports or when he's on the train. He's got special plugs and adaptors for every country on Earth so that he can (5) .... the computer's battery wherever he goes.

At home, he's got another really fast computer with one of those (6) .... screens. He bought a digital camera recently and spends a lot of time uploading photos to his (7) .... drive and then editing them. He downloads a lot of music too and (8) .... the files onto (9) .... so that he can listen to them on his portable disk player. I sometimes wonder if Sam would be able to survive at all if there was a power failure and no batteries!

3 Use of English: word formation (Part 3)

Read the text below. Use the word given in capitals below the text to form a word that fits in each gap. There is an example at the beginning (0).

CLUE: Three words need a negative prefix. Choose from: *de-, dis-, im-, mis-, un-*.

A TECHNOLOGICAL NIGHTMARE

I had a really **(0)** *dreadful*.... weekend last month. In forty-eight hours almost every **(1)** .... appliance in the house broke down. The computer was first. A message appeared saying 'Disk **(2)** ....' and I just had to switch it off and call the **(3)** .... for help. Next was the washing machine. I heard a terrible noise like an **(4)** .... and when I went to check, the laundry was full of smoke. I managed to **(5)** .... the machine just before it caught fire. **(6)** .... as it may seem, the fridge stopped working the same day. It started to **(7)** .... itself for no reason and there was water all over the kitchen floor. By then I was a **(8)** .... wreck, so I decided to lie down for a while. I was just falling **(9)** .... when my electric toothbrush started buzzing **(10)** .... Somehow it had switched itself on!

0 DREAD
1 ELECTRIC
2 FAIL
3 TECHNICAL
4 EXPLODE
5 PLUG
6 BELIEVE
7 FROST
8 NERVE
9 SLEEP
10 LOUD

Listening: multiple matching (Part 3)

Strategy
Look at the statements before you listen and decide if they are positive or negative.

1 You will hear five people talking about how computers have affected our lives. Look at these opinions and decide if they are positive (P) or negative (N)

A They have made it possible to get information immediately. ....
B They have reduced the amount of leisure time people have. ....
C They have provided lots of new kinds of entertainment. ....
D They have made it too easy to spend money. ....
E They have reduced the amount of privacy people have. ....
F They have only affected the lives of some people. ....

2 Now listen to the recording and choose from the options A to F the opinion each speaker expresses. Use the letters only once. There is an extra letter which you do not need to use.

Speaker 1   [| 1]
Speaker 2   [| 2]
Speaker 3   [| 3]
Speaker 4   [| 4]
Speaker 5   [| 5]

Grammar 1: certainty and possibility ▶ *CB page 70*

1 Rewrite these sentences using one of the modal verbs in brackets.

1 It's possible that you will find some information about him on the internet. (*can / might*)

....

2 I am certain it's not illegal to download music. (*can't / mustn't*)

....

3 I am sure he has a webpage. (*could / must*)

....

4 It's quite likely that she will buy a new laptop this week. (*may / can*)

....

5 It's possible that she has her mobile phone switched off. (*must / could*).

....

2 Underline the correct alternatives in the following sentences

A: Is Eva coming to the beach?

B: She wasn't sure. She said she (1) *might / could* have to look after her little brother.

A: Have you heard the weather forecast?

B: Yes, they said it was going to be cold and cloudy and that it (2) *might / must* even rain later.

A: Does Renata speak Italian?

B: She (3) *could / must* speak it. She lived in Rome for fourteen years, after all.

A: Look at this old photograph. There's Dad and that (4) *must / could* be Uncle Richard standing next to him.

B: It (5) *can't / mustn't* be! He's always been much darker than that.

A: Where's Galeana?

B: I'm not sure. She (6) *might / must* be playing tennis. She sometimes does on Saturday afternoons.

A: I stayed up all night working on my assignment.

B: Really? You (7) *must / could* be exhausted. Did you finish it?

A: No, but I (8) *might / can* by this afternoon.

3 **Speaking:** long turn (Part 2)

Strategy

If you are not sure about what is happening in the photographs, you can use modal verbs and other expressions to express uncertainty.

1 Complete the comments below a student made about these photographs.

❝ I don't really know what the connection is between these two photographs but it (1) .... be modern technology or perhaps communication. In the first photograph, the man (2) .... to be talking to himself but I suppose he (3) .... have one of those mobile phones with headphones you plug into the handset. Of course, he (4) .... be singing, though it seems unlikely because he looks a bit angry. He (5) .... be having an argument with the person he's talking to. He's quite well dressed. He (6) .... be a lawyer or perhaps an advertising executive.

The other photograph shows a group of young people in a cyber café. They (7) .... be sending email messages or playing computer games, but I can't see the screens very clearly so I'm not too (8) .... Whatever they're doing, they (9) .... be enjoying it because they're all smiling and laughing. I don't think the photograph was taken in Europe. It (10) .... be somewhere like Thailand or perhaps India. I like playing computer games and sending emails too but I don't usually go to cyber cafés. ❞

 2 Now listen to the recording and check your answers.

Reading: gapped text (Part 2)

1 You are going to read a text about a woman who spent a day with her mobile phone switched off as part of an experiment. Read the text and the sentences that have been removed from the text. Decide which of these titles is the most suitable.

a) My name's Sandra and I'm a mobile phone addict
b) A very difficult 24 hours
c) Yes, I could live without a mobile

2 Read the text and the sentences again. Seven sentences have been removed from the text. Choose from sentences A–H the one which best fits each gap (1–7). There is one extra sentence which you do not need to use.

> **CLUE:** Pay special attention to the underlined words and phrases in the sentences and text.

A Everyone who really needed to managed to get hold of me.

B My phone isn't there, of course.

C My husband agrees with me.

D There are no interruptions and no one demanding long conversations.

E Instead, I record a message explaining that I'm going to be without my phone for two days.

F My brother calls to remind me it's my mother's birthday next week.

G I explain that I'm taking part in an experiment to spend twenty-four hours with my mobile switched off.

H Without mine, I feel liberated and even a bit pleased with myself.

Journalist Sandra Mills took part in an experiment to see if she could get through twenty-four hours without her mobile phone. Here's what happened.

Day 1 Hour 1. My mobile is lying on the bedside table. It's still switched on. The screensaver of my baby son seems to be staring at me in reproach[1]. I'm supposed to have switched it off by now. I will. Just give me a minute.

At 8.30, the phone rings. I don't answer because I'm convinced that it's someone ringing to check up on[2] me. **(1)** .... I give my office and home numbers as alternatives. It's not exactly cheating, but I suppose it is bending the rules slightly. Then I switch it off.

Leaving the phone at home is the first hurdle[3]. What if the train crashes and I need to call my loved ones to say a last goodbye? What if, like the man who got lost in the mountains, I fall down a ravine and the only way out is an SOS message? 'You're being ridiculous!' I tell myself. **(2)** .... I take his advice, leave the phone on the table by the front door and step into the world without it.

When I get to work, the phone on my desk rings. A friend is worried about me and wants to know if everything is alright. **(3)** .... She thinks this sounds terrible. Her mobile isn't working properly, but she's so addicted she can't even get it fixed. Every time she takes it to be repaired, the people in the shop say it's going to take three hours. She can't bear to be without it for that long. I understand how she feels.

At about 11.30, a very strange thing happens. I hear my phone ring. It's definitely mine because I'm the only one in the office with a salsa ring tone. I check my bag. **(4)**.......... . I left it at home. Remember? I hear it ring again and then I realise that it's just my imagination. My phone is haunting[4] me. It's like being in a horror movie.

At lunchtime, I meet up with some friends and they all sit down and put their phones on the table so that they can be sure not so miss a single call or message. It's as if they were physically tied to their phones. **(5)**.......... . It's a bit like when you've given up smoking and you see other people lighting cigarettes. I still keep hearing my phone ringing, but I'm getting used to being without it. It's making me feel quite adventurous[5]. I decide to walk back to the office instead of catching the bus. For a whole ten minutes, no one can contact me.

By the end of the afternoon, I've completely forgotten about my phone. I catch the train home and actually enjoy the journey. I spend Friday evening peacefully with my husband and children. **(6)**.......... . I never thought I'd say it, but it's bliss[6].

The next day, it takes me until lunch to remember to switch the thing back on. There are twelve voicemail messages and a few texts. There's nothing very important though. **(7)**.......... . The others can wait for me to call them back, when it's convenient for me!

3 Look at the numbered words and phrases in the text. Use forms of these words and phrases to complete the following sentences.

1 Exams are a big .... that we all have to face.
2 The memory of her beautiful face seemed to .... him wherever he went.
3 The librarian often walks around to .... just in case we're not actually studying.
4 Lying on a sandy beach under a palm tree is my idea of complete ....
5 I'm quite an .... person. I like travelling on my own and high-risk sports.
6 I won't .... you if you have to leave early. I know you've got a train to catch.

Grammar 2: passives (1)
▶ *CB page 74*

1 There are mistakes with passive forms in some of these sentences. Find the mistakes and correct them.

0 ~~Has~~ *Is* Spanish spoken by more people than Chinese?
1 He was rescue after a terrifying night on the mountain without food or water.
2 It seems ridiculous to me that most computers need to been replaced every three or four years.
3 The message with the virus was forwarded automatically to everyone in her address book.
4 This song was wrote by Norah Jones but many people have recorded it.
5 Are you been met at the airport or will you have to get a taxi?

2 Complete the texts on this page and on page 52 with passive forms of the verbs in brackets.

POLITE NOTICE
This is a garage.
Cars parked here
(1) .... away. (*tow*)

RULES

Smoking
(2) ....
anywhere in the building. (*not permit*)

Food and drink may
(3) .... in the library or computer room. (*not consume*)

ANNOUNCEMENT
Mobile phones may interfere with the aircraft. They must (4) .... before take off. (*switch off*)

Luxury Limos
You (5) .... by our uniformed chauffeur and driven in style to your wedding, birthday party or other celebration. (*pick up*)
Full service only £50 in the London metropolitan area.

APOLOGY
Our overnight loan service (7) .... until further notice. (*suspend*)

CAN YOU HELP?
My bicycle (8) .... from outside Renee's Café last Tuesday afternoon. (*steal*)
Reward offered for information.
I can (9) .... on 0610859412. (*contact*)

WARNING
A £50 fee (6) .... on all flight cancellations. (*charge*)

SORRY FOR THE INCONVENIENCE!
Our reception area (10) ....
Please use the rear entrance. (*repaint*)

3 **Use of English:** open cloze (Part 2)

Read the text below and think of the word which best fits each gap. Use only one word in each gap. There is an example at the beginning (0).

A VERY OVERDUE BOOK

I **(0)** ...*was*... left a little money and a collection of old books by my Uncle Albert when he passed away last year. When the books **(1)** .... delivered, I went through them to try to decide which ones to keep and which ones should **(2)** .... given away or sold. Some of them looked almost brand new, **(3)** .... made me wonder if they had ever been read.

Then I came across a book on Greek mythology which had **(4)** .... published in 1922. It looked **(5)** .... a very rare and valuable book, but the problem was that it didn't seem to **(6)** .... belonged to Uncle Albert at all! It had been borrowed from London University Library. The book had been stamped with the name of the university but the piece of paper with the date of the loan **(7)** .... been torn out, possibly **(8)** .... Uncle Albert himself.

A few months later, I went to London and I decided that the book really should **(9)** .... returned to its owner. I went to the library and gave it to one of the librarians, who looked very worried. Uncle Albert had borrowed the book in 1923 and according to their records they **(10)** .... owed over £4000 as a fine! That was the same amount as my uncle **(11)** .... left me! Fortunately, the librarian said that the huge fine would **(12)** .... cancelled now that I had returned the book. I felt so relieved!

Vocabulary 2: communicating with others ▶ CB page 76

1 Match the sentence halves.

1 She was very unpopular at school because she told
2 The boss said she wanted to have
3 Although I live so far away we keep
4 She's never had a good word
5 Alberto only speaks
6 A lot of rumours are spread
7 I know you really like John but I can't
8 I can't hear a word

☐ a) to say for her son-in-law.
☐ b) his mind when it is really necessary.
☐ c) tales on her classmates.
☐ d) a word with me after work.
☐ e) say that I do.
☐ f) in touch by email.
☐ g) you're saying. Can you speak up a bit?
☐ h) by word of mouth.

2 Underline the correct alternative to complete these sentences.

1 I don't *tell / say* lies if I can help it, but sometimes it's actually better not to *speak / tell* the truth.
2 I wish Carlos wouldn't *speak / talk* shop every time we go out with his friends from the office.
3 *Speak / Talk* up! We can't hear you at the back of the room.
4 I first met Gianni *for / through* a friend of mine in Rome.
5 She *said / told* us a really funny joke about an English class.
6 She doesn't *talk / speak* a word of Spanish though she's lived in Spain for years.
7 Everyone *said / told* they enjoyed my presentation.
8 Don't *say / speak* a word to Simon about the party. It's supposed to be a surprise.

Go to www.iTests.com for interactive exam practice.

Writing: report (Part 2)
▶ *CB page 78*

About the exam: In Paper 2, Part 2, you may be asked to write a report in which you make recommendations about what to do.

Strategy
1 Make sure you use an appropriate formal style.
2 Use headings to organise the information clearly.

1 On the right is a report a student wrote in answer to the task on page 78 of the Coursebook. The language of the report is too informal. The student's teacher has <u>underlined</u> the parts of the report that should be changed. Use the words and phrases below to make the necessary changes and write the corrected report in your notebook.

a) urgently
b) several students and their parents
c) It might be necessary
d) be irritating
e) if a student has transport problems
f) be extremely useful at times
g) Students' parents
h) can become anxious
i) A relative
j) contact them
k) some other emergency may have occurred
l) their son or daughter is late home
m) we do not believe they should be banned
n) I interviewed
o) Nevertheless,

IN DEFENCE OF MOBILE PHONES

Introduction

This report explains why mobile phones are important for students, and makes recommendations for their use in the school. **¹**<u>I had a word with</u> **²**<u>a few students and a couple of parents too.</u>

Why mobile phones are necessary

1 **³**<u>You might need</u> to phone home **⁴**<u>if you miss the bus or something</u>. Some parents **⁵**<u>can get really worried if</u> **⁶**<u>you're not home on time</u>.

2 **⁷**<u>Your parents</u> might need to **⁸**<u>get in touch with you</u> **⁹** <u>in a hurry</u>. **¹⁰**<u>Your uncle or someone like that</u> might have been taken to hospital or **¹¹**<u>something else might have happened</u>.

Recommendations

Everyone agrees that mobile phones can **¹²**<u>get on your nerves</u> but they can **¹³**<u>come in handy sometimes</u>. We recommend that students should check that phones are switched off before classes start. **¹⁴**<u>Still</u>, **¹⁵**<u>we think you should let us bring them to school.</u>

---

2 Now look at this task and the points a student has written down. Group the points into appropriate sections and write your report.

You are a student at a language school. Teachers have complained that some students are spending too much time using the computers with Internet connections to visit chat rooms and send email messages to friends. They say this is not a proper use of the school's equipment and want the Director to ban anyone who does this from using the room.

Write a report for the director of your school explaining why Internet access is important and should be available to everyone. Make recommendations about ways in which the situation can be controlled.

Write your report in **120–180** words.

- some students chat in English and find this helpful
- report explains why access should not be restricted and also suggests how teachers can help
- teachers should check that students are using English
- students should be able to use the computers at lunchtimes and after school.
- interviewed students who use the room
- students need to be able to send emails to family and friends at home

Vocabulary 1: general nouns
▶ *CB page 81*

1 Complete these texts with words from the box.

luxuries	vehicles	advantages	toiletries
facilities	goods	qualifications	utensils
containers	skills	transport	clothing
appliances	equipment		

Bay View Villas

All the (1) .... of country living, right in the centre of the city. One and two-bedroom apartments with modern (2) .... and easy access to public (3) .... Inspections by appointment.

BRIGHT IDEAS FROM *NEDEA*

Store all your kitchen (4) .... in our handy (5) .... or hang them on hooks for easy access.

CLERICAL ASSISTANT

Excellent position for someone with the right (6) .... and experience. Good keyboard and telephone (7) .... essential. Contact Dennis Acton on 0208 92289938

SUMMER SALE

Big discounts on camping (8) .... and outdoor (9) ....

Come in and see our extensive range.

WARNING
(10) .... left parked in this area will be towed away.

Valentine's Day ❤ Gifts ❤

(11) .... for the one you love on the lovers' special day. Handmade Belgian chocolates, designer silk scarves, imported perfumes and (12) .... Free with every order a dozen of the reddest of red roses sent to your loved one on 14th February.

ANNOUNCEMENT
As of 17th November, a value added tax of 15% is to be paid on all consumer (13) .... and electrical (14) ....

2 **Use of English:** word formation (Part 3)

Read the text below. Use the word given in capitals below the text to form a word that fits in each gap. There is an example at the beginning (0).

MY CAREER

All my family are professional (0) *musicians* , but I was different. I wanted to change the world by becoming a (1) .... or an (2) .... I persuaded my parents to buy me some laboratory (3) .... so that I could do some experiments at home. This was not such a good idea! (4) .... I wasn't very good at science, and not at all (5) .... when it came to doing experiments. I remember when I made a (6) .... attempt to create a new perfume for my friend. The (7) .... of ingredients I used must have been wrong, because there was a small (8) .... , followed by a lot of smoke and a horrible smell. After that I decided to study properly to get the right (9) .... to become a chemist. I had a big (10) .... about it with my family who still wanted me to study music – but I won in the end.

0 MUSIC	**3 EQUIP**	**6 DISASTER**	**9 QUALIFY**
1 SCIENCE	**4 FORTUNE**	**7 MIX**	**10 ARGUE**
2 INVENT	**5 SKILL**	**8 EXPLODE**	

Grammar 1: relative clauses
► CB page 82

1 Use the relative pronouns from the box to match the sentence halves and make full sentences. Use each relative pronoun once.

which	whom	where	whose
when	who	~~that~~	

0 The electric light bulb is one of the inventions *that has had a particularly important impact on human existence.*

1 Thomas Edison, ...
....

2 This was a period ....
....

3 One nineteenth century inventor ....
....

4 He lived in Ohio ....
....

5 The person to ....
....

6 The company he founded, ...
....

☐ a) many inventors were extremely active.

☐ b) invented the electric light bulb, lived from 1847 to 1931.

☐ c) inventions are less well known than Edison's is Granville Woods.

☑ d) has had a particularly important impact on human existence.

☐ e) is called Alcoa, is still in business today.

☐ f) Charles Hall sold the patent for aluminium made a fortune from it.

☐ g) Thomas Edison and Charles Hall, the inventor of aluminium, were also born.

2 Some of the sentences in the text on the right need commas. Add them where necessary. Tick (✓) the sentences that do not need commas.

(0) Granville Woods, who was an African American, is not as well known as some other inventors. (1) He invented a telegraph that could transmit messages to and from a moving train. (2) This prevented many train accidents in which many people might have been killed or injured.

(3) Two other famous inventors who lived in Ohio were Orville and Wilbur Wright. (4) They built the first plane which is another invention that has had a huge impact on our lives. (5) If it was not possible to travel by plane it would take me six weeks to get to Australia where my family live. (6) In the late eighteenth century when the first European settlers went to Australia it took even longer than that. (7) Before cheap air travel it must have been terribly sad for people whose relatives went to live in other countries. (8) They must have wondered if there would ever come a time when they would see them again. (9) My mother to whom I wrote almost every week must have felt a bit like that about me.

3 **Use of English: open cloze (Part 2)**

Read the title and the following text, and think of the word which best fits each gap. Use only one word for each gap. There is an example at the beginning (0).

LETTERS FROM HOME

I lived in a very mysterious house at **(0)** *one* stage when I was a student. It was an old house that had **(1)**.......... empty for a couple of months before my college friends and I moved in. The strange thing **(2)**.......... that the people who had lived there before us had left a lot of their belongings behind. There was some old furniture that they must **(3)**.......... decided they didn't want, some old books and even a **(4)**.......... tins of food in the kitchen. But **(5)**.......... strangest thing was a wooden box that I found hidden under the bed in **(6)**.......... of the rooms. It was full of old letters, all of **(7)**.......... had been written by the same woman to her son. He **(8)**.......... apparently been living in New York when he received them, but he had obviously kept them for several years and brought them back to London with **(9)**.......... to this house. The letters were all in neat bundles according **(10)**.......... the date they had been posted. They told a fascinating story and by the time it got dark I had a really clear picture in my mind of the woman **(11)**.......... had written them. What I couldn't understand was how her son could have kept them for **(12)**.......... many years and then just abandoned them like that.

Reading: multiple matching (Part 3)

1 You are going to read four paragraphs about people who made predictions. Read the paragraphs quickly and tick the events that are mentioned.

1 The events of September 11, 2001
2 The invention of the mobile phone
3 The tsunami in December 2005
4 The Moon landing
5 The assassination of John F. Kennedy
6 The economic crisis of 1929
7 The invention of the submarine
8 World War I and II

PREDICTING THE FUTURE?

A Arthur C. Clarke

Arthur C. Clarke began writing science fiction in the 1930s. Many ideas and elements from his stories, which are set on space stations and distant planets, have become reality here on Earth. For example, in a novel he wrote in 1951, Clarke predicted the 1969 Moon landing, though he suggested that this would probably not occur until 1978. Sometimes his abilities to see into the future are uncannily[1] accurate. The orbit for communications satellites is named after him because in 1945 he suggested precisely where it should be located. Nevertheless, Clarke does not believe that he – or anybody else for that matter – can see into the future. Instead, he says, he simply tries 'to outline[2] possible "futures" while pointing out that totally unexpected inventions or events can make any forecasts absurd after a very few years.' In 1999, he did make a list of some of the events that he thought might happen during the 21st century. Most of these were positive developments because he believes that it is always better to be optimistic about the future.

B Jules Verne

Before he died in 1905, Jules Verne wrote almost sixty novels in which he described a world very like the one we live in today. He predicted inventions such as planes, movies, guided missiles, submarines, air conditioning and the fax machine. Between 1865 and 1870, Verne wrote two novels about space exploration in which an aluminium craft launched from central Florida achieves a speed of 24,500 miles per hour, circles the Moon and splashes down in the Pacific. A century later Apollo 8, made of aluminium and travelling at 24,500 miles per hour, did just that. Of course, not all of what Verne predicted has actually become a reality. For example, in *Propeller Island* he wrote about a 10-square-mile island that could be moved from one part of the world to another. He was right about the submarine, though, to the astonishment of his contemporaries[3]. He dismissed their claims that he could see into the future saying that nothing he wrote about was "beyond the bounds of actual scientific knowledge".

C Michel de Nostredame (Nostradamus)

Nostradamus has been given credit for prophesying dozens of important historical episodes, most recently the destruction of the World Trade Centre towers in September 2001. Born in 1503 into a wealthy family, he left home in 1522 to study medicine. He then worked as a physician and invented some effective medicines for the treatment of the bubonic plague. Perhaps as a result of the tragic loss of his wife and children to the plague in 1538, he spent the rest of his life formulating prophecies. Nostradamus claimed an angelic spirit helped him understand the relationship between the movements of the stars and planets and what occurred on Earth. Over the years, Nostradamus followers[4] have noted hundreds of instances where his book, *The Centuries*, apparently describes modern events. Critics say that the way Nostradamus wrote is very vague and imprecise and that his prophecies are of deaths, wars and natural disasters, which, unfortunately, occur again and again throughout history. This makes it easy for people to find what seem like connections between his writings and actual events.

D Edgar Cayce

Edgar Cayce made his name in the first half of the last century as a psychic healer and clairvoyant. According to his followers, he predicted the two world wars and the stock market crash of 1929. More disturbing still were prophecies of geological upheavals[5] that would lead to the destruction of whole areas of the United States' coastline sometime before 1998. Cayce was from a humble[6] background and left school when he was still very young. He claimed that his ability to heal and see into the future came to him via a vision of a winged figure clothed in white. Many people believe Cayce's explanation for his abilities because they consider that such a simple person could not have known many of the things he mentioned in his diagnoses and predictions. Nevertheless, as critics point out, he worked in a bookshop for several years and was a voracious[7] reader. He would inevitably have acquired a good knowledge of a range of subjects during that time.

2   Read the texts again and for the questions below choose from the people (A–D). The people may be chosen more than once.

Which person:

had formally studied a science?	**1** ☐
surprised other people by predicting an invention?	**2** ☐
made use of astrology in his predictions?	**3** ☐
said that it is impossible to make accurate predictions?	**4** ☐
only used scientific facts to make predictions?	**5** ☐
gave his name to a scientific development?	**6** ☐
had a job that helped him learn what he needed to know?	**7** ☐
predicted good things that might happen?	**8** ☐
used language that is easily misinterpreted?	**9** ☐
was exactly right about an important scientific event?	**10** ☐
only predicted bad things?	**11** ☐
wrote only one book?	**12** ☐
had very little formal education?	**13** ☐
was accurate about an event but wrong about the date?	**14** ☐
predicted a terrible event that has not occurred?	**15** ☐

3   Look at the numbered words and phrases in the paragraphs. Which of these definitions best fits each one?

1 **A** strangely
  B not completely
2 **A** give general information without going into detail
  B make absolutely clear
3 **A** members of his family
  B people living at the same time
4 **A** people who were born later
  B people who admire him
5 **A** great changes and movements
  B improvements
6 **A** not rich or of high status
  B famous
7 **A** inefficient
  B very keen

Grammar 2: conditionals (1)
▶ *CB page 86*

1   Match the sentence halves. Four of the B sentence halves are not needed.

A
1 If I spend too long in the sun,
2 If I fail my exams,
3 If I learnt another foreign language,
4 If I had been born a hundred years ago,

B
☐ a) I would get married very young.
☐ b) I go very red.
☐ c) it would probably be Japanese.
☐ d) I would feel sick and dizzy.
☐ e) my parents would be very disappointed.
☐ f) I will get a job much more easily.
☐ g) I'll feel really terrible.
☐ h) I would probably not have been able to go to university.

2   Complete the following sentences using the verbs from the box.

have	invite	learn	buy	promise	pass	
know	live	be	watch			

1 You .... the exam easily if you study hard enough.
2 If I .... how much fun it is learning to drive, I would have started years ago.
3 If you .... one of those new home cinema centres from CineCity, you get three DVDs free.
4 If I lived in such a huge house, I .... my friends to come and stay.
5 If we .... some eggs, we could make a chocolate cake.
6 If I had lived in the nineteenth century, I probably .... an inventor.
7 You can borrow my laptop, if you .... to take good care of it.
8 If I had known it was going to be on TV, I .... *Back to the Future* last night.
9 .... without modern facilities like central heating and hot water if you had to?
10 The world would be a better place if people .... to be less selfish.

3 **Use of English:** key word transformations (Part 4)

Complete the second sentence so that it has a similar meaning to the first sentence, using the word given. Do not change the word given. You must use between two and five words, including the word given. There is an example at the beginning (0).

0 Without the right equipment, I'm sure I can't do the job.
unless
I'm sure I can't do the job ...*unless I have*...... the right equipment.

1 In the event of fire, do not use the lift.
there
Do not use the lift .... a fire.

2 With more time, I would have been able to finish the assignment.
had
I would have been able to finish the assignment .... more time.

3 If we don't buy a sofa-bed, there won't be anywhere for Johanna to sleep.
unless
There won't be anywhere for Johanna to sleep .... a sofa-bed.

4 I live in London because it is one of the most exciting cities in the world.
was
I wouldn't live in London .... one of the most exciting cities in the world.

4 **Speaking:** discussion (Part 4)

1 Here is what two students said in answer to a discussion question. Complete their answers.

Examiner: How are our lives different from those of our ancestors who lived a hundred years ago?

Fatima: I think women's lives were much harder. For example, if I (1) .... born then, I'm sure I (2) .... been able to study medicine.

Stanislao: If you (3) .... living in my country you could have. The thing that I think has changed most is that we write and read more than our great-grandparents did.

Fatima: But if we (4) .... more than our great-grandparents did, then why does everyone criticise young people for being illiterate?

Stanislao: Unless you (5) .... someone around making a note of everything they read and wrote, you probably wouldn't realise.

Fatima: But what about things like healthcare? If penicillin (6) .... discovered, a lot of us probably (7) .... alive today. Now I think that's a really big difference!

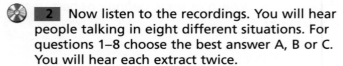 **2** **Listen to the recording to check your answers.**

Listening: extracts (Part 1)

About the exam: In Paper 4, Part 1, you hear eight unrelated extracts and answer one question about each one. You can be asked:
• what the people are talking about
• how they feel
• where they are
• who they are talking to.

1 Look at the questions in Exercise 2 and decide if you are being asked

a) what the people are talking about
b) how they feel
c) where they are
d) who they are talking to.

Label the questions a, b, c or d.

2 Now listen to the recordings. You will hear people talking in eight different situations. For questions 1–8 choose the best answer A, B or C. You will hear each extract twice.

1 You hear part of an interview on the radio
Who is being interviewed?   ...*d*...
A an inventor
B a journalist
C a businesswoman

2 A man speaks to you in the street.
What does he want you to do?   ......
A give him directions
B answer some questions
C donate some money

3 At the bus stop you hear this couple talking.
How is the woman feeling?   ......
A amused
B irritated
C worried

4 You are listening to a radio phone-in.
Why has Susan phoned?   ......
A to ask for advice
B to complain about something
C to suggest something

5 You hear this advertisement on the radio.
What is being emphasised about
the product?   ......
A It is good value.
B It is high quality.
C It is unusual.

6 A woman is talking on her mobile phone.
Where is she phoning?   ......
A a gym
B a college
C a hotel

7 While visiting a national park you hear this
ranger talking.
What features of the park is she
talking about?   ......
A dangers
B history
C research

8 A young man is talking on the phone to a
gallery owner.
What does the man want to do? ......
A buy a painting
B arrange an exhibition
C visit the gallery

Vocabulary 2: collocations
▶ CB page 88

1 There are mistakes with collocations in
some of these sentences. Find the mistakes
and correct them.
0 We're ~~making~~ *doing* some research into what
language the original inhabitants spoke.
1 I don't like it when people make fun of me.
2 He did a big effort and finished in third place.
3 Making housework is incredibly boring.
4 What kind of work does your cousin Pedro
make?
5 The service was so bad we decided to make a
formal complaint.

6 I made my best but I couldn't finish the assignment in
time.
7 It's a pleasure to make business with you.

2 Use of English: multiple-choice cloze (Part 1)

Read the text below and decide which answer (A, B, C
or D) best fits each gap. There is an example at the
beginning (0).

No one can be certain who really (0) *discovered* silk but
according to (1) .... it was a Chinese princess. One day,
this princess watched (2) .... amazement as the
caterpillars on her father's mulberry tree created beautiful silk
thread. Before long, she realised that this thread could be
used to (3) .... cloth. Then, in about 1725 BC, the
Chinese emperor's wife began to (4) .... the cultivation
of silk worms and the manufacture of the cloth. The process
was kept secret, and the Chinese guarded the secret
(5) .... for over 3000 years. They exported the cloth to
many countries and (6) .... the envy of their trading
rivals.

But then the secret got (7) .... Another Chinese
princess married an Indian prince who (8) .... her to tell
him where the silk which her clothes were made from was
produced, and how. He then got some silk worms and the
Indian silk industry was born. At around about the same
(9) .... , two monks (10) .... seeds of the mulberry
tree and silkworm eggs out of China by hiding them in their
(11) .... sticks. They took the secret to Japan, where the
Japanese silk industry boomed – and Japan is still the main
producer and manufacturer of silk today.

Why is silk so popular? It keeps people warm in winter while
keeping them (12) .... in summer. It is hard-wearing and
soft against the skin. Although modern artificial materials are
now available, silk remains the most luxurious of all.

0	A investigated	B invented	C discovered	D founded
1	A fable	B legend	C story	D tale
2	A for	B on	C at	D in
3	A grow	B make	C develop	D do
4	A advertise	B sponsor	C publish	D announce
5	A deeply	B enormously	C carefully	D tightly
6	A attracted	B caused	C led to	D created
7	A away	B through	C out	D over
8	A made	B had	C persuaded	D suggested
9	A time	B period	C age	D moment
10	A exported	B stole	C smuggled	D robbed
11	A walking	B wandering	C climbing	D hiking
12	A chilled	B fresh	C cool	D cold

Writing: essay (Part 2)
▶ *CB page 90*

About the exam: One of the options in Paper 2, Part 2, is an essay in which you present two sides of an argument and say which one you agree with.

Strategy
Organise your ideas into four paragraphs:
Introduction: state the topic
Paragraph 2:   points against the topic
Paragraph 3:   points in favour of the topic
Conclusion: give your own opinion

1 Look at this task and say whether the statements below it are true (T) or false (F).

> Your class has been discussing the value of conserving old parts of your city. Your teacher has now asked you to write a composition giving your opinion of the following statement.
>
> *Too much money is being spent on preserving the old part of town.*
>
> Write your essay in **120–180** words.

1 Your class think preserving the old part of the city is a good idea. ☐
2 You should tell your teacher what you think about this issue. ☐
3 You know what your teacher thinks about this issue. ☐

2 Now look at some points a student has noted down to include in the essay. Decide which points are in favour of conservation (+), which points are against (–); which points would come in the introduction (I) and which points would come in the conclusion (C).

might attract tourists .....
several points of view on the issue .....
very expensive and will cost more than they say .....
old people like going there .....
in favour of conservation because I want my grandchildren to see it .....
young people prefer modern shopping centres .....
young people can learn about their past .....
some of the buildings are dangerous .....

3 Complete this student's essay using the ideas from Exercise 2.

Is investment in preserving the old part of our town money well spent?
(1) ....

Some people claim that the project has already cost a lot of money, and that even more money will have to be spent.
(2) ....
(3) ....

However, other people believe that the town centre is well worth preserving.
(4) ....
(5) ....
(6) ....

To sum up, it seems to me that there are a number of good reasons for going ahead with the conservation project.
(7) ....

8 We are family

Vocabulary 1: adjective suffixes
▶ *CB page 96*

1 Make adjectives from the words in the box to complete these sentences.

create	fury	culture	love	wealth
coward	fun	wash		

1 Are those trousers .... or do you have them dry cleaned?
2 He comes from quite a .... family so he doesn't have to worry about money.
3 I'm sorry, but I don't find that kind of joke .... at all.
4 I thought it was really .... of him to blame the others for what had happened. He was afraid of being punished!
5 Puppies are very .... but they are also a lot of work to look after.
6 People say museums are a good way of preserving our .... heritage.
7 My boss was absolutely .... when I got to work late and missed an important meeting.
8 Sonia is so .... She paints, designs her own clothes and makes wonderful jewellery.

2 <u>Underline</u> the correct alternatives in the following sentences.

1 Everyone agrees that smoking is *harmful / harmless*.
2 She's got a *lovely / lovable* new apartment overlooking the park.
3 Jorge is so *dependable / independent*. He never lets you down.
4 I'm absolutely *hopeful / hopeless* at telling jokes.
5 Alex was a bit *supportive / unsupportive* when I told him I had broken up with Tony.
6 Chicago was *infamous / famous* in the 1920s for its gangsters and organised crime.
7 If you led a more *active / inactive* life, you would probably feel a lot better.

3 **Use of English:** word formation (Part 3)

Read the text below. Use the word given in capitals below the text to form a word that fits in each gap. There is an example at the beginning (0).

TRIPLETS

Unlike most of my friends I grew up in a big, **(0)** *noisy* ...., happy family so **(1)** .... , when I got married, I wanted to have lots of children. The trouble was that my husband and I were not very **(2)** .... In fact we were quite poor so it came as an **(3)** .... shock when I had triplets. Everyone in the family was very **(4)** .... of course and the babies were absolutely **(5)** .... , but it was not easy. Small children are extremely **(6)** .... and three little girls running around the house made me feel **(7)** .... because I was afraid they might hurt themselves. There were **(8)** .... moments of course and we were both extremely **(9)** .... that our children were happy, **(10)** .... , and such good friends for one another. In the end, the money was not important!

---

0 NOISE
1 NATURE
2 WEALTH
3 AWE
4 SUPPORT
5 ADORE
6 ACT
7 NERVE
8 FUN
9 THANK
10 HEALTH

Reading: multiple-choice (Part 1)

About the exam: In Paper 1, Part 1, there is sometimes a question which asks what pronouns (e.g. *it, they*) in the text refer to.

1 Read the article on the right once quickly and choose the best title from the list below.

a) Uncovering family secrets: do you dare?

b) The science of genealogy: new developments

c) A step-by-step guide to researching your family tree

2 Read the article again and answer the multiple-choice questions.

1 What is Maria McLeod's first piece of advice to people researching their family tree?

A 'Don't expect to find out that you are a member of a royal family.'

B 'Be prepared to find out disturbing things about yourself.'

C 'Don't expect to like your relatives in other parts of the world.'

D 'You may find you have serious health problems you didn't know about.'

2 According to Maria McLeod, which of the following is not a valid reason for researching your family tree?

A You think you may have a hereditary illness.

B You want to know if any of your ancestors looked like you.

C You suspect you may have royal relatives.

D You think you may have a similar character to your ancestors.

3 Why might some relatives be reluctant to meet you?

A You bring back bad memories for them.

B You remind them of their younger relatives.

C They think they might have to tell you family secrets.

D They suspect you of having wrong motives.

Genealogy, or researching your family tree, is a hobby that can rapidly develop into an obsession. Before you start looking for your own ancestors, read this advice from genealogist Maria McLeod.

1 The first question to ask yourself is why you want to research your family tree. Genealogy is not about discovering that you are the heir to the throne of an unknown country. It's about finding out more about yourself. For most people the important question is 'why am I like I am?'. You might not look like other members of your immediate family and you want to know where your green eyes or curly hair come from. You may be curious about why you have such a quick temper or are utterly hopeless at mathematics. You may even be suffering from a medical condition and want to know if something in your genetic makeup has caused it.

2 Another common motive for researching your family tree is that you plan to visit the place that your ancestors came from and you secretly hope that you will find some long lost cousins with whom you can share your memories. There can be few more exciting things than meeting a distant cousin who is living on the other side of the globe and finding that she looks just like your younger sister. But you should also bear in mind that they may not necessarily want to have anything to do with you. Sometimes there are skeletons in the cupboard that you and your branch of the family are unaware of, but which are still fresh in the minds of your more distant relatives.

3 This brings up an important aspect of this kind of research that some people do not anticipate. Of course you want to find out about yourself and what makes you 'you', but you may not be so keen on discovering some unpleasant facts about your relatives. Your ancestors were human beings too and there is no reason to expect them to have led blameless lives. It is all part of your own history, after all, and if you are going to do the research, you should accept this fact and understand that you cannot change it.

4 ▶ Once you are clear about your motives, you need to take a moment to think about just how many ancestors you might have and how far back you intend to go. You have, no doubt, thought about your parents' parents and your parents' parents' parents; you may even know quite a bit about them. But go back ten generations and the picture becomes much more complicated. To begin with, many more *line 53* people are involved. You can work *it* out for yourself. You may be descended from no fewer than 1024 people through ten generations and that means there are a lot of different individuals to trace and stories to check. This can mean that you spend hours going through official records, either in person at the records office or on the Internet. Are you prepared for such a huge task?

5 ▶ Simply starting the search can be overwhelming and right now you are probably asking yourself 'Where do I begin?'. I have prepared a report which will put you on the right path to finding your family history. When you get this report, you will have a step-by-step method to follow. The report tells you where to begin and what kind of items you are searching for. It will also provide you with a great way to organise what you find so that future generations will benefit from your search. There will be dead ends and false trails that will have you tearing your hair out but once you start to experience a little success, you will be hooked. And, with my report, you will experience success. I guarantee it!

4 You might have to accept that your ancestors
   A did not want to be found out.
   B were not like you at all.
   C were rather unpleasant.
   D did some things that were wrong.

5 What does Maria McLeod assume that the reader has already done?
   A found out about their family ten generations ago
   B considered the three previous generations
   C decided how far back in time they want to go
   D asked their parents about their grandparents and great grandparents

6 What does the word 'it' in line 53 refer to?
   A how far back you should go in your research
   B how many people you are descended from
   C why doing genealogical research is so complicated
   D when the tenth generation were alive

7 Why might you think twice about researching your family tree?
   A You already know about your great-grandparents.
   B Going back ten generations is too far.
   C You don't have time to do it.
   D You have a lot of relatives.

8 Maria McLeod has written the article to
   A encourage people to research their family history.
   B put people off researching their family's past.
   C share an experience of researching the past.
   D promote instructions on genealogy research.

3   Read the text again and find words or phrases that mean the following.

1 resemble (paragraph 1)   ....
2 combination of biological qualities (paragraph 1)   ....
3 reason for doing something (paragraph 2)   ....
4 shocking and secret events from the past (paragraph 2)   ....
5 without any faults (paragraph 3)   ....
6 find (paragraph 4)   ....
7 searching thoroughly (paragraph 4)   ....
8 very large (paragraph 4)   ....
9 a point from which you can't continue (paragraph 5)   ....
10 unable to stop doing something because you like it so much (paragraph 5)   ....

Grammar 1: gerunds and infinitives ▶ *CB page 95*

1 Complete the following sentences with the correct form of the verb in brackets.

1 I wonder what makes him .... he can get away without studying. (*think*)

2 When the summer ends, I really miss .... to the beach in the afternoons. (*go*)

3 My brother can't bear .... early at the weekend. (*get up*)

4 Would you rather .... soup or salad for lunch? (*have*)

5 I wish you wouldn't keep .... the channel. I want .... the news. (*change, watch*)

6 Do you ever regret .... Australia? (*leave*)

7 He insisted on .... for our meal. (*pay*)

8 The children were pretending .... sumo wrestlers. (*be*)

9 We're considering .... a new car. (*buy*)

10 I really enjoy .... to the cinema on my own. (*go*)

2 There are mistakes with gerunds and infinitives in some of these sentences. Find the mistakes and correct them.

0 She made him ~~to~~ help her with the washing.

1 I stopped to smoke three years ago.

2 Did you remember getting some sugar when you went out?

3 He tried to have warm baths before he went to bed but he still couldn't sleep.

4 We regret to inform you that your application was not successful.

5 I'd like meeting some new people.

6 The children were made to stay indoors during the cold weather.

7 I'll never forget to see The Backstreet Boys play live.

3 Use of English: open cloze (Part 2)

Strategy
Make sure that you read the whole sentence, then concentrate on the words before and after the gap to help you decide on the missing word.

Read the text on the right and think of the word which best fits each gap. Use only one word in each gap. There is an example at the beginning (0).

> **CLUE:** Gap 1: *had* is a past participle and so the missing word is part of the form of a verb.

A HAPPY FAMILY AND A LONG LIFE

When Japan's Kamato Hongo died **(0)** ....*at*........ the age of 116, she was the world's oldest woman. But Mrs Hongo seems to **(1)** .... had a perfectly normal lifestyle, and **(2)** .... seems to be no particular reason for her **(3)** .... have lived so long. She enjoyed things **(4)** .... are sometimes considered to be unhealthy, such as drinking tea, coffee and even a small amount of alcohol every day, although she **(5)** .... not smoke. So what was her secret?

After getting married, she stayed on Kagoshima, the island where she **(6)** .... born, helping her husband on his farm. During her long life, Mrs Hongo gave birth to seven children, lived through three wars, and survived a volcano eruption on Kagoshima **(7)** .... 1914.

Despite her eventful life, she was happy and hated being away **(8)** .... her family. She always kept a close relationship with all seven of her children, and in fact, when she could no longer look **(9)** .... herself, she went to live with one of her daughters, Shizue, and her family.

Then, at the end of her long life Mrs Hongo seemed to think more about her early life **(10)** .... the present, and sometimes failed **(11)** .... recognise close relatives and friends who visited her. She preferred to live in the past, and talk **(12)** .... her very happy childhood. Was happiness the secret of her long life?

4 **Speaking:** giving personal information (Part 1)

Look at the answers a student gave to the questions below. Complete her answers using the verbs from the box.

> go out   travel   think   visit   dance
> make   have   find   spend   research
> manage   use

Examiner: What kinds of social activities do you enjoy?

Candidate: Well, I like (1) .... with friends to the cinema or perhaps to a café or disco. I'm very keen on (2) .... , especially to salsa music, but I don't like parties much. I'd rather (3) .... a small group of friends over for a meal.

Examiner: Do you have any special plans for this weekend?

Candidate: Well, I have to study a bit but I hope (4) .... some time to help my father with a project he's doing. He's trying (5) .... our family history but he's not very good at (6) .... the Internet. It's a really fascinating project and it makes me (7) .... a lot.

Examiner: What are your plans for the future?

Candidate: I'm going to Canada for six months next year. I'm planning (8) .... around Ontario and Quebec but I'd also like (9) .... Alaska if I can (10) .... it. I'm really looking forward to (11) .... new friends but I know I'll miss (12) .... time with my friends here as well.

 5 Now listen to the recording to see if you were right.

Vocabulary 2: relationships ▶ *CB page 97*

1 Complete this crossword with adjectives for describing personality.

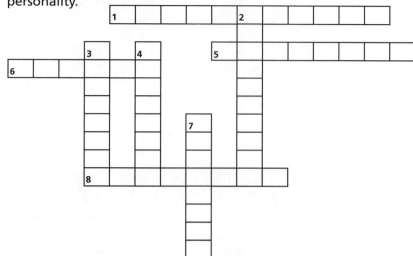

Across

1 People like this will listen to you when you have a problem of some kind.
5 People like this enjoy making new friends and spending time with them.
6 People like this don't boast about their achievements.
8 People like this don't do silly things like staying up all night.

Down

2 People like this remember to visit elderly relatives and friends in hospital.
3 People like this are happy to use their money and time to help others.
4 People like this don't like to change their minds.
7 People like this are always there when you need them.

2 Complete the following sentences using words from the box. There is one word you do not need to use.

> cousins   niece   uncle   grandparents   mother-in-law
> nephew   brother-in-law   aunt   stepbrother

1 Is your .... John your sister's son or your brother's?
2 I get on really well with my new .... since my father married his mother.
3 My .... have twenty-five grandchildren including me.
4 Jules doesn't get along with his own .... , but I'm very fond of my wife's mother.
5 Before my sister married Pierre, I never wanted a .... – but he's great!
6 My father's twin brother is a wonderful .... to me – he takes me to football games every week.
7 I've got two .... who are my mother's sister's children, and we're almost the same age.
8 My .... doesn't have any children but she's very fond of her nieces, especially me.

3 Speaking: long turn (Part 2)

Look at these two photographs and the comments a student made about them and fill in the gaps.

6 These two photos are (1) .... because they both show happy occasions. One is a party and the (2) .... is a wedding (3) .... They were obviously taken at very different times, but it might even be the same couple in the (4) .... photographs. In the first one the couple are probably (5) .... or even great-grandparents. I'm not really (6) .... but I think there are four generations at the party: the couple, their children, their grandchildren and perhaps the babies are their (7) .... The couple still (8) .... very much in love even after such a long time. In the second photograph everyone looks a little (9) .... nervous and shy. The (10) .... is smiling but the (11) .... looks rather serious and the (12) .... are not looking at the camera. I suppose they might all be feeling a little tired after the (13) .... The couple's friends and relatives are all there too. If I (14) .... married, I don't want to spend a lot of money on a big wedding like this. I would prefer to have a small party with some close friends and then go away somewhere really nice on the (15) 9

 4 Now listen to the recording and see if you were right.

Listening: multiple-choice questions (Part 4)

 1 You will hear a man talking about attending a surprise party. For questions 1–7, choose the best answer, A, B or C.

1 One of the people invited to the party
- A had met Charlie in Australia.
- B was related to Charlie.
- C hadn't seen Charlie for twelve years.

2 People were asked
- A to keep the party a secret from Charlie.
- B to send a written reply to the invitation.
- C to give their invitations to others if they couldn't come.

3 The speaker doesn't think Charlie knew about the party because
- A he reacted with real surprise.
- B he wasn't wearing a fancy dress costume.
- C he was angry about the way people were dressed.

4 The speaker thinks his outfit was a success because
- A very few people spoke to him.
- B very few people knew who he was.
- C there were three other people dressed the same way.

5 Charlie went to the disco where the party was held because
- A he knew they played a lot of seventies music.
- B he expected to meet up with some friends there.
- C his girlfriend had bought him a new outfit.

6 One idea the speaker particularly liked was
- A encouraging the guests to bring their cameras.
- B getting the guests to have their photos taken.
- C providing cameras for the guests to take photos.

7 The speaker says that the girl called Lidia he met at the party

  A had just broken up with her boyfriend.

  B is one reason he started to feel better.

  C hasn't been out with him yet.

Grammar 2: expressing hypothetical meanings ▶ *CB page 99*

1 <u>Underline</u> the correct alternatives in the following sentences.

1 I wish I *wouldn't eat / hadn't eaten* so much last week. Now I can't get into my wedding dress.

2 We both wish you *were / had been* here. You'd love it.

3 I wish I *could / would* dance better.

4 I wish you *didn't / wouldn't* keep changing the channel like that. It's driving me mad.

5 If only I *have / had* enough money to buy a better computer.

6 I wish I *had given / could give* up smoking years ago.

7 I wish I *were / would be* a bit taller.

8 If only Eleanor I *had realised / would realise* that Carlo is no good for her.

9 Everything is so brown and dry. If only it *rained / would rain*!

10 I wish I *could / would be able to* come to your party but I'll be away that weekend.

2 Complete the following sentences using the correct form of the verbs in brackets.

1 It's time you .... a few days off. You look really tired. (*take*)

2 Would you rather we .... out to dinner for your birthday or would you like some friends over for a meal here? (*go*)

3 Suppose we .... the lottery. We could spend the rest of our lives travelling. (*win*)

4 Simon would rather his friends .... and watch him play next week. He says it makes him nervous. (*not come*)

5 Everyone says it's high time I .... to drive, but I'm not keen on the idea. (*learn*)

6 I'd rather you .... in here. I don't like the smell. (*not smoke*)

7 Suppose you .... famous. Do you think it would change you much? (*be*)

3 **Use of English:** key word transformations (Part 4)

Complete the second sentence so that it has a similar meaning to the first sentence, using the word given. Do not change the word given. You must use between two and five words, including the word given. There is an example at the beginning (0).

Note: These sentences all focus on hypothetical meaning. In the exam, the same keyword will not appear in more than one sentence.

0 I'm sorry I didn't see that film.

  wish

  I *wish I had seen* .... that film.

1 I really regret inviting him to the party.

  only

  If .... him to the party.

2 It really annoys me the way she does that.

  wish

  I .... that.

3 It was a real mistake not to revise for the exam.

  only

  If .... for the exam.

4 I wish I could rollerskate.

  able

  I would be happy if .... to rollerskate.

5 She sometimes wishes she had never left Australia.

  regrets

  She sometimes .... Australia.

6 You should go to bed now.

  time

  It's .... to bed.

7 I'd prefer you to give me some money for my birthday.

  rather

  I'd .... me some money for my birthday.

8 You might not think it's risky but what if someone saw you do it.

  suppose

  You might not think it's risky but .... you do it.

Writing: article (Part 2)
▶ *CB page 102*

1   Look at this task and the points a student has written down to include in the article. Some of the points don't fit the task. Cross them out.

Young people around the world meet other young people in different places to have fun and talk. Write us an article about where you and your friends go in your town and what you like to do there, explaining why this is a good place for young people to meet and why you enjoy going there. The best articles will be published and the writers will receive £500 each.

- *Young people - same all over the world - want to meet friends.*
- *Where we go - Heraclio Sánchez Street*
- *When we go there (Friday and Saturday nights)*
- *Why we think there should be more places to park*
- *Lots of pubs, cafés, places to sit and talk*
- *First time I went there with Carla and what happened*
- *Lots of university and high school students go there*
- *Disagree with parents who don't like their children going there*
- *People who live in street don't like it but it's still a great place to go.*
- *Coming to La Laguna? Want to meet local young people? Come to Heraclio Sánchez Street*

2   Group the points you have left under these headings in your notebook.

Introducing the topic	Main part of the article	Ending

3   Now look at the two titles and opening paragraphs the student has written. Which one is best?

A

Where my friends and I go in my town

My friends and I are the same as other young people. We like to meet our friends. We go to a street in my town called Heraclio Sánchez Street. Basically, we go there to meet other young people and to have fun and talk. Everyone I know really likes going there. Here are the reasons why.

B

A great place to meet!

Young people all over the world like to be with people their own age, to relax, chat and generally have a good time. We're the same here in La Laguna and we've got a fantastic place to meet our friends and make new ones. It's called Heraclio Sánchez Street. Let me tell you about it.

4   Write your answer to the task in your notebook. You can use the title and the opening paragraph you chose from Exercise 3, or write your own.

UNIT 9 A new look

Grammar 1: present and past habit ▶ *CB page 106*

1 **Cross out the incorrect verb form in each sentence.**

1 At the beginning of the last century many women *wore / used to wear / would wear* extremely uncomfortable underwear, called corsets.

2 Sometimes these were so tight that they *were having / used to have / would have* trouble breathing and *sometimes used to faint / had sometimes fainted / would sometimes faint.*

3 People *used to think / would think / thought* that women only looked attractive if they had tiny waists.

4 Some women *used to have / would have / had* waists that were almost as narrow as their necks.

5 These women *used to need / would need / needed* the help of at least one other person to do the corset up.

6 A servant *used to pull / would pull / was pulling* the laces of the corset until it was so tight that the woman could hardly breathe.

7 Only poor women who couldn't afford servants *didn't use to have to / wouldn't have to / didn't have to* wear corsets.

8 In the 1920s many women *started / were starting / used to start* to dress in comfortable loose-fitting clothes and to wear their hair cut short.

2 **Each of the following sentences has a word missing. Choose a word from the box to complete the sentences.**

had	would	to	used	got	could

0 When I was a child I used⋀hate some of the things my parents made me wear. *(to)*

1 Whenever we had visitors they dress me up in a horrible blue suit.

2 My older brothers and sisters to laugh at me.

3 I beg my mother not to make me wear it but she insisted.

4 Eventually, I used to wearing it.

5 I even began feel quite fond of it.

6 One day I not find the little suit in the wardrobe when I went to look for it.

7 It turned out that my mother given it away to charity the day before.

8 She had bought me a new suit, which I never got used wearing.

3 **Use of English: open cloze (Part 2)**

Read the text below and think of the word that best fits each gap. Use only one word in each gap. There is an example at the beginning (0).

RECYCLED FASHION

I went shopping with my mother the **(0)** ..*other*.. day. I **(1)** .... used to going shopping on my own now but it was my birthday and she said she would buy me some new clothes as a present. I wanted to get a new top and some jeans, **(2)** .... we went to a shop I really like called *Stradivarius*. My mother started to laugh as soon as we got there because almost all the clothes in the window were just **(3)** .... the things that she used **(4)** .... wear when she was young. She told me that she **(5)** .... to have lots of pairs of flared trousers and that very short skirts were also really popular.

Back in the seventies, my mother and her friends **(6)** .... spend every Saturday morning looking round the shops. Of course they **(7)** .... not always afford to buy anything but they used to decorate their old jeans to make them look new. My grandmother is very good at sewing and she **(8)** .... help my mother sew coloured patches onto her old jeans. Apparently, even the hairstyles today **(9)** .... very similar to the way my mother and her friends **(10)** .... to wear their hair.

She says she really likes these styles and so do I – in fact, I'm **(11)** .... used to the idea that my hair looks just **(12)** .... my mother's!

Reading: gapped text (Part 2)

1 You are going to read an article about fashion. Read the article and the sentences that have been removed from the article quickly. Which of these ideas are **not** included?

a) Wearing what suits you rather than wearing what is fashionable.

b) Avoiding wearing clothes that are designed for much older or much younger people.

c) Not buying clothes made by underpaid workers.

d) Spending too much money on clothes.

2 Now read the article and sentences again. Seven sentences have been removed from the article. Choose from sentences A–H the one which best fits each gap (1–7). There is one extra sentence which you do not need to use.

A They throw away perfectly decent things that look good and feel comfortable, and replace them with the latest designer items.

B They will go out in the latest spring fashions even if it is snowing or wear high-heeled shoes to a picnic in the woods.

C There are limits though and if you want to avoid going over them, here's what you should do.

D Fashion victims don't care if they're fat or thin, short or tall.

E They often have favourite styles and are reluctant to give them up even if the trend faded decades earlier.

F This is fine if you happen to have a lot of money, of course.

G In their desperate bid to be in style, they completely miss the most important aspect of being stylish.

H If you wear them all at once, they just compete for attention.

HOW TO SPOT A
FASHION VICTIM
(AND HOW TO AVOID BECOMING ONE YOURSELF)

You've probably heard the term 'fashion victim' on TV and in magazines, but who are these critics referring to and why do they call these people 'victims'?

Fashion victims are people who take a fashion trend and follow it slavishly. They don't care whether it looks good on them or not, whether it is appropriate or whether they are wearing it in excess. **(1)**.......... . This is to customize trends to suit their own body and circumstances.

So what are some telltale signs of a fashion victim? Number one on my list is wearing clothing and accessories that do not suit their body shape. **(2)**.......... . They will snap up the latest trends and wear them proudly to show the world that they know what's in style. Meanwhile, everyone is thinking, 'You may be very trendy, but do you own a mirror?'

Wearing too much of one thing is never a good idea whether it is jewellery, make up, designer clothes or perfume. This is the second area where fashion victims often get it wrong. The right style tactic is to create a single focal point. It might be a designer T-shirt or some unusual boots or perhaps a trendy jacket. **(3)**.......... . Wear one fashion item at a time and keep the rest simple.

A third trap that victims fall into is being so into fashion that they are completely out of touch with the world around them. For these people fashion sense is always more important than common sense. **(4)**.......... . Make sure that you don't sacrifice safety and comfort for the sake of looking good.

Fashions date very quickly and this presents fashion victims with another problem. **(5)**.......... . If you really want to be fashionable, it is important to be alert to the fact that others have stopped dyeing their hair red or wearing long strings of beads or low-rise jeans, and change your style accordingly. At the other extreme are people who buy a completely new wardrobe every season. **(6)**.......... . However, this costs them a fortune and makes it obvious to everyone else that they have fallen prey to an obsession with fashion. Instead, look critically at your clothes and only throw or give away what you haven't worn for over twelve months.

Most people want to look good and for almost everyone this means following fashion trends to some extent. **(7)**.......... . Buy cheap, wear often and invest in classic items that never go out of fashion. Follow the trends that really suit you rather than forcing yourself to fit into them. That way you won't run the risk of becoming a fashion victim.

3 Find words or phrases in the article to complete these definitions.

> **CLUE:** The definitions are in the same order as the text.

1 To copy something very closely without making necessary changes.
2 To make something obvious that you don't want other people to recognise.
3 To buy something very quickly and eagerly.
4 When something changes and you no longer know about it or understand it.
5 To do something in a way that fits the circumstances or situation.
6 To become a victim of a thing or person.

Vocabulary 1: fashion
▶ *CB page 107*

1 Put the words from the box under the correct headings below.

beige	sweater	silk	V-necked	cardigan
velvet	suit	washable	brown	jeans
flared	tight-fitting	wool	top	slip-on
waterproof	mauve	linen	polo-necked	
cotton	grey	sleeveless	polyester	
stretch	navy	T-shirt	turquoise	

Colours	Designs	Qualities	Fabrics	Clothes
cream	long-sleeved	crease-resistant	lycra	shorts
....	....	....	....	....
....	....	....	....	....
....	....		....	....
....	....		....	....
....	....		....	....
....	....		....	....

2 Use words from Exercise 1 to complete these comments people made about the clothes.

1 'I really like that (0) ..*linen*........ suit. It looks great with the (1) .... (2) .... too. You could wear it with those (3) .... -on shoes you bought.'

2 'I want to get a pair of (4) .... jeans like that but I'm not so sure about that (5) .... Things made of (6) .... like that don't really suit me.'

3 'If you're going to be up in the mountains it would be a really good idea to get one of those (7) .... sweaters. I've got one and I just love it. It's machine (8) .... , incredibly light but really warm at the same time.'

4 'Mum might like that pure (9) .... (10) .... they've got in the window there. I looked at them the other day. They come in lots of colours. There's mauve, navy, charcoal (11) .... and turquoise but I think she'd probably like one in chocolate (12) .... best.'

3 Use of English: multiple-choice cloze (Part 1)

Read the text below and decide which answer (A, B, C or D) best fits each gap. There is an example at the beginning (0).

FASHION HURTS

Wearing fashionable clothes can be bad for you! This may surprise you, but it is **(0)** ..*said*.... that some clothes can cause a **(1)** .... of problems. Do you find this **(2)** .... to believe? Well, researchers have discovered that following the latest fashion **(3)** .... can be unhealthy. For example, if you **(4)** .... a scarf or tie too tightly it increases your blood pressure. Tight jeans and trousers, short skirts and even sensible **(5)** .... shoes may all cause **(6)** ....

Experts say that things we wear can also **(7)** .... to stomach problems, rashes, backache and painful feet. Yet how can we explain this? Very tight clothes can **(8)** .... people moving naturally, and this is not good for you. If you wear trousers or skirts that are too tight around the waist, then your stomach does not have **(9)** .... to expand after you have eaten, and this can cause stomachache. Rashes can be caused by an allergic **(10)** .... to synthetic material. And last, but not **(11)** .... – wearing shoes with high heels can lead to foot and back problems. Even practical shoes can cause backache if they don't **(12)** .... you properly.

0	**A** said	**B** spoken	**C** talked	**D** explained
1	**A** variety	**B** group	**C** bundle	**D** collection
2	**A** puzzling	**B** complicated	**C** complex	**D** difficult
3	**A** directions	**B** trends	**C** changes	**D** cultures
4	**A** fasten	**B** fix	**C** tie	**D** install
5	**A** flat	**B** level	**C** smooth	**D** even
6	**A** complaints	**B** conditions	**C** illnesses	**D** sickness
7	**A** move	**B** lead	**C** go	**D** grow
8	**A** prevent	**B** avoid	**C** block	**D** check
9	**A** extent	**B** area	**C** place	**D** room
10	**A** reply	**B** response	**C** reaction	**D** return
11	**A** final	**B** least	**C** end	**D** terminal
12	**A** shape	**B** match	**C** suit	**D** fit

Vocabulary 2: phrasal verbs with up ▶ CB page 108

1   Complete the following sentences using the correct form of the words in the box.

> sew   wrap   close   tidy   gather   drink   save
> finish   zip   wash

1 It's very cold outside, so make sure you .... up warmly if you're going out.
2 I'll clear the table and you can .... up those plates and glasses. OK?
3 If you don't .... up your room, I'm going to throw everything that's on the floor away.
4 The kitten .... up the saucer of milk.
5 He .... up his jacket, put on his helmet and rode off into the sunset.
6 We were .... up for years before we could afford to buy a car.
7 No one could decide where to go so we .... up at Eva's house.
8 The children .... up all the toys they had been playing with and left the beach.
9 We've .... up our apartment in the city for the summer and moved down to the coast.
10 The surgeon .... up the wound so neatly that it didn't leave a scar.

2   Put the words in order to make common phrases with *up*, then match them to their meanings a)–f) below.

1 you   up   it's   to
....
2 the   up   way   wrong   that's
....
3 have   our   downs   and   ups   we
....
4 up   to   going   go   everything's
....
5 to   to   keep   try   date   up
....
6 up   time   is
....

☐ a) It's upside down.
☐ b) It's all going to get more expensive.
☐ c) You have no time left.
☐ d) There are good times and bad times.
☐ e) You have to decide.
☐ f) Don't be old fashioned.

3   Underline the expressions with *up* or *down*, and decide if the meaning is positive (✓) or negative (✗).

0 Things are <u>looking up</u>.   ✓☑
1 I'm feeling a bit down.   ☐
2 She'll be up and about by the end of the week.   ☐
3 The computer's down so I can't do any work.   ☐
4 They look down on their country relations.   ☐
5 He was feeling very down-hearted.   ☐
6 She really looks up to him.   ☐
7 They've got the whole system up and running.   ☐

4   **Use of English:** key word transformations (Part 4)

Complete the second sentence so that it has a similar meaning to the first sentence, using the word given. Do not change the word given. You must use between two and five words, including the word given. There is an example at the beginning (0).

0 A lot of people really admire the president of our country.
look
A lot of people really ......*look up to*...... the president of our country.

1 I've had a few problems at work but things are improving now.
up
I've had a few problems at work but things are .... now.

2 The price of petrol has increased a lot lately.
gone
The price of petrol has .... a lot lately.

3 You've hung that picture upside down.
way
You've hung that picture .... up.

4 It's your decision whether you take the job or not.
up
It's .... whether you take the job or not.

5 The doctor told me I would be able to get up and walk around tomorrow.
about
The doctor told me I would be .... tomorrow.

Listening: sentence completion (Part 2)

1 You will hear an interview with a famous shoe designer. For questions 1–10, complete the sentences. You should use no more than three words.

The person who means the most to Manolo is his
(1) ....
His family own a **(2)** ....
Manolo did not have a **(3)** .... when he was young.
Manolo's sister **(4)** .... with him now.
His parents wanted him to **(5)** ....
He did not finish his **(6)** ....
A famous magazine editor told him he should begin
(7) ....
He went back to England to learn how **(8)** ....
In his house he keeps **(9)** .... of all the shoes he's designed.
In London there was **(10)** .... of his work.

Vocabulary 3: things in the home
▶ *CB page 110*

Speaking: long turn (Part 2)

1 There are eight things wrong with the description of the photograph on the right. Study the photograph and correct the mistakes.

❝ This could be a room in a flat or perhaps it's an artist's studio. It's very small but the person who uses it obviously does different things here. For example, I think the person spends some time reading as there are a lot of books on the shelves. It looks as if he or she also listens to music. I'm not sure, but I think the grey box on one of the small tables could be a CD player. There are no plants in the room but I can see a cat on the sofa. The furniture is very classical. By one wall, there's a kind of low sofa ... I'm not sure what you call it in English ... it's covered in white fabric. Opposite it is a kind of low bed with a patterned cover on it and there are dark coloured blinds on the windows. In the corner of the room there's an armchair. There are no pictures on the walls, which are covered in patterned wallpaper. There is a computer in the photograph but there's no television, so perhaps this person doesn't enjoy watching TV very much. I think I would like to live in a room like this because it is very light. ❞

Grammar 2: participle clauses
▶ *CB page 111*

1 Change the relative clauses in these sentences into participle clauses.

0 Near where I used to live, there was a shop which sold glass beads.
Near where I used to live, there was a shop ......
selling glass beads. ....

1 Under the bed was a wooden box, which contained hundreds of old love letters.
....

2 The meal, which was cooked by a famous chef, was one of the best we had eaten.
....

3 The college, which was founded in 1926, has always attracted the best students.
....

4 A path, which led down to the sea, suddenly came into view.
....

5 The island, which was almost hidden by the mist, seemed to be calling her.
....

6 He returned the camera which belonged to my father.
....

7 All students who wish to see the principal should make an appointment.
....

8 A woman who was chasing her dog, fell over and broke her leg yesterday.
....

2 Use of English: word formation (Part 3)

Strategy

When you have formed a new word, make sure the sentence makes sense. Add a negative prefix (*in-*, *un-*, *dis-*) if you need to.

Read the following text. Use the word given in capitals below the text to form a word that fits in each gap. There is an example at the beginning (0).

DRESS DISTRESS

Does getting dressed in the morning present you with choices that are almost **(0)** *impossible*. to make? If it does, you're not alone. One in five women have **(1)**.......... deciding what to put on each day, according to a recent survey.

The results showed that 28 per cent of women were more **(2)**.......... about their clothes than any other aspect of their lives. This tremendous sense of **(3)**.......... about clothes even causes some 22 per cent of women to arrive late for work. They waste **(4)**.......... time trying on outfits only to take them off again a few minutes later because of a profound lack of **(5)**.......... about what looks good on them and what doesn't.

But do men worry about their **(6)**.........., too? It would appear that they do.

A heightened **(7)**.......... of the role image plays means that many men today also buy fashion magazines, and spend hours shopping and going to the hairdressers. This is not because they find these activities **(8)**.........., however. It is because they realise the way they look has an influence on professional **(9)**.......... . Of course it isn't the only factor, but it does play a role, and this can be a cause of **(10)**.......... for many men as well as women.

0	POSSIBLE	6	APPEAR
1	DIFFICULT	7	AWARE
2	DECIDE	8	ENJOY
3	SECURE	9	SUCCEED
4	VALUE	10	ANXIOUS
5	CONFIDENT		

Writing: report (Part 2) ▶ *CB page 114*

1 Look at this list of DOs and DON'Ts for report writing and the report a student wrote in answer. Put a cross (✗) next to the advice he has ignored and a tick (✓) next to the advice he has followed.

1 DO give your report a heading.
2 DON'T begin *Dear Sir or Madam*.
3 DO use headings like these: *Introduction, Results, Conclusion*.
4 DON'T give your opinion at the beginning.
5 DON'T use informal language.
6 DO use an impersonal style to express your opinion.
7 DO say how you collected the information.

This report is to recommend a room in the school for a student common room. I interviewed a number of students about this issue and the following were their opinions. Many students felt the room that is currently used as classroom 3 would make the best common room. It was pointed out that the new building in Malcolm Street has brand new classrooms so it is probable that classroom 3 will soon not be needed for teaching purposes. It was generally agreed that the room should be painted and that sofas and easy chairs should be bought as well as a small refrigerator. Posters of pop, film and sports stars could be used to give the space a personal touch. Finally, a number of people mentioned the fact that a sink would be very useful for washing up coffee mugs and so on. Although it will be necessary to spend some money doing the room up, it is, in my opinion, the best choice. As was stated earlier, this opinion is shared by many other students.

2 Write the report out again in your notebook, following the advice the student ignored.

3 Now look at the task below and write your answer in your notebook.

The director of the place where you study wants to sell clothing and other gifts for students to buy as souvenirs. You have been asked to write a report saying what items of clothing and gifts should be sold, making suggestions on how the items should be decorated to show that they come from the school.

Write your report in **120–180** words.

Listening: multiple matching (Part 3)

1 You will hear five people talking about learning. Here are some words and phrases, five of which you hear in the recording. Match them to the subjects A–F.

1 … more specialised courses on writing and speaking … ☐

2 Some people I went to school with were terrified of her … ☐

3 ... lots of practice tasks and exercises you could correct yourself. ☐

4 … the speed of the computer was an important thing to think about … ☐

5 … but at least I can hit the ball. ☐

6 … the first time I had to give a patient an injection … ☐

A A physical activity
B A language
C How to use a machine
D A professional skill
E A teacher
F A book

2 Now listen to the recordings and decide which of the sentences in Exercise 1 is <u>not</u> on the recording.

3 Listen again and match the subjects A–F to the speakers. Use the letters only once. There is one extra letter which you do not need to use.

Speaker 1 ☐ **1**
Speaker 2 ☐ **2**
Speaker 3 ☐ **3**
Speaker 4 ☐ **4**
Speaker 5 ☐ **5**

Grammar 1: obligation, necessity and permission ▶ *CB page 117*

1 There are mistakes in some of these sentences. Find the mistakes and correct them.

0 ~~Had~~ you ∧ to wear a uniform when you were at school?
  Did   have

1 She had to get up at five o'clock to be sure of catching the plane.

2 You said I needn't do the test if I didn't want to.

3 We are not allowed using our mobile phones in the library.

4 If you became a member you can come to as many classes as you want.

5 She told me that I could to have my money back if I wasn't completely satisfied.

6 Have you to go? It's still so early.

2 <u>Underline</u> the correct alternatives in the following sentences.

1 He *shouldn't / mustn't* have told Sara how he felt. She's really embarrassed.

2 You *must / need* see that new film. It's really brilliant.

3 We *didn't need to pay / needn't have paid*. The man on the door let us in for free.

4 You *don't have to / mustn't* help with the dishes. They'll only take me a minute.

5 I *have to / must* go to the dentist this afternoon so I won't be able to come to class.

6 We are *supposed to / allowed to* help my father with the housework but he actually does it all himself.

3 **Use of English:** key word transformations (Part 4)

Complete the second sentence so that it has a similar meaning to the first sentence, using the word given. Do not change the word given. You must use between two and five words, including the word given. There is an example at the beginning (0).

0 Club members can bring guests to the club on Thursdays. **permitted**

Club members .._are permitted to bring_.. guests to the club on Thursdays.

1 Could you tell me if I have to bring a sleeping bag? **necessary**

Could you tell me if .... me to bring a sleeping bag.

2 You can't use a personal stereo on a plane. **allowed**

You .... a personal stereo on a plane.

3 We asked if we could move to a quieter room. **possible**

We asked if it .... move to a quieter room.

4 He had to give the money back. **obliged**

He .... give the money back.

5 You mustn't wear dark-soled shoes in the gym. **supposed**

You .... dark soled shoes in the gym.

6 They made me admit that I was wrong. **forced**

I .... that I was wrong.

7 I wanted to go out with my boyfriend, but my parents said I couldn't. **let**

My parents wouldn't .... with my boyfriend.

8 My parents insisted I study the piano. **made**

I was .... the piano by my parents.

Vocabulary 1: expressions with mind ▶ CB page 119

1 Complete the following sentences using the correct form of the words from the box.

| change | read | cross | put | make | in | on |
| off | out | on | | | | |

1 I really liked Toni at first but now I've completely .... my mind about him.

2 Why don't you come out with us tonight? It might take your mind .... things.

3 You look a bit anxious. Have you got something .... your mind?

4 I can't .... your mind, you know! You have to tell me what you want me to do.

5 Eli is telling everyone that I want to steal her boyfriend but the idea never even .... my mind.

6 You must be .... of your mind if you think I'm going to drive across Europe with you in that old car!

7 He can play really well when he .... his mind to it.

8 I wish you'd .... up your mind. Do you want spaghetti for dinner or lasagne?

9 I'm .... two minds about whether or not to go to the party.

10 I was so worried about Ralph that I couldn't keep my mind .... my work.

2 Use expressions with mind from Exercise 1 to replace the underlined words or phrases in these sentences.

1 I don't have the same opinion now about that jacket. I think it does suit you after all.

....

2 She was so excited about going out with Paolo that she couldn't concentrate on the lecture.

....

3 Playing tennis let Juan forget about his problems.

....

4 Nina's been a bit bad-tempered lately. She must be worried about something.

....

5 The idea that he was the one who stole the money didn't occur to me.

....

6 He knew her so well that she sometimes thought he could tell what she was thinking.

....

7 I'm not sure about buying a new car at the moment. I haven't got much money.

....

8 He can write really well when he gives it his full attention.

....

9 One night she's out with me, the next she's out with Lucas. I wish she'd decide which one of us she likes.

....

10 He must be crazy to leave a wonderful girlfriend like Laura.

....

Reading: gapped text (Part 2)

1 You are going to read a text about the man in the photograph. Read the text and the sentences that have been removed from the text. Which of these two titles is the most suitable?

a) THE NOT SO NUTTY PROFESSOR
b) A QUESTION OF MIND OVER MATTER

2 Read the text and the sentences again. Seven sentences have been removed from the text. Choose from sentences A–H the one which best fits each gap (1–7). There is one extra sentence which you do not need to use.

A Nobody knows why, but it certainly gets people talking.

B After the first step, he again found that his foot was fine.

C This was reinforced when he was looking through an issue of the magazine The Physics Teacher.

D Other experiments are quieter though no less dramatic.

E He knew from his mother's example that he would not get burnt fire-walking.

F He was demonstrating a law of Physics to his first-year students in a memorable way.

G The other teachers like the idea, but what do Willey's students think of it all?

H He feels that this is because the principle is demonstrated so clearly in what looks like a very dangerous thing to do.

Fire-walking has been practised as a ritual by people from all parts of the world for thousands of years. The first written reference to it appears in a story from India, dating back to 1200 BC. More recently, however, it has made an appearance in classrooms at the University of Pittsburgh.

David Willey, a lecturer in Physics, recently showed a dramatic video of himself walking barefoot across hot coals in one of his classes. Why did he do this? **(1)**.......... . Willey, chosen as the University's 'Teacher of the Year' last year, believes there is value in starting his lectures with a bang.

Sometimes there is actually a real explosion in one of Willey's classes. To demonstrate the effects of heat, for instance, he has been known to pour liquid nitrogen into a soft-drink bottle and cover it with a plastic rubbish bin. The nitrogen changes into gas, expands and then causes the bottle to explode. **(2)**.......... . For a class on energy and pressure, Willey lay on a bed of nails while others broke a concrete block on his chest.

None of Willey's experiments quite captures the students' attention like walking on hot coals, however. **(3)**………. . He uses his video to demonstrate the difference between temperature and heat, and backs this up with a simple explanation. 'Just because something is at a high temperature, doesn't mean that it has a lot of heat to give out,' he explains. 'Firstly, the burning wood does not conduct heat well and on top of this the walker's feet are only in contact with the burning material for a short time.'

He thought that these two facts made fire-walking useful for teaching. **(4)**………. . There he came across an article entitled 'Fire-walking as a Lesson in Physics' by John R. Taylor. Although traditionally people have seen fire-walking as proof of the power of mind over matter, in his article Taylor explained that controlling pain through concentration has nothing to do with it. The secret of fire-walking lies in physics.

After reading the article, Willey remembered his mother picking up hot coals that had fallen out of the fireplace and throwing them back without burning her hands. **(5)**………. . Nevertheless, he was still hesitant when it actually came to stepping onto a pile of hot coals that he had put down in his back garden. 'The very first time I tried to step on them, my body just said, "No Dave!" and I panicked. The second time I made a much more conscious effort, put my foot on the coals, stepped across them and said to myself, "Wow! I'm OK."'

Having passed his own test on a small pile of coals in private, Willey then decided to try a full fire-walk, and film it. **(6)**………. . Then he made his full walk. Willey has now repeated the stunt on three different occasions but the University administration will not allow him to fire-walk on the campus because they are worried about a possible fire, and insurance.

In spite of this, Willey has posted information about his experiments on his webpage for other physics teachers who might like to use fire-walking or some of his other experiments in the classroom. **(7)**………. . 'They just think it's me being crazy as usual. They're fairly used to me doing strange demonstrations,' he says.

---

3 Find words and phrases in the text and sentences that mean the same as the following.

> **CLUE:** The words are in the same order as the text and sentences.

1 without shoes or socks
2 shows that what he is saying is true (*phrasal verb*)
3 found by chance (*phrasal verb*)
4 nervous and unsure about doing something
5 made stronger
6 easy to remember

Grammar 2: *it is, there is*
▶ *CB page 122*

1 Complete these conversations using it or there.

1 A: Tommy, …………'s after ten o'clock. …………'s time you went to bed.
  B: Can I stay up a bit longer? …………'s a really good movie on TV.

2 A: …………'s so hot outside! I'm really thirsty. Is ………… anything to drink?
  B: Yes, …………'s some orange juice in the fridge.

3 A: Is ………… hard to learn to roller-blade?
  B: No, …………'s easy as long as you've got a good sense of balance.

4 A: Ela thinks you are angry with her.
  B: …………'s no reason for her to think that at all.

5 A: Do you like living here?
  B: Yes, but ………… has been quite difficult for me to learn Spanish.

6 A: Is Ignacio still going out with Margot?
  B: No. …………'s a rumour going round that he and Alba are back together again.

7 A: What did ………… use to be like here when you were a child, Grandpa?
  B: ………… weren't nearly as many cars and ………… was much quieter. People used to be friendlier too.

8 A: Hi. …………'s me. I was just ringing to say that I'll be a bit late.
  B: OK. Is ………… anything special you'd like to have for dinner?

9 A: Hello! Is ………… anybody home?
  B: Yes. I'm in the bath.

2   **Speaking:** long turn (Part 2)

1   Look at these two photos and the comments a student made about them. Seven words have been left out of her comments. Decide where they should go and write them in. There is an example at the beginning.

‘ These two photographs both show people teaching and learning things. In the first photograph, *there* is a group of people learning to do some kind of Oriental martial art. I'm not exactly sure what is. They are all on a basketball court. In the first row of the group is a man doing one of the exercises and they are all watching him so I suppose he might be the instructor. Some of the people seem to be imitating his movements. There people of different ages and nationalities.

The second photograph is very different. It shows a laboratory with some students doing an experiment of some kind. Is difficult to see exactly what they are doing but it seems to involve putting some chemicals in test tubes. One of the students seems to be having some trouble because is an older woman next to her who seems to be explaining what she should do. The main similarity between the photographs is that in both of them is someone who is teaching but the students are also doing something. I suppose you could say that they are learning by doing. In my opinion, is much better to learn like this. ’

 2   Now listen to the recording and check your answers.

3 **Use of English:** open cloze (Part 2)

Read the title and the text, and think of the word which best fits each gap. Use only one word for each gap. There is an example at the beginning (0).

TAI CHI

A couple of years (0).*ago*... , a friend from college asked me if I (1).......... like to come along to a Tai Chi class with her. I had (2).......... people doing Tai Chi, but I didn't know much about it so I decided to look it (3).......... on the Internet. I found out that Tai Chi involves one hundred and eight movements that (4).......... used to develop flexibility and good health. It has been practised in China (5).......... hundreds of years and is now becoming popular (6).......... over the world. There are several different schools of Tai Chi, but (7).......... all follow the same basic principles. The movements are made very slowly and gracefully. Tai Chi can, (8).......... fact, be used as a martial art if the person moves (9).......... quickly, but most people do it just to (10).......... fit. In China and elsewhere, people meet (11).......... parks and public squares to do Tai Chi together, so it's also a great way of meeting people and getting some fresh air. Learning the movements can (12).......... quite a long time, but it's much easier to remember them if you practise in a group.

Vocabulary 2: education ▶ *CB page 123*

1 Find 13 words to do with education in this wordsearch grid. Use the words to complete the sentences in the text on the right.

w	h	e	t	l	h	s	e	p	r	y	o	p
s	u	b	j	e	c	t	s	r	u	e	o	l
e	n	t	b	s	m	u	h	o	i	n	x	f
f	i	c	d	s	p	d	s	j	t	o	h	r
r	v	o	e	o	s	e	q	e	p	q	t	e
p	e	u	g	n	s	n	y	c	e	n	l	v
m	r	r	r	s	t	t	u	t	a	r	k	i
a	s	s	e	s	s	m	e	n	t	s	r	s
r	i	e	e	t	e	a	c	h	e	r	s	i
k	t	o	m	n	p	r	i	m	a	r	y	n
s	y	r	l	e	c	t	u	r	e	s	u	g

My niece Lucy is studying Chemistry at (1) .... After she finishes her (2) .... , she wants to go on to do a postgraduate (3) .... in Medicine. From what she tells me, a lot has changed since I was a university (4) .... Lucy has quite a lot of exams, whereas in my day it was all continuous (5) .... We had to attend all our (6) .... and at the end of the year we had to hand in a (7) .... which we had all worked on in groups. I spent most of my time on that but Lucy seems to spend most of her time (8) .... for exams. She gets really good (9) .... , I must say, usually As or Bs. Of course, she's been a very good student ever since she was at (10) .... school. All her (11) .... loved her because she really seemed to enjoy her (12) .... even if they weren't in (13) .... that she liked or was good at.

2 Use of English: word formation (Part 3)

Use the word given in capitals below the text to form a word that fits in each gap. There is an example at the beginning (0).

TEACHING CHILDREN AT HOME

It is **(0)** compulsory for children to have an education, but you may find it **(1)** .... that the teaching doesn't always have to take place in the school building. As long as they have the **(2)** .... paper **(3)** ...., parents themselves can teach their children at home. They may make the **(4)** .... to do this because they are **(5)** .... with a particular school, or because they feel that they have more **(6)** .... of their own child's needs than teachers at school. However, there may be **(7)** .... of parents who make this **(8)** .... because some people feel that children who are taught at home find it difficult to mix **(9)** .... with young people of their own age. However, **(10)** .... of the idea disagree with this. They think it is a better way of teaching children what is really important.

0	COMPEL		
1	SURPRISE	6	KNOW
2	NECESSITY	7	CRITICIZE
3	QUALIFY	8	CHOOSE
4	DECIDE	9	SOCIAL
5	HAPPY	10	SUPPORT

Writing: article (Part 2)
▶ CB page 126

1 Look at this list of DOs and DON'Ts for article writing. Then read the article a student wrote in answer to the task on page 126 of the Coursebook. Put crosses (✗) next to the advice the student has ignored and ticks (✓) next to the advice he has followed.

1 DO think of an interesting title.
2 DON'T start and finish your article in the same way as a letter.
3 DO use informal language to involve the reader.
4 DO try to involve your readers by using questions in your article.
5 DO finish your article by summarising your main point and giving your opinion or expressing your feelings.

6 DON'T use the same wording as the task.
7 DO divide your article into paragraphs.
8 DON'T forget to check your work for spelling and grammar mistakes.

Everyone has their favourite ways of studying but have you ever stoped to ask yourself how efective these habbits really are? Here are some of things I have learn about ways of studying that help me learn. Lots of my friends go to library. To my mind, that's fine if you like spend a lot of time outside chating. If I really want to get some work made, I study on my own. Another thing my friends say me is that they can study while listening music. I know I can't. When I'm revising, I turn music off so that I can keep my mind on what I'm doing. Finally, a lot of students can't make anything without a computer. Of course computers can be very usefull, but I prefer to switch mine off while I'm studying so that I won't be tempted to look at my email or interesting webpages.

2 Rewrite the article in your notebook.

1 Make changes so that it follows the advice in Exercise 1.
2 Correct the spelling and grammar mistakes which the student's teacher has underlined.

3 Now write your answer to the task below in your notebook.

An international students' magazine is looking for articles on the topic 'What makes a good teacher?'. They are offering a prize of £200 for the best article they receive. Write your article in **180** to **200** words.

UNIT
11 Hard at work

Listening: sentence completion (Part 2)

 1 You will hear a lecture about making a good first impression in a job interview. For questions 1–10, complete the sentences.

GOOD IMPRESSIONS IN JOB INTERVIEWS

Creating a positive or negative impression on an interviewer takes only **(1)**.. .

Eighty to ninety per cent of job interviewees forget **(2)**.. when they go into the interview room.

The way you move at an interview can make you seem either shy or **(3)**.. .

Two gestures that can make you seem defensive are not making eye-contact and **(4)**.. .

Something else that can make a bad impression is constantly touching **(5)**.. .

People who wear red show that **(6)**.. and yellow makes you seem open.

Other colours associated with positive qualities are **(7)**.. .

For job interviews most people choose neutral colours like **(8)**.. .

It may be a good idea to follow tradition and wear a **(9)**.. .

On your way out of the building, it's important not to forget **(10)**.. to anyone you met when you arrived.

"Why were you dismissed from your last job? ..."

Vocabulary 1: employment
▶ *CB page 132*

1 Underline the correct alternatives in this text.

TRAINEE MANAGERS

We are looking for (1) *rather / highly* motivated people with a good knowledge of the European travel market to work as (2) *learner / trainee* managers in our new branches. These are exciting (3) *circumstances / positions* for tourism graduates.

You will be (4) *based / situated* in either our Edinburgh or Barcelona offices, but will have plenty of (5) *possibilities / opportunities* to travel. (6) *Loose / Flexible* working hours also mean that you can continue to (7) *better / upgrade* your skills and (8) *diplomas / qualifications* through our staff development programme.

Other (9) *profits / benefits* include a clothing (10) *permission / allowance* and intensive language instruction in English and/or Catalan.

Excellent prospects for (11) *promotion / improvement*.

(12) *Salary / Money*: €20,000 – €30,000 a year depending on experience.

Contact Julian Turell on + 34 939289938 for an application form.

2 Match the headings to the parts of the text on the right.

a) Date of birth
b) Qualifications
c) Education
d) Employment
e) Sporting achievements
f) Current address
g) Name
h) Hobbies and other interests

Curriculum Vitae

1 ....
Elizabetta Crawford

2 ....
27 March 1983

3 ....
42 Harcourt Gardens, Granley
Tel (home): 0922 289938 (mobile): 0610859412

4 ....
1987–1994 Granley Primary School
1994–1999 Granley Grammar
2000–2003 University of Leeds
October 2003–July 2004, ESADE, Barcelona

5 ....
Bachelor of Science, University of Leeds, 2003
Graduate Diploma in Marketing, ESADE, Barcelona 2004

6 ....
Shop Assistant, Modish Mums, Granley. August–September 1998
Volleyball Instructor, Granley Children's Summer Camp.
August–September 1999
Assistant Manager Pizza Palace, Dartington Place, Leeds. (Part-time position) 2000–2003

7 ....
Junior Girls Champion Granley Tennis Club 1995
Senior Girls Champion Granley Tennis Club 1996

8 ....
I play the guitar and the piano and compose my own songs.
I have also worked as a volunteer taking care of elderly and disabled people in Granley since 1997.

3 **Use of English:** word formation (Part 3)

Read the text below. Use the word given in capitals at the end of each line to form a word that fits in the gap in the same line. There is an example at the beginning (0).

JOB INTERVIEWS

Many people feel very **(0)** .*nervous*....... about job interviews but remember the interviewers must have liked your **(1)** .... , so you only have to live up to their **(2)** .... ! Before you go into the interview room, take a few deep **(3)** .... If you think about something nice, that brings you a feeling of **(4)** .... then you will smile, and give an impression of **(5)** .... Make sure that you take all the right papers with you – if you forget something, you could look **(6)** ....

If they ask why you left your last job, don't give a long **(7)** .... You have a right to your **(8)** .... and so do your previous employers. Any future employer will like it if you show **(9)** .... to your old boss. Take your time to answer questions, and relax. If you follow this **(10)** .... , you have a good chance of getting the job!

0	NERVE
1	APPLY
2	EXPECT
3	BREATHE
4	HAPPY
5	CONFIDENT
6	PROFESSION
7	EXPLAIN
8	PRIVATE
9	LOYAL
10	ADVISE

Grammar 1: ability and possibility
▶ *CB page 132*

1 Some of these sentences have mistakes. Find and correct the mistakes and then tick (✓)the other sentences.

1 My father was able to play the piano when he was five.

2 He could became a concert musician.

3 Unfortunately, his family could not to afford to pay for him to study.

4 He could get a job in the postal service as a trainee postman.

5 He was not able to save very much because he had to help his parents.

6 He began to wonder if he could ever to continue his music studies.

7 He could also play the guitar.

8 He was able to get a part-time job playing the guitar in a restaurant.

9 He earned enough money so that he could actually save some.

10 He saved so much that eventually he could go to London to study at the Guildhall School of Music.

2 Use the words in the box to complete the sentences below.

could	can	be	have	was	had

1 I should able to finish the work by next Tuesday.

2 My father always told us that we to be able to look after ourselves.

3 Tina do most of her homework without my help.

4 I not able to attend the meeting because of ill health.

5 My cousin could become a professional tennis player, if she had had the chance.

6 I can't ride a bicycle but it would be great if you teach me.

3 Use of English: open cloze (Part 2)

Read the text below and think of the word which best fits each gap. Use only one word in each gap. There is an example at the beginning (0).

PAID TO PLAY

The Internet is **(0)** ..*full*.......... of websites which seem to offer dream jobs. There are quotations from people who seem to have succeeded in making large amounts of money without having to **(1)** .... any real work at all. Instead, these lucky people have **(2)** .... able to earn enough to live well by playing various kinds of computer games and then evaluating **(3)** .... It seems too good to **(4)** .... true!

There are also other jobs in **(5)** .... people seem to be paid to play, or to do work that is such good fun it does not seem **(6)** .... work at all. For example, **(7)** .... you like cinema and computer games, then being the manager of a video shop would be very enjoyable, because you have to watch or play with all the latest releases so that you **(8)** .... decide what to buy for the shop.

Obviously, playing a sport like tennis or volleyball professionally is really being paid to play, but even working **(9)** .... a travel guide or doctor on a cruise ship can also be quite good. One of my friends, **(10)** .... had spent years working long hours in hospitals, was **(11)** .... to get work as a doctor with an adventure travel company. She now spends **(12)** .... life trekking in Nepal or white-water rafting in New Zealand – and being paid for it!

Reading: multiple matching (Part 3)

About the exam: In Paper 1, Part 3, you have to answer fifteen questions.

1 You are going to read a magazine article about four people and their first jobs. Match the illustrations to the people (A–D).

2 Now read statements 1–15 and match them to the people (A–D).

Which girl:

was sometimes lonely?	**1**
wanted the job very much?	**2**
had too much responsibility?	**3**
got the job by chance?	**4**
disagreed with her parents over the job?	**5**
found the job more difficult than expected?	**6**
had to write an application for her job?	**7**
thought that the money was unimportant?	**8**
worked with people who were kind to her?	**9**
worked more hours than she was paid for?	**10**
is glad to have left the job?	**11**
developed a special relationship with her employers?	**12**
was unusual in having a job?	**13**
lived where she worked?	**14**
chose to leave the job?	**15**

My first job

A   Eileen

Hardly anyone in my year at school had a job, and if they did, it was only helping their parents with whatever they did, but I really wanted to earn some of my own money and be able to spend it on whatever took my fancy. The trouble was that there weren't a lot of jobs around at the time and even fewer for a teenage girl without any skills or qualifications. My parents had a friend who owned an apple orchard and he was complaining to them one night about how difficult it was to get people to pick the apples. I overheard – and that was how my career as a fruit picker began. The other pickers were almost all women in their thirties and forties so I was the baby of the group. They were nice to me, especially at the beginning when I was very new not just to the orchard but to the whole experience of working. If you wanted to make any money, you had to pick very fast because we weren't paid a wage, but our money was based on the number of wooden crates we filled with apples. The other women, who almost all worked in pairs, filled nine or ten of these a day but my record working on my own was a rather pitiful two. Still I did have a bit of money in my pocket at the end of the week which was what I wanted, after all.

B   Susan

There was no question of having the pony my parents had bought me at home, so we had to pay for her to be kept at a nearby farm. There were a couple of teenage girls working there part-time and it was my dream that the people who managed the farm would offer me a job too. Sure enough, when I turned fifteen they did. My parents were not at all keen on the idea because they said the work was too hard but I loved every second of it. We had to clean the stables, feed and groom the horses and in the spring help with the new-born foals. That was the best part. The money wasn't great, but it really didn't mean anything to me, I just wanted to be with the horses. We didn't actually get to ride them, though, as they were all highly strung and could only really be ridden by very experienced riders like Mr and Mrs Calvin, my employers. Actually I worked there for so long that I think they almost began to think of me as their daughter. When I left school I had to sell Tania – that was my pony's name – and give up the job but I still pop in on the Calvins whenever I'm in town.

C   *Margaret*

My parents had a shop and we lived on the premises so even when we were tiny we were always in the shop with them. Almost as soon as I could walk, I started helping put things on the shelves and so on and then from the age of about nine I used to serve the customers. Of course I wasn't on the payroll, nor did I ever think I should have been. I just accepted that the shop and giving mum and dad a hand in it, was part of normal life. When I was about fifteen, a supermarket company made my parents an offer for the shop which they found very attractive at the time. We could continue to live there as tenants but the supermarket chain would actually own the shop. This new arrangement meant that my parents had to have the shop front painted in the company colours. It also meant that I had to go through the formalities of filling in a lot of forms and going on a training course so that I could continue to work there. It seemed a bit silly since I would have happily done the work for nothing but after that I was also paid a very small wage.

D   *Patricia*

My first real job was in a language school my uncle had set up in Majorca. He needed someone who spoke English, Spanish and the local dialect of Catalan as a manager and I fitted the bill. It was a bit overwhelming for someone like me who had just finished university because I was in complete charge of the school. It was very challenging and I learnt a lot about the business world and also about myself but I doubt whether I would take on a job like that again. There were so many problems I had not anticipated. I was not one of the teachers, so I often felt quite isolated. Still, there were good things about the job. The money was good and I was able to live in Spain for the first time in my life, which was something I had wanted to do since I was a child. I stuck it out for a year but in the end I had to change jobs. The pressure was too much. Then I went to work for a large company in the city and I loved it … particularly the fact that if there was anything I felt uncertain about I could always ask, and I was not in sole charge.

Grammar 2: mixed conditionals
▶ *CB page 135*

1   Complete the following sentences with the most suitable form of the verbs in brackets.

1 If she only .... (*leave*) half an hour ago, she .... (*not be*) home yet.
2 If I .... (*want*) someone to talk to, he .... (*always be*) there when I called.
3 If she .... (*not ever visit*) La Gomera, she .... (*be able*) to go over when she comes at Christmas.
4 If you .... (*feel*) like being alone tonight, you .... (*tell*) me not to come over.
5 If we .... (*not move*) here, we .... (*not be able*) to celebrate your birthday with your family next month.
6 If you .... (*plan*) to withdraw a lot of money from the bank, you .... (*need*) to tell them in advance.
7 If she .... (*not put*) me under so much pressure, I .... (*finish*) the work more quickly.

2   **Use of English: key word transformations (Part 4)**

Complete the second sentence so that it has a similar meaning to the first sentence, using the word given. Do not change the word given. You must use between two and five words, including the word given. There is an example at the beginning (0).

0 If no one else applies, you can have the job.
   provided
   You can have the job .*provided that no-one else*..... applies.
1 If it isn't too hot, we'll go for a walk in the mountains.
   unless
   We'll go for a walk in the mountains .... too hot.
2 I found the film rather frightening but I'm glad I saw it.
   even
   I'm glad I saw the film .... by it.
3 We'll place an order so long as you give us a discount.
   condition
   We'll place an order .... you give us a discount.
4 If you don't put that money in a safe place, you might lose it.
   case
   You should put that money in a safe place .... it.
5 I'll buy that jacket if they have it in my size.
   long
   I'll buy that jacket .... it in my size.

Vocabulary 2: numbers and money ▶ CB page 136

1   Complete these sentences using words from the box.

distance	date	fraction	time
sum	weight	speed	amount
temperature	percentage	number	
decimal			

1   It only took a .... of a second for them to decide she wasn't suitable for the job.

2   What's the .... today? Is it the 20th or the 21st?

3   What .... did you set the alarm for?

4   Don't forget to put in the .... point clearly when you write your answers in the maths exam!

5   He lost a considerable .... of money on the stock exchange.

6   What's the .... of milk a growing child should drink every day?

7   A large .... of students start working before they finish their degrees.

8   What .... of the whole population voted in the election?

9   What's the .... between here and the Isle of Man?

10   What is the average .... limit in a city in your country?

11   What's the average .... in São Paulo at this time of year?

12   What's the average .... for a man, do you think?

2   Match the questions from Exercise 1 to these answers.

☐   a) I think it was about 75%.
☐   b) It's the 22nd, actually.
☐   c) I have no idea – could it be around 90 kilos?
☐   d) About 200 kilometres.
☐   e) 24 degrees Celsius.
☐   f) I'm not sure – I think it's about half a litre.
☐   g) 5 a.m.
☐   h) 50 kilometres an hour, I think.

3   Use of English: multiple-choice cloze (Part 1)

Read the text below and decide which answer (A, B, C or D) best fits each gap. There is an example at the beginning (0).

THE PRICE OF EDUCATION

Recently, more and more students have started to **(0)** _take up_ full-time paid work while they are still studying. This means that some of them end up actually leaving their degree courses because they see the advantages of having a stable **(1)** .... and feel that this is more useful than getting a degree. **(2)** .... a reasonable wage means that they are able to begin to **(3)** .... the debts they have **(4)** .... while they were at college or university. Why do they have these debts?

Sometimes it is because they are not good at managing their money and overspend on entertainment and clothes. Sometimes it is not their **(5)** .... Banks are keen to offer students credit cards and it's very easy to build up a big **(6)** .... It's almost impossible for students to cover all the **(7)** .... of accommodation and other necessary expenses.

It can be depressing to start working life **(8)** .... but that is the way it is for many students. Universities can charge high fees, and the price of a university education is **(9)** .... all the time. Nowadays, not everyone, it seems, is willing to spend that **(10)** .... of money, and in future there may be fewer graduates coming into the **(11)** .... Perhaps instead of **(12)** .... in stocks and shares we should all put more money into subsidising education.

0	**A** take over	**B** take up	**C** take out	**D** take away
1	**A** income	**B** intake	**C** increase	**D** input
2	**A** Winning	**B** Gaining	**C** Earning	**D** Doing
3	**A** pay out	**B** pay in	**C** pay up	**D** pay off
4	**A** run up	**B** run on	**C** run in	**D** run out
5	**A** blame	**B** fault	**C** offence	**D** crime
6	**A** overdraft	**B** statement	**C** balance	**D** withdrawal
7	**A** prices	**B** costs	**C** values	**D** sums
8	**A** in debt	**B** on loan	**C** in credit	**D** on duty
9	**A** rising up	**B** getting up	**C** moving up	**D** going up
10	**A** number	**B** fraction	**C** percentage	**D** amount
11	**A** company	**B** job	**C** workplace	**D** vacancy
12	**A** providing	**B** investing	**C** purchasing	**D** giving

Writing: letter of application
▶ *CB page 140*

About the exam: In Paper 2, Part 1, you may be asked to write a letter of application for a job, scholarship or grant.

Strategy
Read the task through carefully and underline key words and phrases in the advertisement and the notes. Use a formal style and include the following information in this order:
1 Why you are writing, where you saw the advertisement and which position you are applying for.
2 Why you are a suitable candidate (your skills and qualifications).
3 When you will be available and how you can be contacted.

1 Look at this task and the letter of application a student wrote. The sentences are in the wrong order. Put them in the correct order.

You see the following advertisement in an international newspaper.

✪ ANGLO-GREEK BANK ✪

TRAINEE MANAGER

We are looking for an enthusiastic and committed person with a good knowledge of the European financial markets to work as a trainee manager in our new Athens branch. This is a challenging and demanding position for banking and finance graduates.

We offer flexible working hours, a fully-supported staff development programme, a clothing allowance and intensive language instruction in English and/or Greek. Excellent prospects for promotion.

Salary €30,000 – €35,000 a year depending on experience.

Send a handwritten letter of application to:

Stelios Ryder, ANGLO-GREEK BANK, 59 Olympic Gardens, Athens, Greece

---

Write your letter of application in **120–180** words.

---

1 ..... Dear Sir/Madam,

..... I can be contacted by telephone on 01094893214 during the day and in the evenings.

..... I have a working knowledge of Greek and have recently passed the University of Cambridge First Certificate in English Examination.

..... I look forward to receiving your reply.

..... I am writing in reply to your advertisement in last Tuesday's Evening News.

..... I will also complete a degree in Banking and Finance in June and will be available to start work immediately afterwards.

..... I would like to apply for the Trainee Manager position you advertise.

2 Look at these DOs and DON'Ts for job applications and the letter in Exercise 1. Tick (✓) the advice the student has followed.

1 DO say which job you are applying for and where and when you saw it advertised. Invent a newspaper and date if you need to. ☐
2 DO organise your application so that you mention each of the areas in the advertisement. ☐
3 DO say when and how you can be contacted. ☐
4 DON'T forget to mention why you would be suitable. ☐
5 DO begin and end your letter as you would other formal letters. ☐

3 Read the task in Exercise 1 again. Rewrite the student's letter in your notebook, adding all the information required. Remember to divide your letter into paragraphs.

UNIT
12 Strange but true

Writing 1: making your writing more interesting ▶ *CB page 143*

1 Complete these sentences with the most suitable word from the box. Change the form of the word to fit the sentence if necessary.

| pace | creep | stroll |

1 We .... along the beach hand in hand and watched the sun go down.
2 He .... nervously up and down outside the building looking at his watch.
3 The burglar .... around the back of the house without making a sound.

| swallow | bite | chew |

4 The medicine was so bitter I could hardly stand to .... it.
5 The dog sat in the yard contentedly .... a bone.
6 As I .... into the chocolate, the delicious taste of cherry exploded in my mouth.

| imagine | wonder | believe |

7 Have you ever .... what life would have been like if we had never met?
8 I truly .... that if I hadn't heard the phone ringing, I wouldn't have noticed that the kitchen was on fire.
9 I wouldn't .... that he spends much time thinking about his appearance!

| suffocate | gasp | pant |

10 The old man lay on the bed .... for breath.
11 I fell asleep with the blankets over my head and dreamt that someone was trying to .... me.
12 You could see that the dog was tired and thirsty by the way he ....

| peer | glance | stare |

13 She walked straight past me without even .... in my direction.
14 We .... into the darkened room trying to make out the faces of the people inside.
15 The old fishermen spent most of their time sitting on the wall and .... out to sea.

Vocabulary 1: crime and punishment ▶ *CB page 144*

1 Find words in the wordsearch grid to complete the definitions below.

a	f	e	n	l	a	b	n	d	c	f	h
i	l	d	w	h	o	l	o	d	i	o	s
l	b	k	i	d	n	a	p	p	e	r	i
k	u	e	t	l	y	c	t	o	m	g	m
a	r	k	n	e	a	k	c	r	i	e	u
m	g	i	e	n	a	m	l	o	f	r	g
m	l	o	s	s	t	a	b	o	r	e	g
d	a	r	s	o	n	i	s	t	t	e	e
d	r	s	h	o	p	l	i	f	t	e	r
h	i	j	a	c	k	e	r	n	a	g	e
r	i	n	m	p	l	r	g	e	y	o	y
i	p	i	c	k	p	o	c	k	e	t	p

1 A .... steals things from people's pockets in public places.
2 An .... sets fire to buildings to cause damage.
3 A .... is someone who has seen a crime take place and is willing to tell the police or a court about it.
4 A .... steals things from a shop.
5 A .... keeps someone captive in order to demand money from their friends or relatives.
6 A .... threatens people in the street with a weapon to get their money and valuables.
7 A .... makes copies of things in order to deceive people.
8 A .... seizes a plane with its passengers and crew and demands money or the release of prisoners.
9 A .... gets money from people by threatening to reveal their secrets to others.
10 A .... breaks into people's houses and steals things.

2 Use of English: multiple-choice cloze (Part 1)

Read the text below and decide which answer (A, B, C or D) best fits each space. There is an example at the beginning (0).

A STRANGE CASE

When I was doing my law **(0)** ..*degree*.., I got to know a famous criminal lawyer who had defended many people. One week, he was involved in a very controversial murder **(1)** .... and I decided to go along and watch the proceedings.

The defendant was **(2)** .... of having murdered his wife. One night, they had a violent argument. At one point, the man put his hands around the woman's neck. He claimed that he had not been trying to strangle her but that he was acting in self defence. She collapsed and soon afterwards he **(3)** .... asleep from exhaustion. When he woke up and saw his wife, he was horrified to **(4)** .... that she was dead. He phoned the police to **(5)** .... the crime and they came and arrested him. The man was **(6)** .... with murder. If he had been **(7)** .... guilty, he would have received a long prison **(8)** ...., since **(9)** .... punishment had already been abolished, but the crime was still very serious.

Various experts were called to **(10)** .... evidence about the woman's death, but they couldn't agree about exactly how she had died. The **(11)** .... thought the evidence was so confusing that it took them three whole days to **(12)** .... a verdict. In the end, they decided the man was innocent, and he walked away free.

0	**A** career	**B** title	**C** degree	**D** certificate
1	**A** trial	**B** court	**C** judgement	**D** decision
2	**A** blamed	**B** prosecuted	**C** accused	**D** arrested
3	**A** fell	**B** dropped	**C** slid	**D** went
4	**A** establish	**B** prove	**C** confirm	**D** discover
5	**A** state	**B** report	**C** inform	**D** notify
6	**A** judged	**B** sentenced	**C** charged	**D** held
7	**A** found	**B** stated	**C** shown	**D** revealed
8	**A** time	**B** punishment	**C** stay	**D** sentence
9	**A** mortal	**B** capital	**C** fatal	**D** death
10	**A** witness	**B** testify	**C** speak	**D** give
11	**A** jury	**B** team	**C** committee	**D** panel
12	**A** make	**B** arrive	**C** reach	**D** have

Listening: extracts (Part 1)

 1 You will hear people talking in eight different situations. For questions 1–8, choose the best answer A, B or C.

1 You hear part of an interview on the radio. Who is being interviewed?
   A a writer
   B a detective
   C a lawyer

2 A woman telephones you. What does she want you to do?
   A try something out
   B answer some questions
   C give her some information

3 At the railway station you hear this couple talking. How is the man feeling?
   A angry
   B suspicious
   C anxious

4 You are watching a television chat show. Why has Margaret agreed to take part?
   A to give her expert opinion
   B to criticise the government
   C to ask for help

5 You hear this woman talking about something she has bought. What does she like about it?
   A It is modern.
   B It is cheap.
   C It works well.

6 A man is leaving a message on an answer phone. Who is the message for?
   A his flatmate
   B his assistant
   C his boss

7 On a boat trip you hear this guide talking. What aspects of the area is he talking about?
   A tourism
   B the history
   C the customs

8 You hear this announcement in an airport. What do they want passengers to do?
   A wait
   B board the plane
   C collect their luggage

Grammar 1: passives (2)
► *CB page 146*

1 Complete this letter using the appropriate passive or active forms of the verbs in brackets.

Dear Julia,

You'll never guess what (1) .... (happen). Our lovely new car (2) .... (steal)!

One day the week before last, Hugh went out to the beach for a swim and as usual he (3) .... (hide) the car keys in the toe of his shoe. When he came out of the water, he (4) .... (not notice) anything suspicious. It didn't look as if his clothes (5) .... (touch). When he started to put on his shoes, however, he realised that the keys (6) .... (take) and when he got to the car park, of course, the car was gone too.

The police say there is a gang of car thieves who (7) .... (know) to be operating in the area. They think Hugh (8) .... (watch) as he arrived at the beach. The thieves saw where he had parked the car and then where the keys (9) .... (hide).

It was almost two weeks ago and although we hope it (10) .... (find), we're beginning to think we might never see it again.

So that's my news. Write soon and tell me all about your new job.

Love,

Rocio

2 **Use of English:** key word transformations (Part 4)

Complete the second sentence so that it has a similar meaning to the first sentence, using the word given. Do not change the word given. You must use between two and five words, including the word given. There is an example at the beginning (0).

0 They gave him a free meal after he complained about the long delay.

was

After he complained about the long delay, *he was given* ... a free meal.

1 Our dog loves it when you take him for a walk.

taken

Our dog .... for a walk.

2 I was thrilled that they chose me to play the part.

to

I was thrilled .... play the part.

3 They made me feel extremely welcome.

made

I .... extremely welcome.

4 People knew she was an expert.

known

She .... an expert.

5 The cat dislikes it when children pat him.

patted

The cat .... by children.

6 He was angry when someone told him to turn the music down.

about

He was angry .... to turn the music down.

7 He hoped they would let him take the test again.

allowed

He hoped he .... take the test again.

8 People say the castle is over eight hundred years old.

said

The castle .... over eight hundred years old.

Vocabulary 2: nouns linked by *of* ▶ *CB page 150*

1 Put two of the words from the box next to each of the nouns with *of*.

ice	seagulls	bananas	teenagers
sheep	ponies	pickpockets	judges
cards	roses	coins	poems
flats	criminologists	lies	goats

1 a bunch of   ....
2 a flock of   ....
3 a gang of   ....
4 a panel of   ....
5 a collection of ....
6 a pack of   ....
7 a block of   ....
8 a herd of   ....

2 Use phrases with *of* from Exercise 1 to complete these sentences.

1 I think that story she told about having amnesia is a complete ....
2 A .... were discussing how street crime levels could be reduced.
3 .... without anywhere else to go, gather on the street corners in the warm summer evenings.
4 He bought her the most enormous .... for their anniversary.
5 She lives in a large .... just near the corner of Bourke Road and Richardson Street.
6 A .... swooped down and settled on the beach.
7 He's got an enormous .... from almost every country on Earth.
8 The boy and his dog came down the hill with the .... ready for milking.

3 **Speaking:** long turn (Part 2)

1 Look at these comments a student made about the two photographs and correct the mistakes.

❛ Although both these photographs show people working, they are very different in many ways. In the first photograph, a man is working at a very untidy desk. There are rows of papers and books everywhere. I'm not sure exactly what he is doing but he seems to be looking at a bar of stone or something. Perhaps he is an archaeologist.

The second photograph shows a group of people working in a restaurant kitchen. It is much tidier than the office in the first photograph even though everyone is very busy. There are piles of gas jets on each side of the cooker. Each of the chefs is preparing a different dish. The one in the foreground is cutting mushrooms into blocks and the one opposite him could be making an omelette but I'm not sure. They all seem to be enjoying working together. I think it would be fun to work in a kitchen like that. ❜

 2 Now listen to see if you were right.

Grammar 2: *have/get something one* ▶ *CB page 150*

1 Rewrite these sentences using the correct form of *have* + an object + the past participle of an appropriate verb.

0 The hairdresser cut his hair last week.
He *had his hair cut last week.* .

1 Some builders are repairing the roof of our house.
We ....

2 The dressmaker has shortened these trousers for me.
I ....

3 Someone stole all my friend's money while she was on the beach.
My friend ....

4 A photographer took photos of the bridal couple.
The bridal couple ....

5 A famous artist is going to paint her portrait.
She ....

6 A professional mechanic will have to look at our car.
We ....

7 A physiotherapist is treating my arm.
I ....

8 The supermarket can deliver your shopping.
You ....

9 A typist is going to type my assignment for me.
I ....

2 Use of English: key word transformations

Complete the second sentence so that it has a similar meaning to the first sentence, using the word given. Do not change the word given. You must use between two and five words, including the word given. There is an example at the beginning (0).

0 Our house needs painting. **must**
We *must have/get our house* painted.

1 Someone stole their television when they left their front door unlocked. **had**
They .... when they left their front door unlocked.

2 My friend gets a manicurist to paint her nails for her. **has**
My friend .... by a manicurist.

3 A friend checked the car for me before I bought it. **had**
Before I bought it, I .... a friend.

4 Did the storm break those windows? **get**
Did those windows .... the storm?

5 They cut off the king's head. **had**
The king .... off.

Reading: gapped text (Part 2)

1 You are going to read a newspaper article about a famous theft. Read the article and the sentences quickly. Which headline below fits the facts in the article?

a) Missing painting returned after 40 years
b) A reluctant art thief tells his story
c) Photograph reveals art thief's identity

2 Read the article and the sentences again. Seven sentences have been removed from the article. Choose from sentences A–H the one which best fits each gap (1–7). There is one extra sentence which you do not need to use.

Irish company director, Paul Hogan, made front page news across the world when he was photographed walking out of London's Tate Gallery on 12th April 1956 with a French Impressionist masterpiece under his arm. Hogan's plan was never to keep the painting, which was called *Jour d'été*. He and his friend, Bill Fogarty, said they were merely 'borrowing' it. There was some controversy around who owned a particular collection of paintings in the gallery, and they wanted to publicise this.

So what was the dispute about? Hugh Lane, a successful art dealer, had originally bequeathed his collection of modern paintings to Ireland. (1).......... . He made a second will and left everything to London's Tate Gallery. However, Lane must have come to regret his hasty decision. Shortly before he died in a shipwreck in 1915, he wrote yet another will leaving everything to a gallery in Dublin. Because no one witnessed the will, the English courts refused to recognise it as a legal document. As a result, Lane's collection, including *Jour d'été*, hung in the Tate Gallery for the next thirty years.

Despite the controversy over who really owned the paintings, the Irish government made few serious attempts to claim them back. This situation might have continued if Paul Hogan, a student at Dublin College of Art, had not come across a pamphlet written by Lane's aunt. (2).......... . Hogan told Fogarty about his discovery and together they decided that something should be done to get the collection returned to Ireland.

It was not long before the two friends came up with an idea. (3).......... . They chose a date for their 'robbery' and then phoned an Irish news agency in London to tell them to watch the front door of the gallery on their chosen day.

'On that morning we went into the gallery together,' says Hogan. 'In those days, the paintings were hung on the wall on chains and could be easily unhooked.' There were only two from the Lane collection on view, one of which was *Jour d'été*. (4).......... . While Fogarty pretended to make a copy of the painting on a sketchpad, Hogan lifted it off the wall and put it inside the large portfolio he had brought with him for that purpose. They worked quickly and it only took a moment to hide the painting.

The pair then walked as calmly as they could towards the front door of the gallery. Waiting for them there was a photographer from the news agency. He got several shots of them as they hurried down the steps, *Jour d'été* under Hogan's arm. (5).......... . There they waited for the evening newspaper to come out.

They didn't realise how big an impact their actions had made until they saw the headlines. (6).......... . 'When I saw it, I knew we had achieved our aim,' says Hogan. Three days later, a friend handed the painting in to the Irish embassy. 'We didn't want to keep it. The whole point of the robbery was to get people talking about the situation.'

This aim was achieved. In 1959, just three years after the raid, the governments of Ireland and the UK agreed that the ownership of the paintings should be shared. (7).......... . Hogan, who has rarely discussed his role in the famous theft, insists that he has no regrets. 'Because of what we did, some of the most famous paintings in the world now hang in their rightful place, the Hugh Lane Gallery in Dublin.'

A Each of the paintings now spends some of the time in London and some in Dublin.

B Hogan fell in love with it immediately and knew that it had to be the one.

C Unfortunately, the Tate Gallery is not happy with this arrangement.

D The theft of the painting had become the big story on the front page.

E In it, she said her nephew had always wanted the paintings to belong to Ireland.

F Angered by the fact that no permanent gallery was built for the collection in Dublin, he changed his mind.

G The young men then jumped into a taxi and drove back to a friend's flat.

H They decided to take one of the paintings from the gallery to attract public attention to the situation.

3 Find words and expressions in the text and the sentences that mean the following.

CLUE: The words and expressions are in the same order as the text.

1 a piece of work, especially art, which is the best of its kind
2 only
3 gave to others after death
4 done too quickly without thinking carefully
5 discovered especially by chance (*phrasal verb*)
6 thought of (*phrasal verb*)
7 a large flat case like a large flat book cover, for carrying drawings, etc.
8 photographs
9 a rapid visit to a place to carry something away secretly or by force

Writing 2: story (Part 2)
▶ CB page 151

1   Look at this story a student has written in answer to the task on page 151 of the Coursebook and put the sentences into the correct order.

.... a) Steve turned his back on them and walked slowly into the house.

.... b) Everyone commented on it, so Steve was astonished when she said she was going to have it all cut off and dyed blue.

.... c) When he went outside, he saw Elena and the boy taking their motorcycle helmets off.

.... d) The boy had bright blue hair and Steve began to suspect that something was going on.

.... e) He hoped he would never see Elena and Martin again.

.... f) Steve and Elena had been inseparable for months.

.... g) Later that same day, he heard a motorcycle screech to a halt outside his house.

.... h) A few days after Elena had told him about her plans, he saw a boy strolling along the street outside a new hairdressing salon called 'Martin's'.

.... i) They now both had bright blue hair.

.... j) He liked everything about her but he adored her long blond hair.

2   Now divide the story into paragraphs.

Paragraph 1:   sentences: ...*f*.... , ... , ...

Paragraph 2:   sentences: .... , ... ,

Paragraph 3:   sentences: .... , ... , ...
           .... , ... ,

3   Look at this task and the ideas a student has written down. Cross out the ideas that you think will make the plot too complicated.

You have been asked to write a story for a student magazine beginning or ending with the words:

Hurriedly, Malcolm stuffed the letter back into the envelope and pushed it into his pocket.

Write your own story in **120–180** words

Why 'hurriedly'? Is someone coming?
Why doesn't Malcolm want them to see the letter?
Why is he putting it in his pocket?
What is in the letter?
Does it contain good or bad news?
Who sent it?
When was it sent?
When did Malcolm receive it?
Is the letter a reply to a letter Malcolm wrote?
Is the letter handwritten or typed?
How does Malcolm feel about the letter?
Has he had time to read it yet?
What had happened before?
Had Martin applied for a job?

4   Now write a plan and your answer to the task in your notebook.

Go to www.iTests.com for interactive exam practice.

UNIT 13 Natural wonders

Vocabulary 1: animals ▶ CB page 156

1 **Speaking:** collaborative task (Part 3)

Look at this task and the discussion two students had about it, and fill in the gaps.

❝ I'd like you to imagine that a family is considering having a pet to help their children become more responsible by looking after the animal. Here are some of the options they are considering. First, talk together about the advantages and disadvantages of each option then say which of the pets you think would be easiest to look after. ❞

Anita: Well, if they have children, they would probably like an animal they can play with as well as look after. I think the cat would be good, don't you?

Jerzy: Well, cats have very sharp (1) .... and that might not be so good with a baby. It might (2) .... her. Cats aren't very easy to look after, either.

Anita: Yes, I suppose you're right. What about a dog?

Jerzy: I think that's a better idea. Dogs are great for children to play with – and they can have the responsibility of taking the dog for walks.

Anita: The trouble is they might not have enough space for a dog if they live in the centre of the city. They wouldn't have anywhere to (3) .... it out for walks.

Jerzy: Yes and if they go out to work every day and the children go to school, the dog will probably be lonely and it might (4) .... or (5) .... the furniture. Perhaps a pet like the parrot would be better.

Anita: I'm sorry, but I think the parrot might be a bit dangerous with the baby as well. They can bite with their big (6) .... I know they are easy to look after – but they're not much fun! I think the rabbit would be the best choice.

Jerzy: Well, they have lovely soft (7) .... but you can't really let them (8) .... around in a flat. They're a bit messy inside so it would have to be kept in a (9) .... I don't think that's fair to the rabbit! How about a fish?

Anita: You do have to remember to clean their (10) .... but they're probably less work than all the other animals. So they'd be easy for the children to look after.

Jerzy: That's true …

Examiner: Have you reached a decision?

Anita: Yes, we have.

Jerzy: We think the fish is the best choice if they live in the city because the children would have to remember to look after them – but the dog would also be good if the family have more space.

 2 **Now listen to the recording to see if you were right.**

Listening: sentence completion (Part 2)

1   Guillermo Quick had an experience that changed the way he thought about the environment. You will hear an interview with him. First read through the notes and think about the type of information needed for each gap.

Guillermo was walking along a jungle path on his way to **(1)** .... when he heard a loud noise.

At first he thought someone was trying **(2)** .... him but then he realised the noise was coming from the tops of the trees.

The trees were covered with **(3)** .... and were impossible to climb.

Hard wooden shells were falling from the trees and they were **(4)** ...., which made the noise.

The shells were shaped **(5)** ....

Guillermo returned to Spain and told **(6)** .... about the shells.

He had to find a way of collecting 500,000 shells in **(7)** ....

He employed **(8)** .... to help him collect the shells and eventually reached his target.

He uses the shells to make **(9)** ....

He hopes that the proceeds from sales can be used to raise money for **(10)** ....

   2   Now listen to the recording and complete the sentences.

Grammar 1: *so, such, too, enough, very* ▶ *CB page 158*

1   <u>Underline</u> the correct alternatives in these sentences.

1 Guillermo was *so / such* terrified that he hid behind a tree.
2 The shells bore *so / such* a striking resemblance to tiny dolphins that he could hardly believe it.
3 He thought distributing the dolphins with the magazines was a *too / very* good opportunity.
4 Five hundred thousand shells were *too / so* many for one person to collect.
5 With the help of local families he was able to collect *too many / enough* shells by the deadline.
6 Everyone likes the dolphin necklaces because they are *so / such* exotic.
7 Making jewellery like that can be *too / very* hard work.
8 I'm not *so much creative / creative enough* to design jewellery.
9 I have *so much / so* spare time now that I can start to write a book.

2   There are mistakes in most of these sentences. Find the mistakes and correct them.

0 It was ~~a so~~ *such an* expensive car that we couldn't afford to buy it.
1 It was enough cold to turn on the central heating.
2 It was such hot that you could hardly move.
3 The jeans were much too tight for her.
4 Are you too strong to lift that table on your own?
5 The music was very loud for us to be able to talk.
6 Her parents said she was so young to go off travelling on her own.
7 They were so nice people we asked them to come and stay with us.
8 Will you have time enough to visit me when you come to Poland?
9 It was such cold that we couldn't go outside.

3 Use of English: open cloze (Part 2)

Read the title and the text, and think of the word which best fits each gap. Use only one word for each gap. There is an example at the beginning (0).

UNWELCOME FREEDOM

Some animals become famous and manage (0) *to* capture the public imagination. One of (1)......... was Keiko, the killer whale. Keiko was captured when he was only two years (2)......... and then taken from his home in Iceland to California. There he became the star of a series of successful movies (3)......... *Free Willy* about a killer whale that was kept in a tank in a marine zoo. The tank was (4)......... small that he couldn't even swim around. In the films, people fight to free the whale and return him to the open sea, something they eventually succeed (5)......... doing. Many people wanted Keiko to be set free just as Willy had (6)......... in the movies. Eventually, enough money was raised to transport him to Iceland, (7)......... natural home. There he was to live in an enclosure while he was prepared (8)......... life at sea with other whales. But (9)......... was a problem. Keiko was too shy. Every (10)......... he met a group of whales, he would only spend a little while with (11)......... before swimming back to his enclosure. Sadly, Keiko had spent (12)......... long in captivity to adjust to living in the wild again.

Grammar 2: emphasis with *what*
▶ *CB page 161*

1 These sentences have been scrambled. Put the words into the right order.

1 about the winter can't stand what I the rain is

....
....

2 like most what I is about Bill sense of humour his

....
....

3 need I what is rest a long

....
....

4 should you do what is tell can't come you them

....
....

5 with water have to you what do fill is the tank

....
....

2 Rewrite these sentences starting with the words given.

1 The thing that has changed most about zoos is that the animals are better cared for.

What has changed ....

....

....

2 The thing that interested people like Stamford Raffles most was research.

What interested people ....

....

....

3 The reason most people were attracted to zoos in the past was curiosity.

What attracted most people ....

....

....

4 The unusual thing about those clouds is their shape.

What is unusual ....

....

....

5 The cause of earthquakes is pressure beneath the Earth's surface.

What causes ....

....

....

6 The thing that would frighten me more than anything else would be a tsunami.

What would ....

....

....

Reading: multiple matching (Part 3)

1   You are going to read an article about research into animal intelligence. Read the article quickly. Which topics are **not** mentioned?

a) birds
b) animal communication
c) cruelty to animals
d) animals' emotions
e) dolphins
f) chimps
g) training circus animals

2   Read the article again. For questions 1–15, choose from the people A–D. You can choose each person more than once.

Which scientist:

investigated an animal that many people think is unintelligent?	**1**
used animals held in captivity in the experiment?	**2**
used several different recording devices?	**3**
demonstrated that the animal had abilities thought to be exclusive to other species?	**4**
knew that these animals could do something young humans could not do?	**5**
put something on the animals' bodies?	**6**
divided the animals into three groups?	**7**
showed that these animals have strong feelings?	**8**
observed how these animals reacted to sound?	**9**
observed how these animals reacted to touch?	**10**
wanted to find out more about something interesting these animals did?	**11**
used an entertaining game to test animal intelligence?	**12**
needs a sophisticated device to interpret the animals' behaviour?	**13**
worked with a group of researchers?	**14**
put something into the animals' bodies?	**15**

ANIMAL INTELLIGENCE

Everyone knows that animals are intelligent, but do they really think? Four scientists might have the answer to that question.

A Lisa Parr

Lisa Parr has been observing chimps as they watch TV to see if they think about others emotionally and recognise emotional states. Parr recently tested the chimps by showing them video clips of other chimps getting injections from the vet or treats like fruit juice. The test chimps could put each scene into a category by using a button on a computer monitor. 'A vet scene is negative and they match it to a negative facial expression like a scream face,' explains Parr. 'A positive scene is matched to a positive expression like a playful, smiling face.' The chimps put nearly every scene into the right category, which means they understood what they saw on TV. In a second study, Parr monitored the chimps' brain activity while they watched ten-minute scenes of play and aggression. To do this she placed thermometers in the chimps' ears to measure brain temperature. Like humans watching horror movies, the right side of the chimp's brain heats up during scary[1] scenes. During happy, playful moments, the left hemisphere gets warm. These studies show that chimps almost certainly understand the emotions of others and feel strong emotions themselves.

B Diana Reiss

Self-recognition is a clear sign of intelligence, but until recently researchers thought most animals couldn't identify their own reflection. Now Diana Reiss of the Wildlife Conservation Society has shown that bottlenose dolphins do know themselves. She and another scientist had been told that dolphins at a nearby marine laboratory seemed to gaze[2] at themselves in the shiny tank walls. The two researchers decided to conduct an experiment. They used odourless[3] marker pens to draw lines on the bodies of the dolphins at the laboratory. Some of the marker pens they used were black, others were filled with water and some dolphins were not marked at all. The point was to see if dolphins who felt the marker pens on their bodies would check themselves in mirrors. And they did. 'The dolphins that felt the marker were very motivated to look,' says Reiss. They inspected the markings closely, using the mirror to examine body parts they could not otherwise[4] see. The conclusion to be drawn is that dolphins are the first animals apart from primates to show the ability to recognise themselves.

C Con Slobodchikoff

Another telltale sign of intelligence is the ability to communicate. Prairie dogs warn their colony of approaching danger with a language of chirps that includes more than one hundred 'words', according to researcher Con Slobodchikoff, who discovered the prairie-dog language. These little animals even use 'adjective' and 'verb' chirps to communicate information as complex as 'large black dog moving slowly'. Sitting in an observation tower near a prairie-dog colony, Slobodchikoff uses a powerful microphone, tape recorder and video camera to capture prairie dog sights and sounds. A computer program then turns the sounds into digital information that is translated into sound charts which let Slobodchikoff see patterns in otherwise indecipherable[5] noise. By ear, Slobodchikoff can understand some chirps, like 'hawk' or 'dog', but he relies on the computer to translate whole sentences.

D Chris Evans

Chickens are often considered to be rather stupid, but Dr Chris Evans and his team have shown that they are actually very sophisticated communicators. To investigate what the birds are capable of telling each other, the Evans team played food calls to adult hens. The scientists discovered that the high-pitched[6] 'tck, tck' sound that the birds make actually means 'here is some food.' Tests on seventeen birds showed that the calls made fellow hens scratch around to look for feed, but only if they had not recently discovered food, that is, only when the signal provided new information. The hens even have different calls for food they particularly like. But chickens do more than just indicate to one another that some especially tasty[7] food is available. As Evans points out, other researchers have shown that the birds have the ability to understand that an object, when taken away and hidden, still exists, something that small children can't grasp[8].

---

3 Match the numbered words or phrases in the article to these definitions.

a) understand
b) with a meaning you cannot understand
c) in other conditions
d) with a good strong taste
e) look at something for a long time
f) without a smell
g) (of a sound) not low or deep
h) frightening

Vocabulary 2: the natural world
▶ *CB page 162*

1 Unjumble the words in the box and add them to the most suitable group of words below.

ruartepmeet	zerebe	reshow
mrostrednuth	stim	temlica	storf
zildrez	gninthlig	laeg	gof	lahi

1 wind   ....
2 cloud   ....
3 weather   ....
4 snow   ....
5 thunder   ....
6 rain   ....

2 Use words from Exercise 1 to complete these sentences.

1 There were very thick black .... in the morning and then late in the afternoon the most torrential .... I have ever seen in my life.

2 I have always preferred to live in a tropical .... with very little change in .... from one season to another.

3 Last night there was a very violent .... and I thought the house had been struck by .... at one point.

4 When I went outside, a dense .... had descended on the valley and you could hardly see your hand in front of your face.

5 It was terribly hot during the day but in the evening there was a lovely cool ....

6 The ground was covered with thick .... which was several feet deep in places.

3   Use of English: key word transformations (Part 4)

Complete the second sentence so that it has a similar meaning to the first sentence, using the word given. Do not change the word given. You must use between two and five words, including the word given.

1 I have too much work to do at the moment.

snowed

I .... work at the moment.

2 The doctor told me I would be perfectly all right in the morning.

rain

The doctor told me I would be .... in the morning.

3 We were all crying by the end of the movie.

floods

We were all in .... by the end of the movie.

4 I have no problems at all at the moment.

cloud

There isn't .... for me at the moment.

5 Many people disagreed strongly with the new law.

storm

There was .... about the new law.

4   Use of English: multiple-choice cloze (Part 1)

Read the text below and decide which answer (A, B, C or D) best fits each gap. There is an example at the beginning (0).

A DRAMATIC STORM

On 31st March 2002 I had my only **(0)** *first-hand* experience of a fairly small natural disaster, when, within four hours, about 224 litres of water per square metre **(1)** .... on the city of Santa Cruz de Tenerife, where I live.

The evening before we noticed some unusual cloud formations that looked as if they were carrying a huge volume of water. It didn't rain during the night but in the morning we noticed that the air was hot and **(2)** .... At around midday it began to **(3)** .... but this quickly developed into quite a **(4)** .... downpour. It didn't stop. The rain continued to **(5)** .... down until about five o'clock when there was a brief pause. We didn't go outside as we were too busy **(6)** .... all the water that had come in through small cracks in the roof. The people who did, soon discovered that they were mistaken if they thought the storm had **(7)** .... Instead there was thunder and lightning and more torrential rain. Cars were swept **(8)** ...., houses flooded and seven people **(9)** .... their lives.

After the storm, many people spent days without either electricity or water and others were **(10)** .... in temporary shelters until the roads could be **(11)** .... of the mud and fallen trees. It seems strange that in a place where there is a volcano that could **(12)** .... and where there are occasional earth tremors, the first real natural disaster I experienced was a flood!!

0	**A** first-hand	**B** first-rate	**C** first-class	**D** first-born
1	**A** dropped	**B** felt	**C** fell	**D** showered
2	**A** humid	**B** damp	**C** wet	**D** moist
3	**A** spot	**B** drizzle	**C** drop	**D** drip
4	**A** strong	**B** dense	**C** heavy	**D** large
5	**A** spill	**B** go	**C** put	**D** pour
6	**A** mopping up	**B** getting out	**C** making up	**D** going through
7	**A** gone out	**B** moved through	**C** blown over	**D** passed up
8	**A** off	**B** away	**C** over	**D** down
9	**A** lost	**B** missed	**C** mislaid	**D** finished
10	**A** put out	**B** put up	**C** put in	**D** put down
11	**A** cleared	**B** cleaned	**C** freed	**D** tidied
12	**A** explode	**B** light	**C** burn	**D** erupt

Writing: informal letter (Part 2) ▶ *CB page 164*

About the exam: You might have the option of writing an informal letter in Paper 2, Part 2.

1 Look at the extracts below and decide if they are from formal or informal letters. Write F (formal) or I (informal).

1 ....

> I wouldn't come in the spring if I were you. It can be very wet and cold but what we all find really hard to put up with is the wind.

2 ....

> We loved the night safari! You could almost reach out and touch the animals. Thanks so much for letting us know about it. I'm sure we never would have come across it on our own.

3 ....

> There is reasonable public transport to most places on the island. Nevertheless, I recommend that you hire a car for the first few days so that you can see as much as possible. The car can be collected and returned to either of the two airports at the end of your stay.

4 ....

> Sonia met this really cool guy at the disco on Saturday. His name is Carlos and she thinks he's the best thing since sliced bread.

2 Underline and label examples of the following in the extracts.

a) contractions
b) passive forms
c) shorter sentences
d) colloquial expressions
e) phrasal verbs
f) formal connectors
g) informal connectors

3 Here are some comments a teacher made about letters students wrote in answer to the task on page 164 of the Coursebook. Which of her comments were about the letter below?

1

> Some of the language you use in your letter is too formal. For example, you could use 'I think it would be better' instead of 'my personal preference'. Also, you use the passive quite a lot and it's not necessary in a letter to a friend. Finally, you don't finish a letter to a friend in this way.

2

> You've missed some of the points in the task. For example, you should suggest some things for your visitors to do during their stay and you haven't given them any advice about accommodation or transport.

> Dear Pat,
>
> Thank you for your letter. ¹I am delighted to learn that you will be visiting my country.
>
> Firstly I would advise you to come by plane, taking one of the many charter flights ²that are currently available. ³With regard to the choice between February and September, ⁴my personal preference would be September as the weather is still warm then. ⁵Furthermore, many of the native bird species can be seen in the wetlands near the coast ⁶at that time. ⁷It is also, therefore an excellent time for bird watching.
>
> ⁸If it is your intention to spend most of your time in the countryside, ⁹might I suggest that you stay with my cousin who has a large country house. If this sounds suitable, please ¹⁰contact me by letter and the necessary arrangements will be made.
>
> Yours sincerely,
>
> Aviva Amanpour

4 Make changes to the underlined parts of the student's letter so that it is a good answer to the task. Use the following words and phrases. Write out the improved version in your notebook.

a) you can get now
b) if you plan
c) I'm really pleased to hear
d) write back and I'll arrange it
e) you could stay
f) when it comes to choosing
g) then
h) I prefer
i) what's more
j) so it's also

Reading: multiple-choice questions (Part 1)

1 You are going to read a text about a group of women who went on an expedition in the Arctic circle. Read the text on the right once quickly and say which of the items in the list is <u>not</u> mentioned.

1 choosing the group members
2 preparations for the trip
3 weather conditions
4 preparing food
5 protective clothing
6 feelings and relationships

2 Read the text again. For questions 1–7, choose the answer (A, B, C or D) which you think fits best according to the text.

1 What was so extraordinary about the expedition?
- **A** There was no one to lead it.
- **B** The women did not have any men with them.
- **C** It was a new experience for most of the women.
- **D** The women had not met one another before.

POLAR PURPOSE

In 1997, a group of twenty British women made history. Working in five teams with four women in each team, they walked to the North Pole. Apart from one experienced female guide, the other women were all ordinary people who had never done anything like this in their lives before. They managed to survive in an environment which had defeated several very experienced men during the same few spring months of that year. Who were these women and how did they succeed where others failed?

In the summer of 1995, an advertisement was put in several British newspapers: 'Adventurers are being sought for the formation of an all-woman team to walk to the North Pole. Applications are invited from women of any age, background and occupation who are willing to put up with real pain and discomfort to achieve an important goal.'

Nearly one hundred women took part in the first selection weekend and then, after several training expeditions designed to weed out unsuitable applicants, twenty women were chosen. The youngest of *line 28* these was twenty-one and the oldest fifty-one. In the group there was a mother of triplets, a teacher, a flight attendant, a policewoman and even a film producer.

They were a very mixed bunch but they all really wanted to take part in the venture and make it a success. Each of the women agreed to raise the £2500 needed for expenses and the airfare to Canada, where the expedition began. They also committed themselves to following an intensive physical training programme before leaving the UK so that they were fit enough to take part in the expedition without endangering their own or others' lives.

The women set off as soon as they were ready. Once on the ice, each woman had to ski along while dragging a sledge weighing over 50 kilos. This would not have been too bad on a smooth surface, but for long stretches, the Arctic ice is pushed up into huge mounds two or three metres high and the sledges had to be hauled up one side and carefully let down the other so that they didn't smash. The temperature was always below freezing point and sometimes strong winds made walking while pulling so much weight almost impossible. It was also very difficult to put up their tents when they stopped each night.

In such conditions the women were making good progress if they covered fourteen or fifteen kilometres a day. But there was another problem. Part of the journey was across a frozen sea with moving water underneath the ice and at some points the team would drift back more than five kilometres during the night. That meant that after walking in these very harsh conditions for ten hours on one day, they had to spend part of the next day covering the same ground again. Furthermore, each day it would take three hours from waking up to setting off and another three hours every evening to set up the camp and prepare the evening meal.

So, how did they manage to succeed? They realised that they were part of a team. If any one of them didn't pull her sledge or get her job done, she would be jeopardising the success of the whole expedition. Any form of selfishness could result in the efforts of everyone else being completely wasted, so personal feelings had to be put to one side. At the end of their journey, the women agreed that it was mental effort far more than physical fitness that got them to the North Pole.

2 Why were the women who took part in the expedition chosen?
   A They were the only ones who answered the advertisement.
   B They had done a weekend training course.
   C They were still in the group after others had been eliminated.
   D They came from very diverse backgrounds.

3 What did the women who answered the advertisement have in common?
   A They were about the same age.
   B They had all suffered pain and discomfort.
   C They all had plenty of money.
   D They all wanted to achieve a goal.

4 What does 'these' refer to in line 28?
   A all the applicants
   B the training expeditions
   C the women who went on the trip
   D the unsuitable applicants

5 What did each woman have to do before the start of the expedition?
   A visit Canada
   B get fit
   C learn to ski
   D meet the other women

6 On the expedition, the women had to be careful to avoid
   A falling over on the ice.
   B being left behind.
   C damaging the sledges.
   D getting too cold at night.

7 It was difficult for the women to cover 15 kilometres a day because
   A they got too tired.
   B the ice was moving.
   C they kept getting lost.
   D the temperatures were too low.

8 What is the main message of the text?
   A Motivation and teamwork achieve goals.
   B Women can do anything they want.
   C It is sometimes good to experience difficult conditions.
   D Arctic conditions are very harsh.

3 Practise transferring your answers to the answer sheet.

	A	B	C	D	E	F	G	H	I
1	A	B	C	D	E	F	G	H	I
2	A	B	C	D	E	F	G	H	I
3	A	B	C	D	E	F	G	H	I
4	A	B	C	D	E	F	G	H	I
5	A	B	C	D	E	F	G	H	I
6	A	B	C	D	E	F	G	H	I
7	A	B	C	D	E	F	G	H	I
8	A	B	C	D	E	F	G	H	I

4 Find words or phrases in the text that mean the same as the following.

> **CLUE:** The words and phrases are in the same order as the text.

a) wanted ....
b) eliminate ....
c) varied group ....
d) project ....
e) piles ....
f) pulled ....
g) beginning a journey ....
h) putting at risk ....

Vocabulary 1: hopes and ambitions ▶ CB page 168

1 Underline the correct alternative in the following sentences.

1 How many goals did Beckham *score / hit* in last night's match?
2 One ambition I still *have / take* is to visit India.
3 She couldn't *hit / meet* the deadline for the article.
4 Do you think you will be able to *meet / fulfil* all your dreams in the next five years?
5 Every night I *have / meet* the strangest dreams.
6 Ready. *Achieve / Take* aim and fire!
7 He *hit / achieved* the bull's eye the first time he fired.
8 The most important goal to *score / achieve* in life is to be happy!

2 Complete this text using the correct prepositions.

After John had been missing for several days, Helen realised that she might have to face (1) .... to the fact that he would never return. Her friends advised her to give (2) .... looking for him and to get (3) .... with her own life.

She ignored their advice and hired a private detective who had dealt (4) .... these kinds of mystery disappearances before. He searched John's apartment and came (5) .... a note hidden behind a picture. The note said: 'Something has come (6) .... We need to talk (7) .... your proposal again. Call me. 0209 733459.'

The detective traced the number to a company that dealt (8) .... forged passports. John had changed his identity and left the country. Helen never discovered why, and whenever his name was brought (9) .... by friends, she would finish (10) .... the conversation quickly or change the subject immediately. She thought she would never trust another man again.

3 **Use of English:** key word transformations (Part 4)

Complete the second sentence so that it has a similar meaning to the first sentence, using the word given. Do not change the word given. You must use between two and five words, including the word given. There is an example at the beginning (0).

CLUE: You will need to use a phrasal verb in each sentence.

0 To make progress in life you have to make plans. **get**
To ....*get on*............ in life you have to make plans.

1 He never abandoned hope of meeting another girl like Sophie. **gave**
He .... hope of meeting another girl like Sophie.

2 Unexpected problems can arise even if you are well-prepared. **come**
Unexpected problems can .... even if you are well-prepared.

3 He found it difficult to accept his own limitations. **face**
He found it difficult to .... his own limitations.

4 Susan always knows how to do what is necessary in a difficult situation. **deal**
Susan always knows how to .... a difficult situation.

5 We found a very cheap and pleasant hotel completely by chance. **came**
We .... a very cheap and pleasant hotel completely by chance.

6 It's a good idea to discuss your ideas with someone older. **through**
It's a good idea to .... your ideas with someone older.

Listening: multiple matching (Part 3)

1 You will hear five people giving opinions about travelling. For questions 1–5, choose from the list A–F which of the opinions each person mentions. Use the letters only once. There is one extra letter which you do not need to use.

A There are no real travellers any more.
B I would prefer to stay at home.
C Being comfortable is essential.
D I wouldn't go anywhere without a guidebook.
E It is too expensive.
F The best trips are for work or study purposes.

Speaker 1 **1**
Speaker 2 **2**
Speaker 3 **3**
Speaker 4 **4**
Speaker 5 **5**

2 Practise transferring your answers to the answer sheet.

1	A	B	C	D	E	F
2	A	B	C	D	E	F
3	A	B	C	D	E	F
4	A	B	C	D	E	F
5	A	B	C	D	E	F

Vocabulary 2: holidays and travel
▶ *CB page 172*

1 Choose the best alternative to complete these sentences.

1 Most .... stay in the cheap youth hostels and guesthouses near the central coach station.
   A rucksackers **B** backpackers **C** hitchhikers

2 At any given time, there are several hundred passenger ships .... the Mediterranean.
   A drifting **B** cruising **C** sailing

3 The .... guide on the bus was very knowledgeable about the city's history.
   A travel **B** tour **C** trip

4 He decided to do a holiday creative writing ....
   A education **B** training **C** course

5 My parents went on a weekend city- .... to Paris.
   A gap **B** break **C** pause

6 Some people like the convenience of .... holidays because they don't have to worry about transport, accommodation and meals.
   A package **B** organised **C** group

7 It's been one of my dreams to go .... in Nepal.
   A hiking **B** trotting **C** trekking

8 On .... to the North Pole, the members of the group have to ensure a very high calorie intake.
   A explorations **B** exhibitions **C** expeditions

9 I like walking holidays but a .... holiday is out of the question for me. I can't ride a bike!
   A bicycle **B** riding **C** cycling

2 **Speaking:** long turn (Part 2)

1 Use the correct form of words and phrases from Exercise 1 and other words to complete what a student said about the photographs below.

'Both these photographs show groups of people on (1) .... In the first photograph there is a group of (2) .... about to set out on an (3) .... I'm not sure exactly where they are but it could be a country like Nepal or India. Something that this photograph has in common with the other photograph is that there is a (4) .... leading the group.

The tourists in the second picture are on a (5) .... and they will be travelling around by coach whereas the first group of tourists will be (6) .... They will probably have to carry their own (7) .... but the people on the (8) .... ship have all their luggage on board and don't have to worry about carrying it from place to place.

Another (9) .... is that in the first photograph it is obviously very cold – everyone is wearing anoraks and big boots. In the second photograph, on the other (10) .... , it seems to be either spring or summer as the people are wearing light clothing like T-shirts and sleeveless dresses. Personally, I would prefer to be with the people in the first photograph. I think that is real travelling. '

2 Now listen to the recording to see if you were right.

3   **Use of English:** multiple-choice cloze (Part 1)

Read the text below and decide which answer (A, B, C or D) best fits each gap. There is an example at the beginning (0).

TRAVELLERS ON A LONELY PLANET

Tony Wheeler and his wife Maureen started the **(0)** *company* known as *Lonely Planet* after a year-long journey across Asia in 1973. They were amazed to find that their friends were **(1)** .... to read their accounts of the **(2)** .... , which had taken them well off the **(3)** .... track.

It was not long before they formed a company and began publishing guides to independent travel. In their early books they **(4)** .... to write about those destinations for which there were no existing guidebooks. Since then, they've **(5)** .... the company and have published more than four hundred guides which cover everything from **(6)** .... exploration to more luxurious adventures. Even today, the *Lonely Planet Guide to Mongolia* is the only one of its **(7)** ....

Tony says it was easier to write the first guide than later ones because they had actually done the trips they were writing about. Nevertheless, the guides remain very popular and include information on every **(8)** .... of travelling, from what brand of insect repellent to use, to where to get a haircut or have your clothes washed.

Tony and Maureen are **(9)** .... of all of their guides but say their favourite is the guide to India. The couple have not stopped travelling – they still **(10)** .... backpacking themselves, and usually **(11)** .... for the Himalayas, which they love. **(12)** .... enough, on these trips Tony and Maureen take the *Lonely Planet Guide to India* with them!

0	**A** enterprise	**B** business	**C** company	**D** endeavour
1	**A** eager	**B** enthusiastic	**C** motivated	**D** committed
2	**A** travel	**B** voyage	**C** trip	**D** tour
3	**A** followed	**B** usual	**C** known	**D** beaten
4	**A** set out	**B** went in	**C** made for	**D** took off
5	**A** extended	**B** expanded	**C** increased	**D** broadened
6	**A** low-budget	**B** small-pocket	**C** cheap-cost	**D** little-money
7	**A** sort	**B** nature	**C** character	**D** kind
8	**A** subject	**B** matter	**C** aspect	**D** concern
9	**A** pleased	**B** excited	**C** keen	**D** proud
10	**A** do	**B** make	**C** go	**D** have
11	**A** head	**B** take	**C** go	**D** fly
12	**A** Normally	**B** Usually	**C** Generally	**D** Naturally

4   Practise transferring your answers to the answer sheet.

	A	B	C	D
1	A	B	C	D
2	A	B	C	D
3	A	B	C	D
4	A	B	C	D
5	A	B	C	D
6	A	B	C	D
7	A	B	C	D
8	A	B	C	D
9	A	B	C	D
10	A	B	C	D
11	A	B	C	D
12	A	B	C	D

Grammar: ways of giving advice ▶ *CB page 173*

1   There are mistakes with ways of giving advice in some of these sentences. Find the mistakes and correct them.

1 It's advisable applying insect repellent.
2 You should also to sleep under a mosquito net.
3 If you go walking in the mountains, make sure to telling people where you are going and when to expect you back.
4 The language is quite hard to master but you ought try to learn a few basic words and phrases.
5 Make sure your passport is valid for more than six months.
6 The tour guide advised that we shouldn't walk around alone at night.
7 He recommended to go out in a group instead.
8 Don't attempt seeing the whole city in a weekend. You will need at least a week.
9 It's unwise to snorkel without wearing protective clothing of some kind.
10 I would wearing a money belt if I were you.

2 Use of English: open cloze (Part 2)

Read the text below and think of the word which best fits each gap. Use only one word in each gap. There is an example at the beginning (0).

SNORKELLING AND DIVING IN THAILAND

Thailand offers near perfect conditions for snorkelling and diving among the beautiful coral reefs.
(0) ..*There*...... are many resorts where you can rent equipment or sign **(1)** .... for a diving course. Whether you're snorkelling or diving you should be aware of your effect **(2)** .... the reef structure. Too **(3)** .... human contact with the reefs damages them in a very real way so if you are really concerned about saving these delicate ecosystems, you should try not to visit them at **(4)** .... However, very **(5)** .... people are that committed to environmental concerns so **(6)** .... best way to minimise your impact is by not touching the reefs or by asking your boatman not to anchor in the middle of **(7)** .... Don't buy coral souvenirs, **(8)** .... tourist demand only encourages local people to destroy the reefs **(9)** .... as to obtain the coral.
As far as snorkelling equipment goes, the **(10)** .... important thing to do is buy or rent a mask that fits. Before you pay **(11)** .... a diving course or expedition you should check that the diving centre is authorised, **(12)** .... ask other people who have done the course what they thought of it.

3 Now practise transferring your answers to the answer sheet.

1		
2		
3		
4		
5		
6		
7		
8		
9		
10		
11		
12		

4 Speaking: collaborative task (Part 3)

Read what two students said in response to the task on page 174 of the Coursebook. Try to complete the dialogue and then listen to the recording to see if you were right.

Daniella: I think we should (1) .... a mobile phone. If we have an accident or get lost, we can always call and tell someone we are in trouble.

Loukas: Yes, I agree. They're quite light anyway and (2) .... in that kind of situation. I think the camera would be a bit too heavy, don't you?

Daniella: It depends. A lot of the new digital cameras are tiny. Perhaps (3) .... one of those mobile phones that is also a camera.

Loukas: That's a good idea. It (4) .... to go on a trip like that and not be able to take any photos, but I'm (5) .... the weight – we don't want to carry too much – and if we're going to carry a torch …

Daniella: Are we going to take the torch?

Loukas: I (6) .... on a camping trip without a torch. It is very dark in the mountains at night, and we could also use it to attract attention if we get lost.

Daniella: I'm sure you don't think that taking a laptop computer is a good idea then.

Loukas: Why (7) .... take a laptop computer with us?

Daniella: Well, it's a long camping trip so we might want to write letters or keep a diary or something. (8) .... we wouldn't be able to recharge the battery up there in the mountains. Some binoculars would be good though. We could use them to watch birds and animals.

Loukas: In my opinion they're (9) .... and they're too heavy to carry.

Daniella: OK we'll leave the binoculars behind, but I want to bring my personal CD player. It hardly weighs (10) .... and I love music.

Loukas: I think we should (11) .... more important things like sunscreen, but if you really want to take it then that's up to you.

Daniella: So, we want to take the mobile phone, the torch, the sunscreen and what about the chocolate?

Loukas: I love chocolate so (12) .... to take that!

Writing: essay (Part 2)
▶ *CB page 175*

Strategy (1)
In the first paragraph of your essay, summarise the task question **in your own words**.

1　Look at these task topics and match them to the first paragraphs of students' answers below. There is one extra task topic which you do not need to use.

1 It is a good idea for young people to take some time off to travel before they start work or university.
2 Tourists do more harm than good.
3 Students benefit from having part-time jobs.
4 Should parents limit the amount of television their children watch?
5 Modern technology prevents real communication taking place.

....　a) Older people often complain that devices such as mobile phones and computers stop us being able to talk or write to one another as we used to.

....　b) Working in the evenings or at the weekends while you are studying has both advantages and disadvantages.

....　c) Places that receive a large number of visitors usually benefit economically but there are also some disadvantages.

....　d) It is often said that travel broadens the mind but should young people spend a period of time travelling before settling down to work or study?

Strategy (2)
Your essay should include a paragraph supporting the statement or question and another in which you offer the opposite point of view.

2　Look at these points a student has written down to include in an essay about task 1 from Exercise 1. Decide if the points support the statement or offer the opposite point of view. Mark them ☺ or ☹.

Travelling is fun and you can have lots of adventures. ☐

It can be difficult to settle down when you come back. ☐

You can get to know other cultures. ☐

You can make friends with people from all over the world. ☐

You can feel homesick. ☐

Travelling can be exhausting and even dangerous. ☐

3　Combine the points into two paragraphs using the linking words below.

There are several obvious benefits of taking some time off to travel. Firstly and perhaps most obviously, (1) .... In addition, (2) .... and this may help you in later life. Another benefit is that (3) .... and even learn their languages.
Nevertheless, some young travellers experience difficulties. Unfortunately, (4) .... particularly if you travel alone. Furthermore, if you don't have travelling companions, (5) ....
A third disadvantage is that (6) .... and this may affect your studies or your work.

Strategy (3)
Express your opinion in the conclusion.

4 Decide which of these two conclusions would be best for the essay in Exercise 3.

A

Taking a year off to travel has advantages and disadvantages for young people who are about to start working or studying. It can be enjoyable but it can also be risky, and rather lonely.

B

Despite the fact that they are not all positive, the experiences you have when you travel help you to become more mature. In my opinion it is, therefore, a very good idea for young people to see the world before they settle down

Strategy (4)
Read your work through carefully and check for errors with punctuation, spelling, grammar, vocabulary and linking words.

5 Look at the essay on the right that a student wrote in answer to the task on page 175 of the Coursebook. The student's teacher has <u>underlined</u> some errors in the essay. Correct the errors.

6 Choose one of the tasks from Exercise 1 and write your essay in your notebook.

People sometimes <u>belief</u> that they have not really had a <u>propper</u> holiday unless they have spent it in <u>other</u> country. Although you can <u>proffit</u> from visiting new countries, there are also some negative aspects to consider.

First of all, you may find that the food <u>is not agree</u> with you or that you simply <u>don't like</u>. If you don't speak the language, you may find that people are not very friendly towards you. Of course trips abroad cost a lot as well. If you try to do your <u>travel</u> on the cheap, you may even find yourself in difficult or dangerous situations.

The benefits of travelling are very varied. You can <u>experiment</u> new cultures and have a complete break from your normal routine. This can be very relaxing, obviously you'll get to see a lot of famous and <u>unnusual</u> places and these will provide you with wonderful memories later.

On <u>ballance</u> I would say that holidays spent in other countries have more advantages than disadvantages. In <u>addition</u>, holidays spent in one's own country can also be a good break.

Practice exam

Part 1

You are going to read part of a magazine article about family life today. For questions **1–8**, choose the answer (**A,B, C** or **D**) which you think fits best according to the text.

Mark your answers **on the separate answer sheet**.

The best of friends

The evidence for harmony in the family may not be obvious in some households. But it seems that four out of five young people now get on with their parents, which is the opposite of the popularly-held image of sullen teenagers locked in their room after endless family rows.

An important new study into teenage attitudes surprisingly reveals that their family life is more harmonious than it has ever been in the past: more than half of 13 to 18-year-olds get on with their brothers and sisters; and one in three has not argued with their parents during the past twelve months. Eighty-five per cent of 13 to 18-year-olds agree with the statement 'I'm happy with my family life,' while a majority said their lives were 'happy', 'fun' and 'carefree'. Only one in ten said they definitely did not get on with their parents.

'We were surprised by just how positive today's young people seem to be about their families,' said one member of the research team. 'They're expected to be rebellious and selfish but actually they have other things on their minds; they want a car and material goods, and they worry about whether school is serving them well. There's more negotiation and discussion between parents and children, and children expect to participate in the family decision-making process. They don't want to rock the boat.'

So it seems that this generation of parents is much more likely than parents of 30 years ago to treat their children as friends rather than subordinates. There are actual statements to back this up. 'My parents are happy to discuss things with me and make compromises,' says 17-year-old Daniel Lazall. 'I always tell them when I'm going out clubbing, or which girl I'm going out with. As long as they know what I'm doing, they're fine with it.'

Susan Crome, who is now 21, agrees. 'Looking back on the last ten years, there was a lot of what you could call

negotiation … or you might have called it bribery. But as long as I'd done all my homework, I could go out on a Saturday night. But I think my grandparents were a lot stricter with my parents than that. I don't think they were that flexible with their children.' But maybe this positive view of family life should not be unexpected. It is possible that ideas of adolescence being a difficult time are not rooted in real facts. A psychologist comments, 'Our surprise that teenagers say they get along well with their parents comes because of a brief period in our social history when teenagers were identified as different beings. But that idea of rebelling and breaking away from their parents really only happened during that one time in the 1960s when everyone rebelled. The normal situation throughout history has been a smooth transition from helping out with the family business to taking it over.'

'The present generation has grown up in a period of economic growth, and as a result teenagers appear to believe much more in individualism and self-reliance than in the past. That has contributed to their confidence in the fairness of life, and thus to a general peace within the family unit.'   *line 54*

But is life really fair? Nine out of ten young people think 'if you work hard enough, you will get just rewards.' However, some recognised that this was not actually inevitable – and not always fair. 'If you have fewer opportunities and live in an inner city,' one 15-year-old boy told researchers, 'you've got to work 110 per cent. Otherwise you can work 50 per cent and get away with it.'

But greater family stability has to be a good place for young people to start out in life, and the findings of the study support this. In spite of some gloomy forecasts about the decline of the family, the future looks good!

* Your teacher will give you a copy of the answer sheet.

1 What is important about the study into teenage attitudes?

  A It confirms previous findings.
  B It gives actual figures for its results.
  C It shows that most teenagers do not get on with their parents.
  D It identifies unexpected facts about family relationships.

2 What is surprising about young people today, according to the research team?

  A They worry about being rebellious.
  B They think that education is important.
  C They negotiate with their parents.
  D They discuss things with their family.

3 According to the results of the survey, parents today differ from their own parents because they

  A listen to what their children say.
  B talk to their children more than before.
  C respect their children more as equals.
  D always compromise with their children.

4 Daniel Lazall and Susan Crome

  A have very different opinions about parents.
  B could both talk to their parents honestly.
  C had no limits placed on what they were allowed to do.
  D are both very responsible.

5 The writer says that 'the positive view of family life should not be unexpected' because

  A a happy family is the normal situation.
  B this view comes from a specific time in the past.
  C parents allow children a lot of freedom nowadays.
  D children can be bribed to behave well.

6 What does 'that' refer to in line 54?

  A a period of economic growth
  B a belief in individualism and self reliance
  C an attitude held only in the past
  D a confidence in the fairness of life

7 What do some young people believe about life today?

  A It always gives everyone a fair chance.
  B Making money is the most important goal.
  C Some people have to work longer than others.
  D Not everyone has equal opportunities.

8 The purpose of the article is to

  A help people improve family relationships.
  B show young people how to choose a career.
  C demonstrate that popular ideas about relationships may be false.
  D suggest ways of educating children in developing relationships.

Part 2

You are going to read an article about a man who discovered that he had a dangerous allergy. Seven sentences have been removed from the article. Choose from the paragraphs **A–H** the one which fits each gap (**9–15**). There is one extra paragraph which you do not need to use. There is an example at the beginning (**0**).

Mark your answers **on the separate answer sheet**.

The day my life changed

It was a bright and sunny Saturday afternoon when events conspired against me to rearrange the rest of my life, in a manner I could never have foreseen. My intention had in fact been to rearrange my life – but I had planned to do it in a very different way.

What I had in mind was winning a lot of money so that I could leave my job, and go and live somewhere warm and sunny. **(9)**………. . I did this almost every weekend and seldom won anything, but as they say, 'You never know'.

While I was standing in the queue to buy my chance of a new life, I decided to get myself something nice for supper. **(10)**………. . Some tasty sandwiches would be just the thing with a cup of cocoa a little later on. It was acting on this impulse that proved to be my downfall.

That evening, while I was eagerly anticipating the results of the lottery draw, I made myself the promised peanut butter sandwich and sat down in front of the television to relax. But very soon I realised that all was not well. Very strange things were happening to me. **(11)**………. . Within minutes it had spread to the rest of my face and my throat felt constricted. When I looked in the mirror, I could see that my face had gone very red and a rash was spreading over my entire body.

Although I had no idea what was actually wrong with me, the link with the peanut butter sandwich was obvious. **(12)**………. . I assumed that the jar I had bought was 'off', but when I

checked the sell-by date, it was fixed for nine months ahead. So that wasn't the problem. It had to be me.

I was beginning to feel a lot worse so I called a taxi to take me to the casualty department of the local hospital. After a battery of tests, I was called in to the consulting room. There I was given the diagnosis. **(13)**………. . The specialists explained to me that although it was impossible to tell whether this was a mild or severe form of the allergy, I should assume that my condition was serious. They said that for the rest of my life I would have to carry a special syringe with me so that I could inject myself with adrenaline if I came into contact with peanuts by accident.

It was this information that changed my life and now I look at everything I eat with great care. **(14)**………. . I now diligently study labels on packets and jars for the warning 'May contain traces of nuts'.

Sadly, many people who are free of the problem don't take a nut allergy seriously. Even some of my friends see it has a bit of a joke, in spite of the problems it causes me in many different situations, some serious, some less so. **(15)**………. . But I have no desire to experience the symptoms of nut allergy again – so I shall have to accept the rearrangement of my everyday life as a permanent feature.

A I feel embarrassed when I have to ask waiters if the food I'm choosing from the menu is nut free or remind a friend who has invited me to dinner that I am unable to eat nuts.

B The first thing I became aware of was a tingling in my gums and then in my lips.

C It's surprising how popular an ingredient nuts actually are in many different types of food and how careful people like me have to be with whatever they put in their mouths.

D I looked around the shelves and on the spur of the moment decided to buy myself a jar of peanut butter.

E It seemed that I was one of a growing number of people with an allergy to peanuts.

F I tried to find information about it on the Internet, but found that most people are diagnosed early in life rather than as adults.

G To this end, I walked to my local corner shop that morning to buy a ticket for the lottery.

H I had eaten nothing else for hours and there could be no other explanation for my symptoms.

Part 3

You are going to read some information about unusual and dangerous activities that some people enjoy. For questions **16–30**, choose from the activities (**A–E**). Some of the activities may be chosen more than once. When more than one answer is required, these may be given in any order. There is an example at the beginning (**0**).

Mark your answers **on the separate answer sheet**.

Which activity

is expensive? **16** ☐

began as something other than a sport? **17** ☐

is compared to another sport? **18** ☐

may put the natural environment at risk? **19** ☐

is a new activity? **20** ☐

has been going for about ten years? **21** ☐

needs personalised equipment? **22** ☐

has surprising benefits? **23** ☐

is not always considered to be dangerous? **24** ☐

will never attract large numbers of people? **25** ☐

has unexpected risks? **26** ☐

should be done with a teacher? **27** ☐

is less dangerous than it seems? **28** ☐

is more dangerous in certain weather conditions? **29** ☐

involves animals that may be dangerous? **30** ☐

The things people do for fun!

*Ray Thomas reports on different and unusual ways
some people find excitement and danger.*

A Gorge walking

At its most intense, gorge-walking requires even more nerve than something as obviously daunting as bungee jumping. It should never be done alone, and the ratio of instructor to client should not exceed 6:1. Often the route that you take follows the course of a young river, going where the water goes, which means when you encounter a waterfall with a deep enough pool, you jump – sometimes as much as 12 metres. Gorge-walking is always exhausting, drenching and challenging to your courage – or lack of it. Surprisingly, no serious incidents have yet been reported from commercial companies who organise the sport, although it is not yet well-established and is potentially very dangerous; the routes often have real hazards, perhaps making you zip across a narrow ravine faster than you ever thought you wanted to go, your legs dangling in the void.

B Diving with sharks

Nothing in the sea fascinates people like great white sharks, and off an island 200 miles north west of Tahiti, divers are guaranteed to see dozens of them. The diving centre prides itself on taking small groups of divers out to the area where the sharks come to breed and feed, but this is not without risk – there are strong water currents and groups of divers must be small. But what about the risks from the sharks themselves? Shark divers are apparently rarely a target for sharks, but certain species do have to be treated with special caution – among them the great whites. Commercial companies have been running shark feeding dives for more than a decade without serious incident; in fact, some believe that human activities are more of a threat to the sharks rather than vice versa. Even so, it is not for the fainthearted!

C Ice boating

Sailing on ice started in Europe in the 1600s, when sailing boats were fitted with runners and used for moving cargo on frozen canals in the Netherlands. Now it is the fastest sailing and non-powered sport in the world. In temperatures of about minus 11°C, the speed that these craft can reach sailing over the ice means that the wind-chill factor is minus 43°C – and frostbite is a real danger. The pilot lies almost flat on his back, pinned to his seat by a speed that can increase from 60–110 mph in two seconds – faster than a Formula One car. But unlike car drivers, there are no brakes, the pilot has no seatbelt or protection of any kind. Less than 5 mm of fibreglass separates him from destruction – and weather conditions play an important part. Yet many are prepared to risk it.

D Canoeing down waterfalls

Place a blunt tube over a vertical drop with tons of water cascading over it, and then let yourself go. Those who have done it say that going over a waterfall in a canoe, or kayak, is an amazing experience, although full of danger. Every item of equipment has to be specially manufactured or customised for the individual, and spinal injury is the biggest risk. Even if the fall itself does not cause injury, there are hidden dangers from rocks or trees in the waterfall itself. Iceland, with its hundreds of waterfalls and rapids, offers many exciting challenges to the extreme white water kayaker – but this is an activity limited to a very small number of adventurers who are prepared to take the very real risk.

E Travelling with dogs in the Yukon

The Yukon lies between Alaska and the Canadian Arctic, and has a population of only 31,000 people, but 185 caribou, 50,000 moose and 17,000 bears. It is also a huge playground for those adventurous types who want to explore this wilderness of ice and snow, and the best way for them to do it is standing on a sled being pulled by dogs. Travelling like this is now big business, and there are plenty of people prepared to pay a lot for it. Speeding through the snowy landscape for hours without seeing another person provides an unexpected escape from the stresses of life. However, even after initial instruction, it's still dangerous, cold and not as easy as some films make it look, yet sledding remains an exhilarating and unusual experience

Paper 2 Writing

Part 1

You **must** answer this question.

1   You recently booked a holiday and have just received this letter from the travel agency confirming your arrangements. Read the letter, on which you have made some notes. Then, using all the information in your notes, write a suitable reply.

We are writing to confirm the details of the holiday you booked with us recently.

| Outgoing flight | FT 457 from Manchester | 21.50 |
| Inbound flight | FT 458 from Funchal | 08.30 |

different time – why?

Could you please let us know if you would like to have the inflight meal, and whether you would like to prebook your seats on the plane. There is a charge for both these services.

Tell them

Your hotel is the Lido, and you have booked for half board. Unfortunately there is no room with sea view available. Would you prefer to have a room overlooking the pool or the garden? You should be aware from the brochure that there may be some noise from the road if you choose to overlook the garden.

Change to full board?

Say which and why

Please don't hesitate to contact us if you have any further questions.

Arrangements for transfer from airport to hotel

Yours sincerely

Jane Thompson

Jane Thompson
Getaway holidays

Write a **letter** of between **120** and **180** words in an appropriate style. Do not write any postal addresses.

Part 2

Write an answer to **one** of the questions **2–5** in this part. Write your answer in **120–180** words in an appropriate style.

2   After a class discussion on the part played by mobile phones in life today, your teacher has asked you to write a composition, giving your opinions on the following statement:

Life was much easier and less stressful before mobile phones were invented.

Write your **composition**.

3   You see this announcement in an international magazine.

Why not write an article for us?

We want our readers to send us an article on:

The best job in the world

What would be your ideal job? Why would you enjoy it so much?

The writer of the best article will win a prize,
and the article will be published in next month's issue!

Write your **article**.

4   Your school Director is worried about untidiness inside and outside the school buildings, and has asked your class to submit a report on what students think needs to be done and the best way to do it.
Write your **report**.

5   Answer one of the following questions based on your reading of one of your set books.

Either

(a) Your English penfriend has asked for your suggestions for a book you have read that they could take on holiday with them to read on the beach. Write a **letter** to your penfriend, giving your opinion of the book you have read and saying why you would recommend it. Do not write any addresses.

Or

(b) 'This is such an exciting story that it would make a wonderful film.' Write an **article** for your college magazine, saying whether you agree with this statement about the book or one of the short stories you have read.

Paper 3 Use of English

Part 1

For questions **1–12**, read the text below and decide which word **A**, **B**, **C** or **D** best fits each gap. There is an example at the beginning (**0**).

Mark your answers **on the separate answer sheet**.

Example:

0   **A**   remember   **B**   remind   **C**   memorise   **D**   recognise

0	A	B	C	D
	▬	▭	▭	▭

WHAT MAKES SOMEONE INTELLIGENT?

Some people claim that only humans are truly intelligent. But what about animals – are they intelligent too? They can certainly learn and (**0**) .... However, many of their actions are instinctive, even (**1**) .... they may look intentional. Generally, animals cannot (**2**) .... one crucial test of self awareness – they are unable to identify themselves in a mirror.

In fact, we're not really sure exactly what intelligence is or how to measure it. In the competitive (**3**) .... market, IQ scores and formal (**4**) .... are used in the selection of employees, although many successful people did not actually do very well at school.

So how are education, intelligence and success (**5**) ....? It is generally agreed that intelligence is all about the ability to learn, solve problems and be successful in life. But is there more (**6**) .... it than that? What about the (**7**) .... of emotions?

Successful people often show a (**8**) .... level of 'emotional intelligence'. This is described as self awareness – they can understand their feelings, organise and (**9**) .... them. And above (**10**) .... , this understanding means that they can motivate themselves, which seems to be the (**11**) .... to success.

So is there any (**12**) .... in teaching emotional intelligence in schools? It would seem that there is – if only we knew how.

1	A	since	B	though	C	but	D	that
2	A	get	B	succeed	C	win	D	pass
3	A	occupation	B	work	C	job	D	business
4	A	certificates	B	abilities	C	qualifications	D	talents
5	A	connected	B	joined	C	united	D	tied
6	A	for	B	to	C	at	D	with
7	A	role	B	part	C	situation	D	work
8	A	big	B	high	C	tall	D	huge
9	A	manage	B	deal	C	administer	D	command
10	A	all	B	each	C	every	D	whole
11	A	lock	B	handle	C	key	D	door
12	A	reason	B	worth	C	use	D	point

Part 2

For questions **13–24**, read the text below and think of a word which best fits each gap. Use only **one** word in each gap. There is an example at the beginning (**0**).

Write your answers **on the separate answer sheet**.

Example: | 0 | *a* |

THE WORLD OF THE COMMERCIAL DIVER

Being a commercial diver is (**0**) ..*a*.... well-paid job. And (**13**) .... needs to be, because diving is not an easy way to earn a living. The training is intense. In addition to having diving skills, divers need advanced training (**14**) .... using heavy equipment, and have to (**15**) .... able to perform skilled tasks underwater. They need to understand (**16**) .... the human body works under pressure, and work (**17**) .... part of a team. But (**18**) .... kind of work do they do? (**19**) .... over the world, they regularly brave dark, deep waters to mend broken pipes or build and maintain oil platforms. They lay underwater telephone cables and repair (**20**) .... when things go wrong. It's only in the last 40 years that this kind of work has (**21**) .... possible in such deep water – and the dangers don't stop once the work is finished. Divers (**22**) .... to wait for hours in special chambers before they can return to the surface because of the effects of pressure on their bodies. (**23**) .... it may seem sensible for companies nowadays to use robots to do deep diving work – after all, they don't need to breathe! – but it seems unlikely that they will ever take (**24**) .... from real divers because robots cannot think for themselves in dangerous situations. Skilled divers will always be in demand.

Part 3

For questions **25–34**, read the text below. Use the word given in capitals at the end of each line to form a word that fits in the gap in the same line. There is an example at the beginning (**0**).

Write your answers **on the separate answer sheet**.   **Example:** | 0 | *extremely* |

THE IMPORTANCE OF PETS

Having friends is (**0**) ..*extremely*....... important, and most people spend a lot of time with	**EXTREME**
them. But is there another important type of (**25**) .... that they may be	**FRIEND**
missing out on? Would having a pet be just as good? There is some (**26**) .... to	**EVIDENT**
support this interesting (**27**) .... It is well-known that dogs can form strong	**SUGGEST**
bonds with people, and can show signs of (**28**) .... if their owner suddenly	**HAPPY**
leaves (**29**) .... In the same way, some people feel as close to their pets as	**EXPECTED**
to their human friends, gaining (**30**) .... and comfort from their animals.	**STRONG**
It seems that the (**31**) .... between animals and people goes deeper than might	**CONNECT**
be expected. Studies into the (**32**) .... of gorillas show that these creatures have	**BEHAVE**
(**33**) .... relationships that are not so different from our own. So although	**EMOTION**
a pet may never (**34**) .... replace a friend, there is clearly a place for both.	**COMPLETE**

Part 4

For questions **35–42**, complete the second sentence so that it has a similar meaning to the first sentence, using the word given. **Do not change the word given**. You must use between **two** and **five** words, including the word given. Here is an example (**0**).

Example:

0 This coffee is too hot to drink.

not

This coffee *is not cool enough to* drink.

Write **only the missing words on the separate answer sheet**.

---

35 I have never seen such an exciting film before.

first

It's the .... seen such an exciting film.

36 'Where do you work now, Sue?' asked Pete.

know

Pete wanted .... now.

37 It's very easy to maintain contact with friends nowadays.

touch

It's very easy .... with friends nowadays.

38 I live in New York because it is a very exciting place.

if

I wouldn't live in New York .... a very exciting place.

39 It was a mistake not to buy a better car.

only

If .... a better car.

40 They had to cancel the game because of the rain.

off

The game .... because of the rain.

41 I wish I could speak Italian.

love

I would .... speak Italian.

42 You have to decide whether to accept the job.

up

It's .... accept the job.

Paper 4 Listening

Part 1

You will hear people talking in eight different situations. For questions **1–8**, choose the best answer **A**, **B** or **C**.

1 In a theatre box office, you hear this conversation. What does the man want to do?
  A buy extra tickets for a different day
  B get a refund on his friend's ticket   **1**
  C exchange his tickets

2 You hear someone talking on the radio. What is the programme about?
  A saving the environment
  B using energy   **2**
  C studying natural history

3 You hear someone talking on the telephone. Who is she talking to?
  A her accountant
  B her secretary   **3**
  C her new client

4 You hear someone talking in a café. What is the speaker doing?
  A disagreeing with a point of view
  B making a recommendation   **4**
  C blaming someone for a mistake

5 You overhear two people talking. What are they talking about?
  A a film
  B a DVD   **5**
  C a live concert

6 You hear a man talking about his plans for next year. What does he intend to do?
  A go to university
  B change his job   **6**
  C travel abroad

7 You hear two people talking in a café. What is the relationship of the man to the woman?
  A husband
  B boss   **7**
  C colleague

8 You hear a guide talking to a group of tourists. Where are they?
  A in a museum
  B in an amusement park   **8**
  C in a library

Part 2

You will hear part of an interview with Luke Harding, a young student. For questions **9–18**, complete the sentences.

Luke says his film studies course is just as

[**9**] as traditional

courses such as English or History.

Students on the course must have ideas about the films they see which they can

[**10**] with proof.

Most of the films studied in the second year are

chosen by the [**11**].

About 20 per cent of the first-year course is

[**12**] work.

The course includes studying

[**13**] films like

Harry Potter.

Students have to find out about people who have

[**14**] in the film

world.

Students who don't pass the first year exam have to

[**15**].

In the second year, students have to study a

[**16**] of films,

including those made in other languages.

Students have to write, shoot and

[**17**] a short film.

Luke says the course has increased his

[**18**].

Part 3

You will hear five people explaining what they think about crime prevention. For questions **19–23**, choose which of the opinions **A–F** each speaker expresses. Use the letters only once. There is one extra letter you do not need to use.

A Police can't be expected to fight crime without support.

Speaker 1 [ ] **19**

B Some people have their priorities wrong when it comes to preventing crime.

Speaker 2 [ ] **20**

C Education can change people's chance of being the victim of crime.

Speaker 3 [ ] **21**

D Not everyone knows what difficulties the police face.

Speaker 4 [ ] **22**

E People may not be aware of all the facilities that are available.

Speaker 5 [ ] **23**

F It's not really a serious problem.

Part 4

You will hear an interview with an expert on different senses. For questions **24–30**, choose the best answer **A**, **B** or **C**.

24 Jane studied the sense of smell because

  A she had always been interested in it.
  B it was part of her course.
  C she found it easy to understand.

25 The sense of smell used to be important for

  A identifying danger.
  B finding food.
  C encouraging eating.

26 Jane thinks that people react to smells

  A sensibly.
  B logically.
  C emotionally.

27 The smells of autumn can

  A make everyone feel depressed.
  B bring back memories.
  C remind people that winter days are dark.

28 Perfume companies use different marketing techniques to

  A sell an image.
  B make people feel good.
  C create associations.

29 What is special about the sense of smell?

  A It makes things more memorable.
  B It changes when we eat food.
  C It is the most enjoyable sense.

30 The speaker's favourite smell is because of

  A family holidays.
  B exciting travel.
  C a sense of belonging.

Paper 5 Speaking

Part 1

The Interlocutor will ask you and the other candidate some questions about yourselves.

 Listen to the recording and answer the questions. Pause the recording after each bleep and give your answer.

Part 2

The Interlocutor will ask you and the other candidate to talk on your own about some photographs.

 Listen to the recording and answer the questions. When you hear two bleeps, pause the recording for two minutes and answer the question. Then start the recording again. When you hear one bleep, pause the recording for 20 seconds and answer the question.

Candidate A

Candidate B

Part 3

The Interlocutor will ask you and the other candidate to discuss something together.

🔘 Look at the pictures and listen to the Interlocutor's instructions. When you hear the bleep, pause the recording for three minutes and complete the task.

Part 4

The Interlocutor will ask you and the other candidate questions related to the topic of Part 3.

🔘 Listen to the recording and answer the Interlocutor's questions. Pause the recording when you hear each bleep and discuss the question with the other candidate.

Answer key

UNIT *1*

Vocabulary 1 p.7

1 1 role   2 script   3 lines   4 characters
5 performance   6 preview   7 released   8 star

2 People: actor, screenwriter, cast
Story: climax, plot, dialogue, character
Film-making: scene, shot, aerial view, cut,
make-up, premiere
Parts of cinema: screen, box office, aisle

3 1 aisle   2 cut   3 screenwriter   4 premiere
5 aerial view   6 dialogue   7 cast   8 make-up

4 1 A   2 B   3 C   4 C   5 A   6 B   7 C   8 C   9 A
10 A

Grammar 1 p.8

1 1 did she start – d
2 has Antonio Banderas known – e
3 did she grow up – f
4 have there been – c
5 does David Beckham appear – a
6 has the average British person been – g
7 is the worst place – b
8 you last – h

2 1 I last saw a film in July.
2 The last time I saw a good movie on TV was
months ago.
3 We didn't buy a DVD player until Nicholas got
his new job.
4 I have never been to the cinema on my own
before.
5 I can't remember when I started wearing my
hair like this.
6 This is the first time I have been to Rome.

3 1 been   2 were   3 the   4 at   5 ago   6 with
7 they   8 had   9 Over   10 have   11 of
12 what

Reading p.10

1 a) T   b) F

2 1 D   2 A   3 B   4 B   5 D   6 C   7 A   8 C
9 D   10 B   11 C   12 D   13 B   14 A

3 a) axed   b) a loyal following   c) pitfalls
d) exploits   e) affectionately   f) editing
g) outlasted   h) dispute   i) fictitious   j) scope

Grammar 2 p.11

1 1 have you ever wondered   2 are able
3 has been living   4 has not managed   5 has
recently registered   6 has been appearing
7 has promised   8 have begun   9 has made
10 has also spoilt

2 The mistakes are as follows:
Yes, I ~~am~~ *have been* living
… and they ~~have~~ lived there when they first got
married
~~am having~~ *have* two brothers and a sister.
They ~~are~~ *have* all *been* studying at university for
several years now.
I've always ~~been liking~~ *liked* all my school subjects …
On Friday night, I ~~am going~~ *go* out with friends.
On Saturdays I ~~am~~ normally ~~playing~~ *play* football …

Vocabulary 2 p.12

1 1 enjoyment   2 enjoyable   3 disappointment
4 disappointingly   5 preparation   6 explanation
7 survivor   8 survive   9 donation   10 financial
11 financially

2 1 enjoyment   2 survivor   3 donations
4 preparation   5 disappointing   6 explain
7 financial

3 1 disappointment   2 enjoyable
3 advertisements   4 financial   5 survival
6 electricity   7 preparation   8 explanation
9 successful   10 performance

Listening p.13

1 The students were not asked question 1.

2 1 at lunchtime   2 150 students   3 going out
with friends   4 watching TV   5 watching sport
6 going to the theatre   7 a problem
8 on entertainment   9 there is no transport
10 half an hour

Tapescript

L=Leo   S=Suzie

L: That was The Red Hot Chilli Peppers and this is Leo
Hernández on Three Triple X campus radio. Next
up Suzie Chu has the results of the entertainment
survey she did last week with our students here at
the university. So tell me, Suzy! Are we a bunch of
boring old couch potatoes who just do nothing
here at Barnett College?

S: Hi Leo. I think I can certainly say that Barnett College students are definitely not couch potatoes. We went into the student union here on the campus at lunchtime last Thursday, the twenty-fifth of March and interviewed just about everyone we could find – a grand total of 150 students. They all seemed keen on helping us – and their answers were very interesting. 70% of the people we talked to said that they liked going out with friends more than anything else. That surprised me – I had expected them to say doing sport or listening to music or something like that. Next on the list … and I wasn't the least bit surprised about this … was watching TV. Even the most studious types spend an incredible 15 hours a week doing that, though they were also watching videos and DVDs as well as soaps and reality shows. Going to the cinema was pretty popular too and so was watching sport but something that surprised me was that some people consider shopping to be entertainment.

L: You must be joking! I hate shopping. So what don't people like doing?

S: Well, although quite a lot of people like acting and even belong to the drama club, surprisingly enough going to the theatre was not very popular at all. In fact, it came bottom of the list! I was amazed that over 95% of people we asked said they hadn't seen a play in the last six months.

L: Is money the problem, do you think?

S: It could be because a lot of students really do have financial problems. Most people spend between £20 and £35 a week on entertainment but this represents about a quarter of their total budget. Half goes on accommodation, 25% goes on transport, food, books, stationery and things like that and the rest goes on entertainment. The other problem is that there's no transport into the town so it's hard getting to the theatre. In fact a lot of people complained about that, so it would be great if there was some way a theatre could be built or even just a space set aside for performances here in the student union. People do really like the games room in the union building, though – that came out on top. Most students spend at least half an hour every week in there.

L: Really! Thanks for that Suzy. And our next track is for all those computer game fans. It's … .

Writing p.14

1 1 b   2 a   3 b   4 a   5 a   6 b

2 1 a   2 b   3 a   4 b   5 a   6 a   7 b   8 b
   9 a   10 a   11 b   12 a   13 a   14 b

3 A Sentences: 2, 7, 11   B Sentences: 3, 6, 12
   C Sentences: 4, 8, 9, 14   D Sentences: 1, 5, 10, 13

4 Model letters:

1 To whom it may concern,
   I am writing to express my concern about the closure of the Westgarth Cinema. Many people in the area enjoy being able to see films in the original version there and we are horrified that this will not be possible any more.

   I understand that the cinema is being closed to make way for a shopping mall. I can appreciate that local business people want to open new shops but I do not think they are really necessary. Furthermore, the Westgarth Cinema is not the right place for them.

   I am sure another solution can be found and I look forward to receiving your reply.

   Yours faithfully,
   Ana González

2 Hi Gloria,
   I got your message and I thought I should let you know about our plans for next Friday.

   We finally managed to get tickets for the festival. They're quite good seats too so we should be able to see the musicians really well. They were a bit less expensive than we had expected as well, so Sam says he owes you some money.

   We're going to meet up for a drink and something to eat just before the festival starts at 7.30. It's being held at the Concert Hall and Friday is the first night.

   See you outside the entrance at 6 p.m.

   Love,
   Ana

3 Dear Dr Barnes,
   Thank you for letting me know about the grants for young filmmakers. I am planning to send in my application this week.

   I have to get someone who has known me for at least two years to write a reference for me. I wondered if you would be willing to do this. You would need to give your opinion about my ability to use the money sensibly and to complete a film project.

   If you do not feel that you know me well enough, I will understand, of course. I would be very grateful if you could let me know, though, as I will need to find another referee.

   Please give my best wishes to Mr Barnes and to Eleanor and Ursula.

   With kind regards,
   Ana González

4 Dear Nicolas,

It was a lovely surprise to hear from you after all this time. I am really glad that you and your family are finally going to have a chance to see something of my country.

You asked about places to visit. It depends a bit on the weather but I would definitely recommend trying to see some of the wonderful birdlife near the lakes in the north. The villages and towns in this region are also full of interest and there are lots of good hotels and guesthouses.

I hope you will also have time to come and visit me and my family here in the city. We would really love to see you.

Write back soon and let me know when you will be arriving.

Best wishes,

Ana

UNIT *2*

Listening p.15

1 **A** RD   **B** RD   **C** RD   **D** RD   **E** RR   **F** RR
2 Speaker 1 D   Speaker 2 C   Speaker 3 E
Speaker 4 F   Speaker 5 A

Tapescript

Extract 1
There was a sign on the door saying the lock didn't work properly but I didn't see it until after I'd pulled the door closed. I wasn't really worried at first because I was pretty sure there were still some other people in the building but after I'd spent about half an hour making as much noise as I could … shouting at the top of my voice, banging on the door with my shoe – that didn't work! – I realised everyone else must have gone home. Then I had a few moments panic before I remembered I had my mobile. I rang my friend and … well, eventually I got out.

Extract 2
The night before, I'd packed a rucksack with water, chocolate, a plastic jacket and so on. Someone had given Alan a whistle because that could be used to attract attention if we were in trouble – and luckily he had that with him as well. When he fell and hurt his ankle, I tried to use the mobile phone but it wouldn't work in the mountains. It was cold and damp but we kept warm and dry with the jackets. Strangely enough, I didn't give up hope – I wasn't even afraid of animals. I knew someone would find us. We waited and I kept blowing on the whistle and eventually the rescue people came.

Extract 3
Susan warned us not to go into the water because there was a very strong current but it was the first day of our holiday and I couldn't resist. Then it all happened so quickly. Eddie and I were swept quite a long way out to sea before we noticed. I knew he wasn't a strong swimmer and I could see he was beginning to panic – so I just said to him very firmly 'Trust me'. I used the surf rescue technique I'd been taught and managed to get us both back to the beach. It was only then I realised how brave I'd been. It was just an automatic reaction.

Extract 4
No one remembered the last place we'd seen him but we all set out to look for him around the area of the picnic ground. It wasn't a very well-organized search and it was getting dark. We searched all night and by morning things were looking bad. And then we heard a noise – a crying sound. I thought it was an animal. Then I realised it was a child calling. We ran forwards and then saw him. He'd fallen into a hole and broken his leg – but he seemed to be all right apart from the pain.

Extract 5
Hardly anyone used the pool in the winter and that day was so cold even the caretaker had gone inside to have a cup of tea or something. The trouble was he'd taken away the ladders that you use to get out of the pool. I didn't notice until I decided to get out. I tried to lift myself out but my arms weren't strong enough. After trying for ten minutes without success I was getting very cold. I tried to keep swimming but I couldn't breathe properly and it was difficult to move my arms and legs. I had swallowed quite a lot of water, and then I actually thought I was going to die. Then the caretaker came back and pulled me out – just in time!

Vocabulary 1 p.15

1 1 –   2 –   3 +   4 –   5 –   6 –   7 +   8 –

2 1 confused   2 irritated   3 frustrating
4 flattered   5 depressed   6 annoying
7 interested   8 frightened   9 encouraging
10 frustrated   11 flattering   12 interesting
13 annoyed

3 1 concerned   2 soothing   3 embarrassed
4 insulting   5 relieved   6 humiliating

4 1 There is nothing more irritating than email advertising.   2 She feels insulted by people not taking her advice.   3 The crowd were so thrilled by the match that they wouldn't stop cheering.   4 The gentle music was soothing for her nerves.   5 A lot of people are frightened by the idea of flying.

Reading p.16

1 False

2 1 C   2 A   3 C   4 B   5 C

3 a) greet   b) single-handed   c) hardships
   d) updates   e) struggle   f) helm   g) biography
   h) sponsors

Grammar 1 p.18

1 1 higher   2 the most physically demanding
   3 easier   4 the worst   5 the most international

2 1 a) Surfing because there are ~~most~~ *more* potential
      risks in the ocean than there are on a
      mountain.
   0 b) The United States has won the ~~more~~ *most*
      gold medals in men's swimming events, closely
      followed by Australia.
   2 c) They are all demanding in different ways but
      rowing is the ~~most tough~~ *toughest* because
      you push and pull with the lower and upper
      part of the body.
   3 d) The level of difficulty is about the same but
      you don't usually get as ~~colder~~ *cold* and as
      wet roller-blading.
   5 e) Everyone knows that cricket is *the* least
      international. Swimming is next but football is
      played in every nation on Earth.
   4 f) Cyclists are more likely to suffer ~~seriouser~~ *more
      serious* injuries than either downhill ski racers
      or windsurfers.

3 1 nearly   2 to study   3 do   4 than   5 far
   6 much   7 a lot   8 better   9 no

Vocabulary 2 p.19

1 1 insecure   2 incapable   3 inexperienced
   4 impossible   5 unfortunate   6 unconscious
   7 unhealthy   8 misunderstand   9 miscalculate
   10 disapprove   11 disobey

2 1 experience   2 fortune   3 unable   4 ✓
   5 misunderstanding   6 impossible
   7 insecurity   8 conscious   9 miscalculated

3 1 adventurous   2 understanding   3 activities
   4 ability   5 miscalculation   6 disobey
   7 disapproval   8 insecure   9 possibility
   10 fearless

Grammar 2 p.20

1 1 –   2 –   3 the   4 –   5 –   6 the   7 –   8 –
   9 –   10 –   11 The   12 the   13 an   14 A
   15 –   16 –   17 the   18 –   19 –   20 –   21 –
   22 –   23 The   24 –   25 –   26 The   27 the
   28 the   29 –   30 –   31 –   32 –   33 –
   34 The   35 the   36 a   37 the

2.1 1 part   2 think   3 chance   4 sure   5 idea
   6 take   7 through

2.2 1 it   2 do   3 like   4 has   5 spends   6 sure
   7 through   8 also   9 after   10 being   11 fun
   12 against

Writing p.22

1 1 I would like to stay with a family.   2 I would be
   interesting in learning to play a musical instrument.
   3 Would it be possible to spend an extra week in
   Australia?   4 Could you tell me what clothes I need to
   bring?   5 I would like to know what the weather will
   be like in October.   6 I would prefer to do the
   grammar and vocabulary course.   7 I would be
   grateful if you could save me a place with the group
   making a class website.

2 & 3 Model answer

Dear Ms Riley,

Thank you for the letter and brochure you sent about
the sport and study programme.

I would be interested in taking part in the programme
but I would like to know a few things. First of all, could
you tell me what nationalities the other students are? I
am Argentinian and I would prefer not to be with a lot
of other Spanish speakers.

I would like to know more about the English courses. I
need to improve my English, so I would be grateful if
you could reserve a place for me on one of your
courses.

Would it be possible for me to study more than one
sport in the afternoons? I like tennis and football and it
will be hard to choose between them. I would like to
know who the trainers are for tennis and football. This
might help me to decide.

I look forward to hearing from you.

Yours sincerely

Guillermo Torres

4 1 F   2 F   3 F   4 T

5 Model answer:

Dear Ms Dupont,

I am writing to enquire about the advertisement for
tour guides you placed in last Tuesday's Chronicle. I am
very interested in these positions but have some
questions I would like to ask.

First of all, I would like to know if I would be working
on my own or with other tour guides. Secondly, I
wonder what level of English you expect the guides

to have. Finally, although you say that guides would not have to spend any of their own money, you do not mention how much we would be paid. Could you tell me whether we would actually earn any money?

I look forward to receiving your reply,

Yours sincerely,

Marek Kosmynka

UNIT *3*

Vocabulary 1 p.23

1 1 d   2 c   3 e   4 b   5 a

2 1 back   2 out   3 round   4 over   5 through
6 from   7 about

3 1 We decided to spend the afternoon <u>looking round</u> the shops.   2 I haven't had a chance <u>to look through</u> the documents for the meeting yet.
3 I <u>heard about</u> the scholarship from a friend of mine.   4 I will always <u>look back on</u> that year as a very happy one.   5 I don't understand why he couldn't <u>see through</u> her.   6 I shouted at him to <u>look out</u> but he still ran across the road without looking.

Reading p.24

1 1 the group of contestants   2 Denise   3 a musical career   4 his first single

2 1 B   2 F   3 E   4 A   5 D   6 C

3 1 aerial   2 common knowledge   3 without trace   4 macabre   5 intrigued   6 unharmed   7 take their word for it

Grammar 1 p.25

1 1 You seem ~~like~~ familiar.   2 Do ~~like~~ *as* I say.
3 She works ~~like~~ *as* a press officer for one of the biggest charities.   4 (correct)   5 ~~Like~~ *As* I told you, Simon and Natalie aren't going out together anymore.
6 I like to do relaxing things at the weekend ~~as~~ *like* going for walks in the mountains.   7 I have always thought of Santa Cruz ~~like~~ *as* my home.   8 How's the weather ~~like~~ in September?   9 Do you feel ~~as~~ *like* going out for a pizza tonight or would you rather get a take away.

2 1 What's   2 as   3 though   4 like   5 as
6 As   7 like   8 similar   9 like   10 seems
11 as   12 like

Tapescript

Part 1

C=Candidate   E=Examiner

C: … here in Barcelona.

E: How long have you lived here?

C: Nearly two years.

E: What's it like living here?

C: It's great. I think of it as my home now.

E: It certainly sounds as though you enjoy it. What would you like to do when you finish university?

C: I want to work as an interpreter. As I explained before, I am going to do a course at a university in Australia. I've always wanted to do something involving foreign languages like translating or interpreting.

E: Which languages do you speak …

Part 2

These photographs are similar because they both show people reading but they are very different in other ways. In the first photograph there are two women reading on a crowded train. It looks like a London underground train but I'm not really sure if it is or not. It seems to be winter because most of the people are wearing coats and the blonde woman looks as though she is very interested in the book. The man in the second photograph is probably somewhere like Jamaica or Barbados. It's a very beautiful beach and he is obviously very relaxed. He doesn't seem to have anyone …

3 1 like   2 as   3 seem   4 in   5 when   6 as
7 as   8 though / if   9 like   10 like   11 more
12 like

Listening p.27

1 1 A   2 B   3 C   4 C   5 A   6 A   7 A

Tapescript

A=Alice   I=Interviewer

I: Today we're talking to novelist, Alice Fenstreet. Alice, you're now a very successful published novelist … have you always wanted to be a writer?

A: I can't remember a time when I didn't write. Once I started school, I spent all my spare time writing and I always knew I wanted to be a professional writer one day. I don't know where it came from because there were no other writers in the family. My aunt is a painter but she's the only one without an ordinary routine kind of job.

I: Do you feel you always knew how to write or did you have to learn how to do it?

A: Oh I definitely had to learn and it was just as tough as everyone said it would be because you have to be your own teacher. I've done courses and they're helpful up to a point especially when you can talk to other writers but in the end it's really up to you. You have to just get on with the writing. You learn as you go along.

I: Would you say that you enjoy all the aspects of your job?

A: I don't particularly enjoy talking about my work in public – you know, getting it known. I'm just not very good at it. I do love the actual writing, though, except of course when the computer crashes on you and you lose all your work. I've been using a computer for longer than most people I know and I still have problems. Everyone does. Even my editor and she's fantastic with everything technical.

I: So you don't enjoy being a celebrity?

A: Oh I do. It's very flattering and it can be great fun but it's not something I wanted when I started out. What I've always loved is that writing isn't a job. I mean you can do it whenever you want to because you do it because you want to. I sometimes stay up all night writing because I'm so involved and interested in what I'm doing. There's no one telling me what to do and when to do it.

I: But surely there are pressures from the publisher and so on.

A: Well yes. They want to see their books sell and so do I. I've been very lucky and my books have done very well so I don't really have to worry about money – I've got more than enough to live on! – but I do try not to spend it all, though. You just never know whether the next book will sell as well so it makes sense to be a bit careful.

I: You're here in London this week and you're flying to New York on Saturday. How do you feel about travel?

A: I love it but unfortunately even though I always take my laptop, it's really hard for me to get much writing done when I'm on the road. There's too much to see and do. I'd love to be able to do more travel but my writing schedules mean I often have to say 'no' to invitations to talk about my work abroad.

I: What advice would you give to a young writer starting out?

A: I'd tell them how much fun it is but I'd remind them that not everyone earns enough from their writing to survive. If they really want to make a lot of money, they should think about another career. In my case, I really think I didn't have any choice. I don't think I would have been any good at anything else. Other jobs seem so much more difficult to me.

Grammar 2 p.28

1 1 badly   2 better   3 worse   4 harder
5 in a very unfriendly way   6 still   7 straight
8 louder   9 automatically   10 late   11 highly
12 lately   13 hardly   14 free

2 1 I think it's <u>highly unlikely (that)</u> the concert will take place.
2 Make sure you wear clothes that <u>allow you to move</u> freely.
3 You can <u>get into that museum (for)</u> free.
4 People who <u>try harder</u> usually do better than others.

5 I thought he <u>behaved in a very silly</u> way.
6 He <u>went straight</u> home.

3 *Student A:* Well, I think that young people <u>usually</u> enjoy reading magazines more than books. What do you think?
Student B: My parents are <u>always</u> buying books and my brother and I <u>sometimes</u> borrow them and read them.
Student A: I <u>certainly</u> don't mean that young people <u>never</u> read books, just that magazines are probably more popular. Don't you agree?
Student B: I suppose so but I <u>still</u> think it's important to remember that books are important too. It seems to me that a new bookshop opens somewhere in town <u>almost every day</u>.
Student A: Yes, and as well as that it's very easy to order books on the Internet <u>nowadays</u>.

Vocabulary 2 p.29

1 1 U   2 G   3 G   4 U   5 G   6 G   7 U   8 G

2 1 terribly   2 quite   3 really   4 extremely
5 incredibly   6 really   7 just   8 quite   9 totally

Grammar 3 p.29

1 1 was walking   2 saw   3 was waving
4 didn't hesitate   5 ran   6 had done   7 was
8 swam   9 had seen   10 got   11 had disappeared
12 looked   13 was   14 was feeling
15 got   16 saw   17 was standing   18 were
laughing   19 turned   20 was   21 had lost
22 had not seen

2 1 endings   2 unusual   3 collection   4 mysterious
5 description   6 darkness   7 seriously   8 amusing
9 disappearance   10 existence

Writing p.30

1 1 C   2 A   3 B   4 C   5 B   6 A   7 C

2 & 4

<u>At first</u>, I could hardly believe it when my father (1) ~~had told~~ *told* us that we (2) *were going* to visit my aunt in Miami. I ~~always~~ (3) ~~wanted~~ *had always wanted* to go there and now my dream (4) *was* about to come true.

<u>The night before</u>, Dad (5) ~~was ordering~~ *had ordered* a taxi to take us to the airport so we (6) *hadn't needed* to take our car. In the taxi we were all so excited about our holiday that nobody (7) ~~was noticing~~ *noticed* that it (8) *seemed* to be taking much longer than usual to get to the airport. My father (9) ~~had~~ *asked* the driver why it (10) *was taking* so long and he (11) *said* that this (12) *was* his first day as a taxi driver and he (13) *wasn't* really sure how to get there.

It was only then that my father (14) *realised* how far away from the airport we (15) ~~had been~~ were at that moment. It was at least an hour away, and our plane (16) *was leaving* in an hour and a half.

Finally my father (17) *persuaded* the taxi driver to let him drive and eventually we (18) ~~had~~ arrived at the international terminal. We all (19) *rushed* to the check in with our suitcases, but as soon as we got there we discovered that the flight (20) ~~was being cancelled~~ *had been cancelled* due to bad weather. Our frantic rush (21) *had been* for nothing.

3 1 b 2 a 3 d 4 c

5 1 c 2 a 3 c 4 d 5 b 6 b 7 a 8 c

6 Model answer:

A good day to stay in bed

I knew it was going to be a bad day as soon as I heard the phone ringing at 6 a.m.. I had gone to bed quite late the night before because I had an essay to finish for university.

I picked up the phone and heard my brother's voice on the end of the line. He lives in New Zealand and had got confused about the time difference. By the time we finished talking it was quite late and I had to really hurry to get ready to go out. I was supposed to be meeting some friends and going on a picnic.

As soon as I stepped outside the front door, I realised that the weather had changed completely. The day before had been sunny and warm but now it was cloudy and quite cold. While I was waiting for the bus it started to rain.

It definitely wasn't a good day for a picnic so I decided to go home and get some sleep instead.

UNIT *4*

Vocabulary 1 p.32

1 a beetroot b batter c aubergine d beans
e yolk f seafood g mince h cucumber

2 1 yolk 2 beetroot 3 seafood 4 beans
5 batter 6 aubergine 7 cucumber 8 mince

3 1 B 2 C 3 A 4 D 5 C 6 A 7 C 8 B
9 C 10 B

Listening p.33

1 1 ✓ 2 ~~on~~ *in* 3 ~~sychology~~ *psychology*
4 ~~advices~~ *advises* 5 ~~get~~ *getting* to know
6 three ~~time~~ *times* 7 ✓ 8 the ~~equipments~~
equipment 9 ~~carrers~~ *careers* in sport
10 ~~the~~ next week

2 1 chef 2 in 1998 3 physical education 4 ✓
5 ✓ 6 twice a week 7 two-month
8 the client 9 ✓ 10 next year

Tapescript

P=Presenter   J=John

P: People all over the UK are beginning to hire personal trainers to help them look and feel better. In the studio with me I have John King, who has worked as a personal trainer both here and in the United States and has recently opened a gym here in London. Tell me, how did you become involved in the personal training profession?

J: Well before I started in the fitness game I was actually a chef – that was my first job, and I made pizzas! I had been thinking of starting my own restaurant, but then I realised I would rather help people get fit. So I opened a gym instead.

P: When was that?

J: That was back in 1998.

P: But you had worked as a personal trainer before that?

J: Informally, yes – I started doing some personal training while I was a student at the University of Southern Florida.

P: What course were you doing there?

J: Oh, Physical education, but I was also in the university's athletics team.

P: Right. So what kind of services do you offer in your gym?

J: Well, we obviously give clients a programme of exercises to follow. Most people want to lose a few centimetres here and there and also to strengthen their muscles so the exercises are designed to do that. But the other aspect of our service is in some ways almost more important. That's advice about nutrition. There's a good reason for this – if people don't learn to eat well, there's not a lot we can do to improve their fitness.

P: You obviously find your work very satisfying. What do you enjoy most about it?

J: Oh – that's an easy question – it's getting to know the clients. Everybody is different and it is really fascinating to find out what their interests and needs are. You really have to see the client quite frequently at the beginning to assess them physically and emotionally. That's why I usually recommend that they start their training by seeing a trainer twice a week.

P: What kind of cost are we talking about?

J: Personal training is not cheap, I'm afraid. A two-month training period can cost as much as €2000 but it really is worth it. You're learning about your own body. What better investment could you make?

P: And do you guarantee success?

J: No. The trainer can't do that. How successful a fitness training programme is, is always down to the client. If they aren't willing to do the exercises and follow the nutritional advice, then there is very little the trainer can do.

P: You told me before I came on the air that you sometimes spend more than twelve hours a day at the gym. Do you have time for anything else apart from your work?

J: Not much but then I really enjoy my work so I don't usually feel tired. Many professional trainers combine their work with careers in sport and I'm no different. I'm a marathon runner and I spend a lot of my free time training. I'm hoping to compete in the London Marathon next year and ...

Vocabulary 2 p.33

1 on   2 in   3 in   4 up   5 on   6 in   7 to   8 at / for / in   9 up   10 among

Reading p.34

1   a
3   1 A   2 C   3 A   4 C   5 C   6 A
4   1 a   2 a   3 a   4 a

Grammar 1 p.35

1   1 some   2 new clothes   3 has   4 is   5 pair of trousers   6 scissors, They're   7 some   8 luggage   9 aerobics   10 any

2   1 few   2 A few   3 a little   4 a little   5 little   6 a few   7 a little   8 Few

3   1 miserable   2 reactions   3 knowledge   4 majority   5 difficulty   6 sickness   7 immediately   8 professional   9 alarming   10 intolerance

Grammar 2 p.36

1   1 That coffee *will* spill if you're not careful   2 I *am/'m* going to apply for a job as a chef.   3 ✓   4 A coffee for me and my friend *will* have an orange juice.   5 By the time you get back, I *will* have finished cleaning the flat.   6 ✓   7 I can't come to class next week. I *will* be in New York.

2   1 I'll be doing   2 I'll be studying   3 Will you   4 I'm going to live   5 I'll come   6 don't   7 will be   8 will be living   9 we are going to   10 are having

Vocabulary 3 p.37

1   1 nose   2 leg   3 hand   4 finger   5 stomach   6 foot   7 eyes   8 shoulder

2   1 sore   2 broken   3 chubby   4 flat   5 strong   6 weak   7 swollen   8 nimble

3   1 Would you mind <u>giving me a hand with</u> this sofa?   2 I've <u>got my finger in</u> a lot of pies at the moment.   3 When I needed <u>a shoulder to cry on</u>, Bill was always there.   4 Since I met him, I <u>have only had eyes for</u> Mark.   5 He was playing so well it seemed he couldn't <u>put a foot</u> wrong.

Writing p.38

1   1 For example   2 as well   3 Unfortunately
2   1 G   2 G   3 S   4 S   5 G   6 S
3   The correct order is: b, d, c, a
4   But have young people exchanged healthier foods for mass-produced rubbish?
5   Model answer:

Healthy eating: have we forgotten what it means?

Hamburgers, crisps, soft drink and sweets: most of us enjoy these things and we eat them from time to time. But have young people exchanged healthier foods for mass-produced rubbish? Many people think that they have.

Of course there are a lot of teenagers and young adults who really enjoy this kind of food. Nevertheless, some of us are very concerned about a healthy diet. We prefer to eat natural foods like fruit and cereals. Others are probably fairly careful about their diet, though they might go out for a pizza or perhaps eat chocolate from time to time. People like this often point out that some so-called junk food is actually quite nutritious.

In balance, although some young people do eat snacks and sweets that are not particularly good for them, others are quite health conscious.

UNIT 5

Vocabulary 1 p.39

1   1 ✓   2 ~~lounched~~ *launched*   3 ~~campains~~ *campaigns*   4 ~~Consummer~~ *Consumer*   5 ✓   6 ~~advertisments~~ *advertisements*   7 ✓

2   1 C   2 B   3 C   4 A   5 A   6 D   7 A   8 A   9 C   10 A

Reading p.40

1   a F   b T

2   1 D   2 A   3 C   4 A   5 D   6 C   7 B   8 B   9 C   10 C   11 C

3   1 patent   2 caught on   3 fad   4 showcase   5 ploy   6 catchy   7 brainchild   8 overtaken

Vocabulary 2 p.41

1   1 Prices   2 selection   3 discounts   4 compact   5 handy   6 control   7 appearance   8 offer   9 sample

2   1 need ~~for~~ *to*   2 ✓   3 useful ~~to~~ *for*   4 gift ~~to~~ *for*   5 ideal ~~for~~ *as*   6 ✓   7 designed ~~for~~ *to*

Grammar 1 p.42

1 1 She asked her how often she went shopping.
  2 She asked her when she last went shopping.
  3 She asked her if she went alone or with someone else.
  4 She asked her if there was a shopping centre near where she lived.
  5 She asked her if she preferred to shop there or in the town centre.
  6 She asked her if she had ever bought anything on the Internet.
  7 She asked her if she could access the Internet from home.
  8 She asked her if she was confident that Internet shopping was safe.
  9 She asked her if she would be making her next important purchase in a shop or online.

2 a) 9 b) 6 c) 1 d) 0 e) 2 f) 3 g) 5 h) 7 i) 8 j) 4

3 1 was 2 went shopping 3 she had last been/gone 4 was 5 lived 6 preferred 7 had bought 8 couldn't access 9 went 10 was going to buy 11 would

4 1 She wanted to <u>know where I bought</u> most of my clothes.
  2 He asked me <u>if he could borrow</u> my leather jacket.
  3 She said <u>that she had to get</u> a new lap-top the next day.
  4 She explained that she <u>wouldn't be there</u> the following week.
  5 She announced <u>that they were going</u> to paint the living room yellow.
  6 She explained that <u>she had never been</u> on a plane before.
  7 He wanted to <u>know who we had seen</u> at the party.
  8 She asked him <u>if he had been living</u> in London when he met Celià.

Listening p.43

2 1 C 2 A 3 B 4 C 5 A 6 A 7 B

Tapescript

I=Interviewer T=Tim

I: In today's edition of 'Working Lunch', we're talking to Tim Whitmore, advertising executive for one of London's top agencies: Bradley and Finch. Was it always your ambition to work in an advertising agency, Tim, or did you have other plans when you finished university?

T: Actually, I started writing poetry when I was a little boy and I even had some of my work published when I was a student. So poetry was my first love,

but you can't expect to survive as a poet – I needed some money! – so I started looking around for something else to do. One of my cousins was working for an agency and he suggested I apply for a job there.

I: It must be very different from the life of a poet.

T: Yes and no. I mean a lot of the writing is actually very like writing poetry but the work environment is completely different. When you're trying to come up with a catchy slogan, everyone shouts out ideas. It's absolute chaos. Some people like working in a group like that but I'm much better off on my own. The best slogans I've written are all things I've thought of after work when I'm by myself.

I: What makes a good slogan?

T: It's hard to say. They need to be short and to have rhythm. Humour is sometimes important too though that depends a lot on the product. But the most important thing is that they need to sound natural. That's why they sometimes go out of date quite quickly. People change the way they speak and then the slogan sounds old-fashioned.

I: What do you like and dislike most about your work?

T: As I said, writing slogans is similar to writing poetry and that's the best thing for me. I really like using words in an original way. Unfortunately, it's a very competitive environment and sometimes there's quite a lot of jealousy and resentment, especially if you're successful.

I: Do you compare your work with the advertisements that come out of other agencies?

T: I try not to. In fact while I'm working on a campaign I rarely turn on the TV in my house just in case I see a commercial and start to think it's better than mine. When I go on holiday though I really like to see TV advertising in the country I'm visiting. I find it really fascinating.

I: So do you see yourself working in the advertising industry for the foreseeable future?

T: I'm getting a bit tired of working for someone else so I'd like to have more independence. I'm thinking of getting together with someone at work and setting up our own business. We would probably still do campaigns but we'd also like to get into other things like helping companies prepare all their publications.

I: Don't you want to get away from the pressure of the advertising industry?

T: A lot of people say that it's a very stressful job and that you need to get out of it before you turn thirty-five. I disagree. I think being interested in what you do keeps you young even if you do sometimes feel tired or hurt by other people's criticism. I keep fit by going to a gym two days …

Grammar 2 p.44

1 1 ~~staying~~ *to stay*   2 ~~that he had taken~~ *of taking*
3 ~~giving~~ *to give* me a lift   4 accepted ~~being~~ *that
she was* wrong   5 ✓   6 ~~told that~~ *told us that*
7 agreed ~~meeting~~ *to meet*   8 suggested ~~us to see~~
that we should see   9 ✓

2 1 She <u>recommended that I (should) eat</u> more fruit.
2 Nigel <u>invited me</u> for a coffee.
3 He <u>denied being</u> anywhere near the bank that day.
4 She <u>explained that she wouldn't</u> be able to finish
the assignment.
5 She <u>refused to let him</u> in.
6 The coach <u>congratulated them on winning</u> the
match.
7 The man downstairs <u>threatened to call</u> the police if
we didn't turn the music down.
8 The teacher <u>warned us not to walk</u> around alone
after dark.

3 1 her   2 been   3 for   4 that   5 their
6 all   7 had   8 to   9 At   10 but
11 him   12 of

Vocabulary 3 p.45

1 1 B   2 D   3 B   4 D   5 B   6 D   7 A
8 D   9 A   10 B

2 1 leisure   2 seems   3 library   4 shelves
5 magazines   6 clear   7 librarian   8 borrow
9 trolley   10 fountains/slides
11 slides/fountains   12 sure

Writing p.46

1 The correct order is: c, e, g, d, f, b, a

2 Why you are writing: sentence c
The problem: sentences e, g, d, f, b
What you want the person to do: sentence a

3 1 First of all, the advertisement said that they had
the widest selection of DVD players in town but in
fact they only had three brands.

2 They also claimed that their players would show
DVDs bought anywhere in the world. However,
they wouldn't show the DVDs we had bought in
Australia.

3 To make matters worse, they offered a choice of
three free DVDs from their huge range of classics
and recent hits but we had to take what they gave
us.

4 Finally, in the advertisement they promised to give
our money back if we were not completely
satisfied whereas they refused to give us a refund
and told us that we had to choose another
machine.

4 Model answer:
I am writing to complain about the advertisement for
DVD Depot which appeared in your newspaper last
Tuesday. There were a number of inaccuracies in the
advertisement.

I think you should contact DVD Depot and ask them to
correct the facts in their advertisement before you publish
it again. Otherwise, people like myself might be misled.

UNIT 6

Vocabulary 1 p.47

1 1 engaged   2 mouse   3 monitor   4 keypad
5 focus   6 plug   7 files, drive   8 email

2 1 downloads   2 screen   3 laptop   4 check
5 recharge   6 flat   7 hard   8 saves   9 CD

3 1 electrical   2 failure   3 technician   4 explosion
5 unplug   6 Unbelievable   7 defrost   8 nervous
9 asleep   10 loudly

Listening p.48

1 A P   B N   C P   D N   E N   F N

2 1 F   2 D   3 A   4 C   5 B

Tapescript

Extract 1
I think a lot of people forget that the majority of
computer owners are in places like the United States,
Asia or Europe, and even in those countries there are
still plenty of people who have never used a computer
at all and certainly don't have one for entertainment
at home. After all, they're not cheap to buy! And in
some places there are communities who don't have
running water, let alone electricity or computers. It's
very unjust, if you ask me.

Extract 2
I think it's a real temptation for some people – it's too
easy when you use a computer – you're looking for a
birthday present for a friend and then you notice that
you can get a cheap digital camera or perhaps some
new jeans and before you know it you're typing in
your credit card number and buying a couple of
hundred euros worth of goods. Of course there are
also dangers in giving private information on the
Internet – it's all a nightmare really.

Extract 3
I just don't know how people did school projects and
things like that before the age of the computer – it
must have taken up all their spare time! Our teachers
expect us to do a lot of research and it would take
ages if we had to go to a library and look things up in
books. Now the answer to almost any question is at
your fingertips. I think it's fantastic!

Extract 4

We've got cable now so we're actually connected to the Internet all the time. We listen to the radio, the children play games. Since we've got one of those new flat screens we also download a lot of movies and watch them on the computer. I actually bought it originally so that I could bring work home from the office not for entertainment – but I don't get much done with all these new possibilities.

Extract 5

I don't have a computer at home – it's too expensive! – and I try to leave the laptop in the office at the weekend. If I didn't do that, I really don't think I'd get any rest. I know lots of people of my age who work every weekend, answering emails, preparing presentations and doing Internet searches and so on. It can seem like quite good fun but it's still work and I think a lot of people forget that.

Grammar 1 p.48

1 1 You might find some information about him on the Internet.
2 It can't be illegal to download music.
3 He must have a webpage.
4 She may buy a new laptop this week.
5 She could have her mobile phone switched off.

2 1 might   2 might   3 must   4 must   5 can't
6 might   7 must   8 might

3.1 1 could   2 seems   3 must   4 could   5 might
6 might   7 could   8 sure   9 must   10 might

Tapescript

I don't really know what the connection is between these two photographs but it could be modern technology or perhaps communication. In the first photograph, the man seems to be talking to himself but I suppose he must have one of those mobile phones with headphones you plug into the handset. Of course, he could be singing, though it seems unlikely because he looks a bit angry. He might be having an argument with the person he's talking to. He's quite well dressed. He might be a lawyer or perhaps an advertising executive.

The other photograph shows a group of young people in a cyber café. They could be sending email messages or playing computer games, but I can't see the screens very clearly so I'm not too sure. Whatever they're doing, they must be enjoying it because they're all smiling and laughing. I don't think the photograph was taken in Europe. It might be somewhere like Thailand or perhaps India. I like playing computer games and sending emails too but I don't usually go to cyber cafés.

Reading p.50

1 The best title is c) Yes, I could live without a mobile

2 1 E   2 C   3 G   4 B   5 H   6 D   7 A

3 1 hurdle   2 haunt   3 check up on us   4 bliss
5 adventurous   6 reproach

Grammar 2 p.51

1 1 was ~~rescue~~ *rescued*   2 need to ~~been~~ *be* replaced
3 ✓   4 was ~~wrote~~ *written*   5 Are you ~~been~~ *being* met

2 1 will be towed   2 is not permitted   3 not be consumed   4 be switched off   5 will be picked up
6 is charged/will be charged   7 has been suspended
8 was stolen   9 be contacted   10 is being repainted

3 1 were   2 be   3 which   4 been   5 like   6 have
7 had   8 by   9 be   10 were   11 had   12 be

Vocabulary 2 p.52

1 1 c   2 d   3 f   4 a   5 b   6 h   7 e   8 g
2 1 tell, tell   2 talk   3 Speak   4 through   5 told
6 speak   7 said   8 say

Writing p.53

1 1 n   2 b   3 c   4 e   5 h   6 l   7 g   8 j
9 a   10 i   11 k   12 d   13 f   14 o   15 m
2 Model answer:

Internet access in the computer room

This report explains why Internet access in the computer room should not be restricted. It also suggests how teachers can help to ensure that computers are available to any students needing to complete written work.

I interviewed students who use the room to find out about their needs. Almost everybody said that they needed to send email to family and friends at home. Some students also chat in English and find this very helpful. Many students, however, feel that teachers should check that students are using English and not just chatting in their own languages. Everyone felt that Internet access should be available at lunchtimes and after school.

To sum up, because most students make valuable use of the Internet, they should be able to use it outside class time. Teachers could help by encouraging everyone to use English

UNIT 7

Vocabulary 1 p.54

1 1 advantages   2 facilities   3 transport   4 utensils
5 containers   6 qualifications   7 skills   8
equipment   9 clothing   10 vehicles   11 Luxuries
12 toiletries   13 goods   14 appliances

2 1 scientist   2 inventor   3 equipment
4 Unfortunately   5 skilful   6 disastrous   7 mixture
8 explosion   9 qualifications   10 argument

Grammar 1 p.55

1 1 b) Thomas Edison, *who* invented the electric light
bulb, lived from 1847 to 1931.   2 a) This was a
period *when* many inventors were extremely active.
3 c) One nineteenth century inventor *whose*
inventions are less well known than Edison's is
Granville Woods.   4 g) He lived in Ohio *where*
Thomas Edison and Charles Hall, the inventor of
aluminium, were also born.   5 f) The person to
whom Charles Hall sold the patent for aluminium
made a fortune from it.   6 e) The company he
founded, *which* is called Alcoa, is still in business
today.

2 1 ✓   2 ✓   3 ✓   4 They built the first plane**,**
which is another invention that has had a huge
impact on our lives.   5 If it was not possible to
travel by plane**,** it would take me six weeks to get to
Australia**,** where my family live.   6 In the late
eighteenth century**,** when the first European settlers
went to Australia**,** it took even longer than that.   7
✓   8 ✓   9 My mother**,** to whom I wrote almost
every week**,** must have felt a bit like that about me.

3 1 been   2 was   3 have   4 few   5 the   6 one
7 which   8 had   9 him   10 to   11 who/that
12 so

Reading p.56

1 1, 4, 6, 7 and 8
2 1 C   2 B   3 C   4 A   5 B   6 A   7 D   8 A   9
C   10 B   11 C   12 C   13 D   14 A   15 D
3 1 A   2 A   3 B   4 B   5 A   6 A   7 B

Grammar 2 p.57

1 1 b   2 g   3 c   4 h

2 1 will pass   2 had known   3 buy   4 would
invite/could invite   5 had   6 would have been
7 promise   8 would have watched
9 Could you live   10 could learn

3 1 Do not use the lift <u>if there is</u> a fire.
2 I would have been able to finish the assignment <u>if I
had had</u> more time.
3 There won't be anywhere for Johanna to sleep
<u>unless we buy</u> a sofa bed.
4 I wouldn't live in London <u>unless it was / if it was not</u>
one of the most exciting cities in the world.

4.1 1 had been   2 would not have   3 had been
4 write and read   5 followed   6 hadn't been
7 wouldn't be

Tapescript

E=Examiner   F=Fatima   S=Stanislao

E: How are our lives different from those of our ancestors
who lived a hundred years ago?

F: I think women's lives were much harder. For example,
if I had been born then, I'm sure I would not have
been able to study medicine.

S: If you had been living in my country, you could have.
The thing that I think has changed most is that we
write and read more than our great-grandparents did.

F: But if we write and read more than our great-
grandparents did, then why does everyone criticise
young people for being illiterate?

S: Unless you followed someone around making a note
of everything they read and wrote, you probably
wouldn't realise.

F: But what about things like healthcare? If penicillin
hadn't been discovered, a lot of us probably wouldn't
be alive today. Now I think that's a really big
difference!

Listening p.58

1 2 a   3 b   4 a   5 a   6 c   7 a   8 a
2 1 A   2 C   3 C   4 A   5 B   6 A   7 A   8 B

Tapescript

Extract 1

A: How did you start your career? What gave you your
first idea?

B: I was sitting in my mother's car doing my homework
while she did the shopping and I thought how
wonderful it would be if people could write in the
dark. I did some research and finally found something
that seemed to work. I actually won an award for it
and there was an article in a national newspaper.

A: How old were you at the time?

B: I was ten when I started but it took me about four
years to get it completely right.

Extract 2

I'm sorry to bother you but I wonder if you could just stop
for a minute – I'm not going to ask you a lot of
questions! I work for the World Wide Fund for Nature –
my office is just around the corner, you may know where

it is – and we're trying to finance a special new campaign to protect the snow leopard. I don't know whether you already give to the WWF but this is a particularly urgent issue and I wondered if you would like to help.

Extract 3

A: I think we should go back and check.

B: I'm sure you wouldn't have left it on. You never do things like that.

A: But I can't actually remember switching it off. Please don't laugh at me – I just can't remember!

B: We can always ring Carla and ask her to pop in and have a look. She has got a key after all.

A: You don't think she'd mind, do you?

Extract 4

Susan, I think this is an interesting idea but I'm not sure that it would appeal to everyone. A lot of young people won't be able to see the usefulness of something like this, so you obviously have to go about marketing your invention very carefully. I would emphasise the safety aspect, if I were you and try to sell it to people who do mountaineering and things like that. They might be very interested in your invention.

Extract 5

Your special and unique memories can be preserved in our luxury time capsules. We use only the strongest materials to ensure that the valuable objects you have chosen to represent your life and times will be in perfect condition 25, 50 or even several hundred years from now. Invest in your future memories with our superb product. If the past and the future are important to you, then price is unimportant. Phone for a free catalogue on 0613 9505595.

Extract 6

OK can we just go over that again. I can come along next Tuesday and try it out and if I'm interested then I pay £15 registration and £50 for the orientation course. After that I pay £50 to use the facilities whenever I want to and I'll also be able to use your centres in other cities. Oh right … and I'm entitled to four guest passes a year so I can bring my friends along as well.

Extract 7

The park has been open to the public since 1979 and we've had our share of problems over the years so I'd just like to run over a few precautions with you. We've taken a lot of trouble to make sure that you will be safe while you are in our park. Keep to the trails because it's easy to get lost and we don't want to have to come and look for you. If you decide to walk on your own, let someone know you are going and when you expect to be back. I'm sure I don't need to remind anybody to take water and protective clothing now, do I?

Extract 8

Will you be inviting the local press along and do you actually want me to say anything at the opening? I mean, I will, if you like … at least people will realise I'm the one who did them. And look I know you're not happy about the prices, but if you're charging a 50% commission on any sales, well they really do have to be that high.

Vocabulary 2 p.59

1 1 ✓   2 ~~did~~ *made* a big effort   3 ~~Making~~ *Doing* housework   4 does your cousin Pedro ~~make~~ *do*   5 ✓   6 ~~made~~ *did* my best   7 ~~make~~ *do* business with you

2 1 B   2 D   3 B   4 B   5 C   6 A   7 C   8 C   9 A   10 C   11 A   12 C

Writing p.60

1 1 F   2 T   3 F

2

might attract tourists	+
several points of view on the issue	I
very expensive and will cost more than they say	–
old people like going there	+
in favour of conservation because I want my grandchildren to see it	C
young people prefer modern shopping centres	–
young people can learn about their past	+
some of the buildings are dangerous	–

3 Model answer:

Our town centre: is it worth preserving?

Is preserving the old part of our town a good investment? There are differing opinions about this issue.

Some people claim that the project has already cost a lot of money, and that even more money will have to be spent. Some of the buildings are actually dangerous and need repairs. This will be very expensive and will almost certainly cost more than the local council say. Furthermore, many young people prefer modern shopping centres and do not even go into the centre of town very often.

However, other people believe that the town centre is well worth preserving. Many believe that once it is renovated it might attract tourists. Furthermore, other people like going there and young people can learn about their past.

To sum up, it seems to me that there are a number of good reasons for going ahead with the conservation project. I am in favour of it because I want my grandchildren to be able to see the old part of the town just as I can today.

UNIT 8

Vocabulary 1 p.61

1 1 washable   2 wealthy   3 funny   4 cowardly
5 lovable   6 cultural   7 furious   8 creative

2 1 harmful   2 lovely   3 dependable   4 hopeless
5 unsupportive   6 infamous   7 active

3 1 naturally   2 wealthy   3 awful   4 supportive
5 adorable   6 active   7 nervous   8 funny
9 thankful   10 healthy

Reading p.62

1 The best title is a) Uncovering family secrets: do you
dare?

2 1 A   2 C   3 A   4 D   5 B   6 B   7 C   8 D

3 1 look like   2 genetic makeup   3 motive
4 skeletons in the cupboard   5 blameless
6 trace   7 going through   8 huge   9 dead end
10 hooked

Grammar 1 p.64

1 1 think   2 going   3 getting up   4 have
5 changing, to watch   6 leaving   7 paying
8 to be   9 buying   10 going

2 1 stopped ~~to smoke~~ *smoking*   2 remember ~~getting~~
to get   3 tried ~~to have~~ *having*   4 ✓   5 like
~~meeting~~ *to meet*   6 ✓   7 forget ~~to see~~ *seeing*

3 1 have   2 there   3 to   4 which/that   5 did
6 was   7 in   8 from   9 after   10 than   11 to
12 about

4 1 going out   2 dancing   3 have   4 to find
5 to research   6 using   7 think   8 to travel
9 to visit   10 manage   11 making   12 spending

Tapescript

E=Examiner   C=Candidate

E: What kinds of social activities do you enjoy?

C: Well I like going out with friends to the cinema or
perhaps to a café or disco. I'm very keen on dancing
especially to salsa music but I don't like parties much.
I'd rather have a small group of friends over for a
meal.

E: Do you have any special plans for this weekend?

C: Well, I have to study a bit but I hope to find some
time to help my father with a project he's doing. He's
trying to research our family history but he's not very
good at using the Internet. It's a really fascinating
project and it makes me think a lot.

E: What are your plans for the future?

C: I'm going to Canada for six months next year. I'm
planning to travel around Ontario and Quebec but

I'd also like to visit Alaska if I can manage it. I'm
really looking forward to making new friends but I
know I'll miss spending time with my friends here as
well.

Vocabulary 2 p.65

1 1 sympathetic   2 thoughtful   3 generous   4
stubborn   5 sociable   6 modest   7 reliable
8 sensible

2 1 nephew   2 stepbrother   3 grandparents
4 mother-in-law   5 brother-in-law   6 uncle
7 cousins   8 aunt

3 1 similar   2 other   3 reception   4 two
5 grandparents   6 sure   7 great-grandchildren
8 look   9 bit   10 bride   11 groom
12 bridesmaids   13 ceremony   14 get
15 honeymoon

Tapescript

These two photos are similar because they both show
happy occasions. One is a wedding anniversary party
and the other is a wedding reception. They were
obviously taken at very different times, but it might even
be the same couple in the two photographs. In the first
one the couple are probably grandparents or even great-
grandparents. I'm not really sure but I think there are
four generations at the party: the couple, their children,
their grandchildren and perhaps the babies are their
great-grandchildren. The couple still look very much in
love even after such a long time. In the second
photograph everyone looks a little bit nervous and shy.
The bride is smiling, but the groom looks rather serious
and the bridesmaids are not looking at the camera. I
suppose they might all be feeling a little tired after the
ceremony. The couple's friends and relatives are all there
too. If I get married, I don't want to spend a lot of
money on a big wedding like this. I would prefer to
have a small party with some close friends and then go
away somewhere really nice on the honeymoon. I hope I
stay married …

Listening p.66

1 1 B   2 A   3 A   4 B   5 B   6 C   7 B

Tapescript

I'd never been to a surprise party in my life so it was all
rather exciting. My friend Charlie's girlfriend Alba sent
out invitations to all of his old friends as well as a cousin
from Australia he hadn't seen since his twelfth birthday
party ten years before. It said on the invitation in huge
letters that it was going to be a surprise and that we
should all make sure we didn't say anything to Charlie
that might give it away. I don't think anyone did
because I'm pretty sure he was genuinely surprised

when he walked in. He looked slightly horrified actually so either he's a very good actor or it really was a surprise. Of course part of the reason he looked so shocked was that it was a fancy dress party and we'd all come along in seventies outfits. I got together with three friends and we dressed up like a seventies pop group in Afro wigs and dark glasses. We looked really funny and hardly anyone recognised us so it was quite a success. Alba and Charlie's family hired a local disco for the night and she told Charlie that they were meeting a couple of friends there. She'd arranged for someone to bring seventies outfits for herself and Charlie so as soon as they got there they went and got changed. The DJ played lots of seventies music as well, of course. Another good idea Alba had was to put those disposable cameras on all the tables so that we could take our own photos. She had them developed and we could all get copies of the ones we liked. Some of the photos were really fantastic, I've even had one of me and my friends enlarged and framed. I only met Charlie a couple of years ago through basketball, so there were quite a lot of people at the party I hadn't met before, but I made a lot of new friends that night, including a really nice girl called Lidia I've seen quite a lot of since. I'd broken up with my girlfriend a couple of weeks before and I had been feeling a bit depressed but Charlie's party and meeting Lidia really cheered me up.

Grammar 2 p.67

1 1 hadn't eaten   2 were   3 could   4 wouldn't
5 had   6 had given   7 were   8 would realise
9 would rain   10 could

2 1 took   2 went   3 won   4 didn't come   5 learnt /
learn   6 didn't smoke   7 were

3 1 If <u>only I hadn't invited</u> him to the party.   2 I <u>wish she wouldn't do</u> that.   3 If <u>only I had revised</u> for the exam.   4 I would be happy if <u>I were able</u> to rollerskate.   5 She sometimes <u>regrets leaving</u> Australia./She sometimes <u>regrets having left</u> Australia.   6 It's <u>time you went</u> to bed.   7 I'd <u>rather you gave</u> me some money for my birthday.
8 You might not think it's risky but <u>suppose someone saw</u> you do it.

Writing p.68

1 The following points should be crossed out:
• When we go there (Friday and Saturday nights)
• Why we think there should be more places to park
• First time I went there with Carla and what happened
• Disagree with parents who don't like their children going there
• People who live in street don't like it but it's still a great place to go

2
Introducing the topic: Young people – same all over the world – want to meet friends
Where we go – Heraclio Sánchez Street
Main part of the article: Lots of pubs, cafés, places to sit and talk
Lots of university and high school students go there
Ending: Coming to La Laguna? Want to meet local young people? Come to Heraclio Sánchez Street

3 The best title and opening paragraph is B.

4 Model answer:

A great meeting point

Young people all over the world like to be with people their own age, to relax, chat and generally have a good time. We're the same here in La Laguna and we've got a fantastic place to meet our friends and make new ones, It's called Heraclio Sánchez Street.

The reason we like the street so much is that there are lots of pubs and cafés and other places to sit and talk. Lots of university and high school students go there. You can be sure that you will meet someone you know and you'll probably make new friends as well.

So if you happen to be coming to La Laguna and you want to meet local young people, why not come to Heraclio Sánchez Street? I know you'll have a really good time!

UNIT 9

Grammar 1 p.69

1 The incorrect form in each sentence is:
1 would wear   2 were having, had sometimes fainted   3 would think   4 would have   5 used to need   6 was pulling   7 didn't use to have to
8 used to start

2 1 Whenever we had visitors they *would* dress me up in a horrible blue suit.   2 My older brothers and sisters *used* to laugh at me.   3 I *would* beg my mother not to make me wear it but she insisted.
4 Eventually, I *got* used to wearing it.   5 I even began *to* feel quite fond of it.   6 One day I *could* not find the little suit in the wardrobe when I went to look for it.   7 It turned out that my mother *had* given it away to charity the day before.   8 She had bought me a new suit, which I never got used *to* wearing.

3 1 am   2 so   3 like   4 to   5 used   6 would
7 could   8 would   9 are   10 used   11 getting
12 like

Reading p.70

1 b) and c)

2 1 G 2 D 3 H 4 B 5 E 6 F 7 C

3 1 slavishly 2 telltale signs 3 snap…up
4 out of touch 5 accordingly 6 fall prey

Vocabulary 1 p.71

1 **Colours**: beige, brown, mauve, grey, navy, turquoise
Designs: V-necked, flared, tight-fitting, slip-on,
polo-necked, sleeveless
Qualities: washable, waterproof, stretch
Fabrics: silk, velvet, wool, linen, cotton, polyester
Clothes: sweater, cardigan, suit, jeans, top, T-shirt

2 1 V-necked 2 T-shirt 3 slip 4 flared 5 top
6 lycra 7 polo-necked 8 washable 9 wool
10 cardigan 11 grey 12 brown

3 1 A 2 D 3 B 4 C 5 A 6 C 7 B 8 A
9 D 10 C 11 B 12 D

Vocabulary 2 p.73

1 1 wrap 2 wash 3 tidy 4 drank 5 zipped
6 saving 7 finished 8 gathered 9 closed
10 sewed

2 1 e) It's up to you.   2 a) That's the wrong way up.
3 d) We have our ups and downs.   4 b) Everything's
going to go up.   5 f) Try to keep up to date.
6 c) Time is up.

3 1 a bit down ✗   2 up and about ✓
3 computer's down ✗   4 look down on ✗
5 feeling very down-hearted ✗   6 looks up to ✓
7 up and running ✓

4 1 I've had a few problems at work but things are
looking up now.   2 The price of petrol has gone up
a lot lately.   3 You've hung that picture the wrong
way up.   4 It's up to you whether you take the job
or not.   5 The doctor told me I would be up and
about tomorrow.

Listening p.74

1 mother 2 banana plantation 3 TV 4 works
5 study law 6 degree course 7 designing shoes
8 to make shoes 9 an example 10 an exhibition

Tapescript

I=Interviewer M=Manolo

I: I'm delighted to welcome Manolo Blahnik, the
famous shoe designer, to our studio this morning.
Mr Blahnik, you were born in the Canary Islands,
weren't you? Do you go back there very often?

M: Every chance I get, which usually means at least a
few months every year. I have certain friends who

are still there – and of course my mother, who is the
most important person in the world for me so I try
to see her as often as I can. She still lives in the
same house where I lived when I was a child,
actually.

I: Can you tell me something about what it was like to
grow up on a small island?

M: I grew up on the banana plantation that's belonged
to my family for generations. I had a wonderful
childhood on that small and quiet island – we had
no TV but I loved the cinema, so I would go as often
as possible. My sister Evangelina and I had lots of
toys, but really I loved chasing her round the banana
trees best! We had great fun playing together. And
now we enjoy our professional life together almost
as much. She works with me now …

I: But your parents didn't want you to be a shoe
designer, did they?

M: No, they had other ideas. They thought I should
study law so they sent me off to the University of
Geneva. I dropped out before I finished my degree
course and went to live in Paris … then London and
then New York. I wanted to be a set designer, you
see, and I was trying to get into set design for
Broadway productions or Hollywood films …

I: But where do the shoes come in?

M: Well, I was showing my portfolio around and when
I showed some of my set designs to Diana Vreeland,
the editor of the magazine *Vogue*; she told me that
what I really should do was start designing shoes. It
isn't very often you get to meet your heroes, let
alone receive advice on your work and career! I
went back to England and began to learn how to
make shoes. Within a year I was making shoes for
my dear friend Ossie Clarke's runway shows. About
one year later, I opened my first shop.

I: And you still have the same boutique today. All sorts
of famous women must be wearing your shoes.

M: You know I never tell anyone who my clients are
because I like to respect people's privacy. At my
house, I have an example of almost every pair of
shoes I've ever made … it's like a shoe museum …
each shoe evokes so many memories for me, they
are like my children!

I: Talking of museums, I saw the exhibition of your
work at the Design Museum here in London in
2003. I believe you are the only shoe designer ever
to have had an entire exhibition like that dedicated
to your work?

M: Really? You may be right … . It was a thrill to be
able to show so much of my work in one place and
try to convey the different influences and
inspirations I have had throughout my career. I never
imagined there would be such a huge and positive
response, so flattering and overwhelming really.

Vocabulary 3 p.74

1 The seven mistakes are as follows:

I think the person ~~spends some time~~ *doesn't spend much time* reading as there are ~~a lot of~~ *no* books on the shelves.

There are ~~no~~ *several* plants in the room.

I can see ~~a cat~~ *two cats* on the sofa.

The furniture is ~~very classical~~ *quite modern*.

there are ~~dark coloured~~ *white* blinds on the windows

There are ~~no~~ *several* pictures on the walls which are ~~covered in patterned wallpaper~~ *painted white*

There is a ~~computer~~ *television* in the photograph but there's no ~~television~~ *computer*, so perhaps this person ~~doesn't enjoy watching TV very much~~ *enjoys watching TV*

Grammar 2 p.74

1 1 Under the bed was a wooden box containing hundreds of old love letters.   2 The meal, cooked by a famous chef, was one of the best we had eaten. 3 The college, founded in 1926, has always attracted the best students.   4 A path leading down to the sea suddenly came into view.   5 The island, almost hidden by the mist, seemed to be calling her.   6 He returned the camera belonging to my father 7 All students wishing to see the principal should make an appointment.   8 A woman chasing her dog, fell over and broke her leg yesterday.

2 1 difficulty   2 indecisive   3 insecurity   4 valuable   5 confidence   6 appearance   7 awareness   8 enjoyable   9 success   10 anxiety

Writing p.75

1 1 ✗ 2 ✓ 3 ✗ 4 ✓ 5 ✓ 6 ✓ 7 ✓

2 Model answer:

Report on the New Common Room

Introduction

This report is to recommend a room in the school for a student common room. I interviewed a number of students about this issue and the following were their opinions.

Results

Many students felt the room that is currently used as classroom 3 would make the best common room. It was pointed out that the new building in Malcolm Street has brand new classrooms so it is probable that classroom 3 will soon not be needed for teaching purposes. It was generally agreed that the room should be painted and that sofas and easy chairs should be bought as well as a small refrigerator. Posters of pop, film and sports stars could be used to give the space a personal touch. Finally, a number of people mentioned the fact that a sink would be very useful for washing up coffee mugs and so on.

Conclusion

Although it will be necessary to spend some money doing the room up, it is, in my opinion, the best choice. As was stated earlier, this is an opinion that is shared by many other students.

3 Model answer:

School Souvenirs

Introduction

I have been asked to write a report on what kinds of clothing and gifts should be sold as souvenirs in the school shop. I interviewed a number of students to find out their opinion on this matter.

Results

Many students suggested that sweatshirts and T-shirts with the name of the school would be a good idea. There could even be a picture of the school building or perhaps the school crest. Other students suggested that coffee mugs and bags would also sell well. Another clever suggestion was to make up posters with photos of typical school scenes like the common room or the new classrooms and to sell these.

Conclusions

Most of the suggestions made were things students could wear or use in some other way. In my opinion, anything of this type would be a success, though the poster idea is also a very good one.

UNIT *10*

Listening p.76

1 1 B   2 E   3 F   4 C   5 A   6 D

2 Sentence 6 is not in the recording.

3 Speaker 1 A   Speaker 2 C   Speaker 3 F   Speaker 4 E   Speaker 5 B

Tapescript

Speaker 1

We did it at school but I didn't like it much, in fact it would be fair to say I hated it. I now think that had more to do with my attitude to things like that than anything else. You know how it is when you're a teenager – you don't want people to see that you're too keen on things. When we went away on holiday to Italy last year I decided I'd give it another try and I really love it now. I have private lessons twice a week and I'm really improving. My serve and backhand are still a bit weak but at least I can hit the ball. My girlfriend and I play most weekends and my coach says I could even enter a tournament next year if I feel like it.

Speaker 2

At the beginning, everyone I knew did a course of some kind. We went to classes for three hours a day every day for two weeks. The instructor was really good. He always gave us some homework and then at the beginning of the next class we'd check it through. That way we could all discuss whatever problems we'd had at home. I can remember him saying that the speed of the computer was an important thing to think about when choosing one to buy – and now I've learned how to use it properly I'm often frustrated because the one I have at home is just too slow – even though I don't use it for work.

Speaker 3

It was a distance training programme so I only had a week of classes right at the beginning of the course. The rest of the time we followed the course manual. It was really excellent. It was divided into twenty units with lots of practice tasks and exercises you could correct yourself. It provided lots of information but it also told you where to look for more both in libraries and on the Internet. We had six assignments which we sent by email and the various subject tutors replied with really helpful comments. They obviously spent a long time reading and thinking about our work. Even so, at the end when they asked us for our opinions about the course, I'm pretty sure everyone mentioned the manual. It really was first class.

Speaker 4

It was in the second year of my law degree, right at the beginning, because we were having a party to welcome new students. I was talking to a group of friends and someone had just said something funny so I was laughing. Suddenly someone tapped me on the shoulder and it was her. I couldn't believe it. She explained she had decided to go back to studying and was going to study law as well – a real change from languages for her! Some people I went to school with used to be terrified of her but I really admired her. She treated us like adults and she was almost the only one who did. I suppose that's why I learnt so much in her classes.

Speaker 5

It was a compulsory course in reading in the second year and then you could continue if you wanted and do more specialised courses on writing and speaking. A lot of people didn't bother with the optional courses because they were more interested in subjects that were more closely connected with psychology – but I wanted to go on and do research and I knew that it would be essential. They say that 90% of the world's scientific publications – books and articles – are in English and for conferences it's vital – even if you memorise your presentation, you still have to talk to people about it afterwards. And you can talk to people socially! I've never regretted studying it.

Grammar 1 p.76

1 1 ✓   2 ✓   3 are not allowed ~~using~~ to use   4 If you ~~became~~ become   5 I could ~~to~~ have   6 ~~Have you~~ Do you have to go?

2 1 shouldn't   2 must   3 didn't need to pay   4 don't have to   5 have to   6 supposed to   7 let me go out   8 made to study

3 1 Could you tell me if <u>it is necessary for</u> me to bring a sleeping bag?   2 You <u>are not allowed to use</u> a personal stereo on a plane.   3 We asked if it <u>would be possible to</u> move to a quieter room.   4 He <u>was obliged to</u> give the money back.   5 You <u>are not supposed to wear</u> dark-soled shoes in the gym.   6 I <u>was forced to admit</u> that I was wrong.

Vocabulary 1 p.77

1 1 changed   2 off   3 on   4 read   5 crossed   6 out   7 puts   8 make   9 in   10 on

2 1 <u>I've changed my mind</u> about that jacket.
   2 She was so excited about going out with Paolo that she couldn't <u>keep her mind</u> on the lecture.
   3 Playing tennis <u>took Juan's mind off his problems</u>.
   4 She must <u>have something on her mind</u>.
   5 The idea that he was the one who stole the money <u>didn't cross my mind</u>.
   6 He knew her so well that she sometimes thought <u>he could read her mind</u>.
   7 <u>I'm in two minds</u> about buying a new car at the moment.
   8 He can write really well when he <u>puts his mind to it</u>.
   9 I wish she'd <u>make up her mind</u> which one of us she likes.
   10 He must be <u>out of his mind</u> to leave a wonderful girlfriend Ike Laura.

Reading p.78

1 1 The most suitable title is
   a) THE NOT SO NUTTY PROFESSOR.

1 A
2 1 F   2 D   3 H   4 C   5 E   6 B   7 G
3 1 barefoot   2 backs this up   3 came across   4 hesitant   5 reinforced   6 memorable

Grammar 2 p.79

1 1 it, It, There   2 It, there, there   3 it, it   4 There   5 it   6 There   7 it, There, it   8 It, there   9 there

2 I'm not exactly sure what *it* is.
   In the first row of the group *there* is a man doing one of the exercises …
   There *are* people of different ages and nationalities.

It is difficult to see exactly what they are doing …
… having some trouble because *there* is an older woman next to her …
… in both of them *there* is someone who is teaching
In my opinion, *it* is much better to learn like this.

Tapescript

These two photographs both show people teaching and learning things. In the first photograph, there is a group of people learning to do some kind of Oriental martial art. I'm not exactly sure what it is. They are all on a basketball court. In the first row of the group there is a man doing one of the exercises and they are all watching him, so I suppose he might be the instructor. Some of the people seem to be imitating his movements. There are people of different ages and nationalities.

The second photograph is very different. It shows a laboratory with some students doing an experiment of some kind. It is difficult to see exactly what they are doing but it seems to involve putting some chemicals in test tubes. One of the students seems to be having some trouble because there is an older woman next to her who seems to be explaining what she should do. The main similarity between the photographs is that in both of them there is someone who is teaching but the students are also doing something. I suppose you could say that they are learning by doing. In my opinion it is much better to learn like this.

3 1 would   2 seen/watched   3 up   4 are   5 for
6 all   7 they   8 in   9 more   10 keep/stay/get
11 in   12 take

Vocabulary 2 p.81

1 1 university   2 course   3 degree   4 student
5 assessment   6 lectures   7 project   8 revising
9 marks   10 primary   11 teachers
12 lessons   13 subjects

2 1 surprising   2 necessary   3 qualifications
4 decision   5 unhappy   6 knowledge   7 critics /
criticism   8 choice   9 socially   10 supporters

Writing p.82

1 1 ✘   2 ✔   3 ✔   4 ✔   5 ✘   6 ✘   7 ✘   8 ✘

2 Model answer:

My Study Dos and Don'ts

We all develop study habits and techniques but have you ever stopped to ask yourself how effective these really are? Here are some things I have learnt about working effectively. Lots of my friends go to the library. To my mind, that's fine if you like to spend a lot of time outside chatting. If I really want to get some work done, I study on my own. Another thing my friends tell

me is that they can study while listening to music. I know I can't. When I am revising, I turn the music off so that I can keep my mind on what I'm doing. Finally, a lot of students can't do anything without a computer. Of course computers can be very useful, but I prefer to switch mine off while I'm studying so that I won't be tempted to look at my email or interesting webpages.

How you learn best is a very personal matter. I think it's important to try things out for yourself and not just listen to other people.

3 Model answer:

Top Teachers

Almost everyone has a favourite teacher, someone they have really liked and admired, but what is it that makes us say that a certain teacher really is fantastic?

Some people think that it is to do with how friendly and nice the teacher is. For me, what is really important is that the teacher is someone you respect. Another comment students often make is that the teacher's classes should be fun. Of course, it's great if you can enjoy learning but I think that a good teacher should help you learn and sometimes that might be a little bit boring. Finally, people say that a good teacher should know a lot. From my point of view, the important thing is that teachers can communicate what they know and help you to develop your own knowledge.

To sum up, friendly teachers whose classes are great fun and who know a lot are obviously good teachers. Nevertheless, the best teachers for me are the ones you respect and who help you to learn and develop what you know yourself.

UNIT *11*

Listening p.83

1 1 a few seconds   2 to smile   3 dependable and honest   4 crossing your arms   5 your clothing or jewellery   6 they have confidence   7 green and orange   8 brown, grey and black   9 navy blue suit
10 to say goodbye

Tapescript

It may seem strange that it should be like this but when you have an interview, your education, knowledge and experience may be less important than the overall impression you make on the people interviewing you. Experts disagree about how long it takes to create a really good – or bad impression, but some estimate it's a few seconds. Many employers check prospective employees for what they call professionalism: this often includes appearance – so make sure you have washed your hair, cleaned your shoes and are wearing the right sort of clothing.

Do you know what 80–90% of candidates never remember to do when they go into the interview room? The answer is *smile*. So make eye contact and smile as soon as you enter the room but follow the interviewer's lead on whether or not to shake hands. Wait to be told where to sit and don't use first names unless the interviewer expects you to.

Try to move in certain ways at an interview – how you move your body or how you sit can indicate what kind of person you are – for example, a certain attitude can make you appear to be shy, or conversely, dependable and honest. It is important to avoid any kind of defensive movement, which may seem strange but it is because doing things like not making eye-contact, or crossing your arms, can seem to be very negative. There are other things that can give a bad impression too, such as turning your body away from the person you're talking to, or constantly touching your clothing or jewellery – all these things give a very bad impression to a person you may be meeting for the first time. You could look as if you don't want to give a straight answer, and so the interviewer might think you're impatient – or maybe even completely untrustworthy.

Believe it or not, the colours you choose to wear may also contribute to the overall impression you make. Colour analysts tell us that people wearing red clothes are showing that they have confidence – that's what the colour signifies – while wearing yellow shows openness. If you choose to wear green, this tells people you're compassionate, while the colour orange conveys happiness. All these are very positive qualities. However, you might not want to go along to a job interview dressed in all the bright colours of the rainbow, and you will probably choose something more neutral: such as brown, grey, and black. Although a traditional navy blue suit can make you seem conservative, it isn't a bad thing to wear one for an important job interview, because this colour also suggests that you're loyal. If it seems a bit dull to you, then add something in another colour to your outfit, perhaps a tie or scarf. Purple is a good choice for this as, according to the experts, this is one of the colours of inspiration.

When the interview is over, remember that people from the company may still be assessing you even after you have left the interview room. So don't forget to say goodbye to the receptionist or anyone else you spoke to when you arrived. Ignoring someone might cost you the job you've tried so hard to get.

Vocabulary 1 p.83

1 1 highly   2 trainee   3 positions   4 based
5 opportunities   6 Flexible   7 upgrade
8 qualifications   9 benefits   10 allowance
11 promotion   12 Salary

2 1 g)   2 a)   3 f)   4 c)   5 b)   6 d)   7 e)   8 h)

3 1 application   2 expectations   3 breaths
4 happiness   5 confidence   6 unprofessional
7 explanation   8 privacy   9 loyalty   10 advice

Grammar 1 p.85

1 1 ~~was able to~~ *could*   2 could ~~became~~ *have become*   3 could not ~~to~~ afford   4 ~~could~~ *was able to*   5 ✓   6 ~~could~~ *would* ever *be able* to continue   7 ✓   8 ✓   9 he ~~could~~ *was* actually *able to* save some   10 he ~~could~~ *was able to* go to London

2 1 I should *be* able to finish the work by next Tuesday.   2 My father always told us that we *had* to be able to look after ourselves.   3 Tina *can* do most of her homework without my help.   4 I *was* not able to attend the meeting because of ill health.   5 My cousin could *have* become a professional tennis player, if she had had the chance.   6 I can't ride a bicycle but it would be great if you *could* teach me.

3 1 do   2 been   3 them   4 be   5 which   6 like
7 if   8 can   9 as   10 who   11 able   12 her

Reading p.86

1 1 D   2 B   3 C   4 A
2 1 D   2 B   3 D   4 A   5 B   6 D   7 C   8 B
9 A   10 C   11 D   12 B   13 A   14 C   15 D

Grammar 2 p.87

1 1 left, won't be   2 wanted, would always be
3 has never visited, will be able   4 feel, should tell
5 don't move, won't be able   6 plan, will need
7 hadn't put, would have finished

2 1 We'll go for a walk in the mountains <u>unless it is</u> too hot.   2 I'm glad I saw the film <u>even though I was frightened</u> by it.   3 We'll place an order <u>on condition that</u> you give us a discount.   4 You should put that money in a safe place <u>in case you lose</u> it.   5 I'll buy that jacket <u>as long as they have</u> it in my size.

Vocabulary 2 p.88

1 1 fraction   2 date   3 time   4 decimal   5 sum
6 amount   7 number   8 percentage   9 distance
10 speed   11 temperature   12 weight

2 a) 8   b) 2   c) 12   d) 9   e) 11   f) 6   g) 3
h) 10

3 1 A   2 C   3 D   4 A   5 B   6 A   7 B   8 A
9 D   10 D   11 C   12 B

Writing p.89

1 The correct order is:
1 Dear Sir/Madam,
2 I am writing in reply to your advertisement in last Tuesday's Evening News.
3 I would like to apply for the Trainee Manager position you advertise.

4 I have a working knowledge of Greek and have recently passed the University of Cambridge First Certificate in English Examination.

5 I will also complete a degree in Banking and Finance in June and will be available to start work immediately afterwards.

6 I can be contacted by telephone on 01094893214 during the day and in the evenings.

7 I look forward to receiving your reply.

2 1 ✓   2 ✓   3 ✓   4 ✗   5 ✗

3 Model answer:

Dear Sir/Madam,

I am writing in reply to your advertisement in last Tuesday's Evening News. I would like to apply for the Trainee Manager position you advertise.

I believe I am a particularly suitable candidate for this position because I enjoy taking on new challenges and have always wanted to live in Athens. Furthermore, I have a working knowledge of Greek and have recently passed the University of Cambridge First Certificate in English Examination. I will also complete a degree in Banking and Finance in June and will be available to start work immediately afterwards.

I can be contacted by telephone on 01094893214 during the day and in the evenings.

I look forward to receiving your reply.

Yours faithfully,

Wendel van Dijk

UNIT *12*

Writing 1 p.90

1 1 strolled   2 paced   3 crept   4 swallow
5 chewing   6 bit   7 wondered   8 believe
9 imagine   10 gasping   11 suffocate
12 panted/was panting   13 glancing   14 peered
15 staring

Vocabulary 1 p.90

1 1 pickpocket   2 arsonist   3 witness
4 shoplifter   5 kidnapper   6 mugger   7 forger
8 hijacker   9 blackmailer   10 burglar

2 1 A   2 C   3 A   4 D   5 B   6 C   7 A   8 D
9 B   10 D   11 A   12 C

Listening p.91

1 1 C   2 A   3 A   4 C   5 C   6 A   7 B   8 B

Tapescript

Extract 1

I=Interviewer   W=Woman

I: What would you say is the most satisfying aspect of your work?

W: Well, I don't have to sit at a desk all day surrounded by piles of papers and computers and so on, though of course I do have to write reports and things like that – but most of my time is spent in court and I really find that very stimulating. I work closely with the police, too.

I: But isn't questioning witnesses quite difficult?

W: Well, of course you have to ask the questions in just the right way so that the evidence comes out and the jury can reach a decision, but it's very satisfying when you get the right verdict.

Extract 2

Good morning. I'm ringing from Calstra telephone services, to inform you of our very special rates on calls made to anywhere in Europe and Latin America. I don't know what you are paying at the moment but I can guarantee that with Calstra you'll make substantial savings on your phone bills. You don't have to decide right away, but why not just take up our special trial period offer and see how much you can save? Give us a call on 0287 983768 and we can deal with any questions you might have. Then once you have registered with us, just dial 1052 before any of your calls and you'll be able to take advantage of the discounts.

Extract 3

A: Did you see that gang of teenagers back there? If you ask me, it's an absolute disgrace.

B: What do you mean? They weren't doing anything – do you think they look suspicious?

A: I don't know – but you'd think in a town this size there would be more for young people to do than just hang around the railway station.

B: Well, I must say they did look a bit like troublemakers – they might make some people feel a bit nervous, I suppose.

A: Oh no – I thought they looked perfectly harmless. It just infuriates me to see that they have nowhere to go.

Extract 4

H=Host   M=Margaret

H: Margaret Mears thank you for being with us this evening.

M: Thank you for inviting me.

H: Your protests against animal experiments are familiar to our viewers but tonight you've got something important you want to say.

M: Yes, that's right. There are thousands of places where animals are still suffering – and in the opinion of the experts it's just not necessary. There are alternatives to using live animals to test cosmetics and drugs. Unfortunately governments don't always see it as a big issue – and without the support of ordinary people our work will never be completed. We need donations to help us to carry on.

H: So viewers if you have any questions for Margaret, or if you think you might be able to give Margaret and her co-workers a hand – phone the number that is coming up on your screen.

Extract 5

And I got some of this in the airport duty free when I came back from holiday last month. My mother used to use it when she was young – though it was a lot cheaper then – but although the price has gone through the roof now – and it comes in fancy modern packaging – I still think it's the best one on the market. It's great for any kind of skin irritation ... insect bites, mild sunburn – you name it, a tiny amount gets rid of any redness or itching. It's not one of these modern creams with long, scientific names, but I still think it's the most effective.

Extract 6

Sorry I missed you this morning, but I had to leave early – I had to go for a dentist's appointment. I meant to leave you a note – you see I forgot to tell you that the computer's not working and I phoned the company and there's a technician coming round to have a look at it this afternoon – at about 2. I've got a lunchtime meeting and I won't be back until three. Would you mind staying in till then, just in case he comes a bit earlier? Give my assistant a ring if you can't, and I'll try to make some other arrangement.

Extract 7

These islands were once covered in pine forests and wheat fields. The Romans actually called them the bread basket of the Mediterranean, because so much of the wheat that was grown there was used for flour that was made into bread that was eaten everywhere. It seems hard to imagine now though – with the arrival of tourism the whole situation changed and most of the agricultural workers went into the hotel and restaurant industries. It's just not the same as it used to be – and even the bread you eat with your meals is probably brought in from the mainland!

Extract 8

Can I have your attention please. This is the final call for those passengers travelling to Mallorca still waiting in the departure lounge. Would the last remaining passengers on flight 766 to Palma de Mallorca please make their way immediately to Boarding Gate 5 where the plane is fully boarded and ready for departure. If you do not present yourself to our staff at the gate immediately, your luggage will be taken off the plane. You will then have to collect it and travel on a later flight.

Grammar 1 p.92

1 1 has happened   2 has been stolen   3 hid
4 didn't notice   5 had been touched   6 had been taken   7 are known   8 was being watched
9 were hidden   10 will be found

2 1 Our dog <u>loves being taken</u> for a walk.   2 I was thrilled <u>to be chosen to</u> play the part.   3 I <u>was made to feel</u> extremely welcome.   4 She <u>was known to be</u> an expert.   5 The cat <u>dislikes being patted</u> by children.
6 He was angry <u>about being told</u> to turn the music down.   7 He hoped he <u>would be allowed to</u> take the test again.   8 The castle <u>is said to be</u> over eight hundred years old.

Vocabulary 2 p.93

1 1 bananas, roses   2 seagulls, sheep   3 teenagers, pickpockets   4 judges, criminologists   5 coins, poems
6 cards, lies   7 ice, flats   8 ponies, goats

2 1 pack of lies   2 panel of criminologists   3 Gangs of teenagers   4 bunch of roses   5 block of flats
6 flock of seagulls   7 collection of coins / coin collection   8 herd of goats

3 ~~rows~~ *piles* of papers and books
~~bar~~ *fragment* of stone
~~piles~~ *rows* of gas jets
mushrooms into ~~blocks~~ *slices*

Tapescript

Although both these photographs show people working, they are very different in many ways. In the first photograph a man is working at a very untidy desk. There are piles of papers and books everywhere. I'm not sure exactly what he is doing but he seems to be looking at a fragment of stone or something. Perhaps he is an archaeologist.

The second photograph shows a group of people working in a restaurant kitchen. It is much tidier than the office in the first photograph even though everyone is very busy. There are rows of gas jets on each side of the cooker. Each of the chefs is preparing a different dish. The one in the foreground is cutting mushrooms into slices and the one opposite him could be making an omelette but I'm not sure. They all seem to be enjoying working together. I think it would be fun to work in a kitchen like that.

Grammar 2 p.94

1 1 We are having the roof of our house repaired.
2 I have had these trousers shortened.
3 My friend had all her money stolen while she was on the beach.   4 The bridal couple were photographed.
5 She is going to have her portrait painted by a famous artist.   6 We will have to have our car looked at.
7 I am having my arm treated.   8 You can have your shopping delivered.   9 I am going to have my assignment typed.

2 1 They <u>had their television stolen</u> when they left their front door unlocked.   2 My friend <u>has her nails painted</u> by a manicurist.   3 Before I bought it, I <u>had my car checked by</u> a friend.   4 Did those windows <u>get broken by</u> the storm?   5 The king <u>had his head cut</u> off.

Reading p.94

1 The best title is b).

2 1 F   2 E   3 H   4 B   5 G   6 D   7 A

3 1 masterpiece   2 merely   3 bequeathed
4 hasty   5 came across   6 came up with
7 portfolio   8 shots   9 raid

Writing 2 p.96

1 1 f   2 j   3 b   4 h   5 d   6 g   7 c   8 i
9 a   10 e

2 Paragraph 1: sentence f, sentence j, sentence b
Paragraph 2: sentence h, sentence d
Paragraph 3: sentence g, sentence c, sentence i,
          sentence a, sentence e

3 Suggested answer:
The following ideas should be crossed out:
Why is he putting it in his pocket?
When was it sent?
When did Malcolm receive it?
Is the letter handwritten or typed?

4 Model answer:

A Change of Direction?

Malcolm had been working at Ibis for nearly five years. At first he had really enjoyed the work, but lately he had begun to feel bored and frustrated. That was why he had applied for a job with Macrodisk, a big computer company.

Naturally, Malcolm hadn't said anything to his boss or his colleagues at Ibis. He didn't think he had a very good chance of getting the Macrodisk job but that morning he found a letter in his mailbox with Macrodisk on the envelope.

Even though there were a lot of people around him at the time, he couldn't resist opening it. He hadn't got the job and he was very glad he hadn't mentioned anything to anyone at Ibis. Hurriedly, Malcolm stuffed the letter back into the envelope and pushed it into his pocket.

UNIT *13*

Vocabulary 1 p.97

1 1 claws   2 scratch   3 take   4 damage
5 scratch   6 beaks   7 fur   8 run   9 hutch
10 tank

Tapescript

A=Anita   J=Jerzy   E=Examiner

A: Well, if they have children, they would probably like an animal they can play with as well as look after. I think the cat would be good, don't you?

J: Well, cats have very sharp claws and that might not be so good with a baby. It might scratch her. Cats aren't very easy to look after, either.

A: Yes, I suppose you're right. What about a dog?

J: I think that's a better idea. Dogs are great for children to play with – and they can have the responsibility of taking the dog for walks.

A: The trouble is they might not have enough space for a dog if they live in the centre of the city. They wouldn't have anywhere to take it out for walks.

J: Yes and if they go out to work every day and the children go to school, the dog will probably be lonely and it might damage or scratch the furniture. Perhaps a pet like the parrot would be better.

A: I'm sorry, but I think the parrot might be a bit dangerous with the baby as well. They can bite with their big beaks. I know they are easy to look after – but they're not much fun! I think the rabbit would be the best choice.

J: Well, they have lovely soft fur, but you can't really let them run around in a flat. They're a bit messy inside so it would have to be kept in a hutch. I don't think that's fair to the rabbit! How about a fish?

A: You do have to remember to clean their bowl but they're probably less work than all the other animals. So they'd be easy for the children to look after.

J: That's true …

E: Have you reached a decision?

A: Yes, we have.

J: We think the fish is the best choice if they live in the city because the children would have to remember to look after them – but the dog would also be good if the family have more space.

Listening p.98

2 1 the beach   2 to shoot   3 sharp thorns
4 bursting open   5 like dolphins   6 a friend/a
magazine editor   7 six months   8 local families
9 jewellery   10 environmental organisations

Tapescript

I=Interviewer   G=Guillermo

I: So you were back in Venezuela on a visit?

G: Yes, that's right. I was walking to the beach along
a jungle path when I heard this noise like a series
of explosions. I immediately suspected that
someone was attempting to shoot me so I ran for
cover. I ducked down behind a fallen tree trunk,
but then I realised that the shots seemed to be
coming straight from the tree tops.

I: You must have been terrified.

G: Of course, but then I realised that the forest there
is almost entirely made up of a tree called the
'Jabillo'. The trunks of these trees are covered in
sharp thorns from the base to the uppermost
branches, so it seemed highly unlikely that
anybody trying to kill me would have gone to such
uncomfortable lengths to get to the top!

I: So what was going on?

G: I had no idea but then I noticed that all these
curved wooden shells had started falling down
from the trees on the ground around me. The
noise wasn't gunfire. It was the explosions made by
the hard woody fruits on the Jabillo trees bursting
open. There were literally thousands of these shells
covering an area of about 50 metres all around me.
But when I picked up one of the shells I was even
more astonished. They looked just like dolphins –
they had the same shape. The resemblance was
uncanny! It seemed as if nature itself were
speaking directly to me warning me about the
threats to the oceans and forests and to the
creatures who live in them.

I: So what did you do?

G: I went back to Spain and talked to a friend there
who was a magazine editor about what I'd seen. I
thought he might like to do a feature on my
experience and on the 'dolphin tree', as I started to
call it, but instead he wanted to give away dolphin
shells with the magazine. He said he would need
the shells for an issue of the magazine that was
going to come out in August. This meant
somehow picking up 500,000 shells in six months.

I: But you couldn't possibly collect so many in such a
short time, could you?

G: Well I hoped I would be able to but I calculated
that I would need to collect about 17,000 shells a
week to meet the deadline and I realised I couldn't
possibly do it alone. After the first week back in
Venezuela I'd only managed to collect about 6000.

The inside joke was: 'Don't worry, we've only got
494,000 to go!' In the end, I decided to pay local
families to gather the shells and somehow we
managed to get the 500,000 packed and ready to be
shipped to Spain by the due date. Everything that
could have gone wrong did, but we managed
somehow.

I: And you still have people collecting the shells for
you, don't you?

G: Yes. I turn them into jewellery. My philosophy is that
the dolphin tree has benefits on three levels. It helps
local communities back in Venezuela. It can be used
as a way of educating people about the damage
we're doing to the environment and finally I hope
that the dolphin jewellery can be sold to increase
funds for environmental organizations.

I: And what are the chances of this happening do you
think?

G: About the same as the chances of collecting half a
million shells in six months!

Grammar 1 p.98

1 1 so   2 such   3 very   4 too   5 enough
6 so   7 very   8 creative enough   9 so much

2 1 was ~~enough cold~~ *cold enough*   2 was ~~such~~ *so* hot
3 ✓   4 Are you ~~too~~ strong *enough*   5 The music
was ~~very~~ *too* loud   6 said she was ~~so~~ *too* young
7 ~~so~~ *such* nice people   8 ~~time enough~~ *enough time*
9 ~~such~~ *so* cold

3 1 these/them   2 old   3 called   4 so   5 in
6 been   7 his   8 for   9 there   10 time
11 them   12 too

Grammar 2 p.99

1 1 What I can't stand about the winter is the rain.
2 What I like most about Bill is his sense of humour.
3 What I need is a long rest.   4 What you should
do is tell them you can't come.   5 What you have
to do is fill the tank with water.

2 1 most about zoos is that the animals are better
cared for.   2 like Stamford Raffles most was
research.   3 to zoos in the past was curiosity.
4 about those clouds is their shape.   5 earthquakes
is pressure beneath the earth's surface.   6 frighten
me more than anything else would be a tsunami.

Reading p.100

1 c) and g)

2 1 D   2 B   3 C   4 B   5 D   6 B   7 B   8 A   9 D
10 B   11 B   12 A   13 C   14 D   15A

3 1 h   2 e   3 f   4 c   5 b   6 g   7 d   8 a

Vocabulary 2 p.101

1 1 breeze, gale   2 mist, fog   3 temperature, climate
4 frost, hail   5 thunderstorm, lightning   6 shower,
drizzle

2 1 clouds, rain   2 climate, temperature
3 thunderstorm, lightning   4 fog   5 breeze
6 snow

3 1 I <u>am snowed under with</u> work at the moment.
2 The doctor told me I would be <u>as right as rain</u> in
the morning.   3 We were all in <u>floods of tears</u> by
the end of the movie.   4 There isn't <u>a cloud in the
sky</u> for me at the moment.   5 There was <u>a storm of
protest</u> about the new law.

4 1 C   2 A   3 B   4 C   5 D   6 A   7 C   8 B
9 A   10 B   11 A   12 D

Writing p.103

1 1 informal   2 informal   3 formal   4 informal

2 a) Extract 1: I <u>wouldn't</u> come in the spring
Extract 2: <u>I'm</u> sure we never would have come
across it on our own
Extract 4: she thinks <u>he's</u> the best thing

b) Extract 3: The car <u>can be collected</u> and <u>returned</u>

c) Extract 2: <u>We loved the night safari!</u>

d) Extract 4: <u>the best thing since sliced bread</u>

e) Extract 1: hard to <u>put up with</u>
Extract 2: I'm sure we never would have <u>come
across</u> it on our own

f) Extract 3: <u>Nevertheless</u>, I recommend that you hire
a car

g) Extract 1: It can be very wet and cold <u>but</u> what we
all find really hard
Extract 3: His name is Carlos <u>and</u> she thinks he's
the best thing

3 The correct comments are: 1

4
Dear Pat,
Thank you for your letter. I'm really pleased to hear
that you will be visiting my country. Firstly I would
advise you to come by plane, taking one of the many
charter flights you can get now. When it comes to
choosing between February and September, I prefer
September as the weather is still warm then. What's
more, many of the native bird species can be seen in
the wetlands near the coast then. So it's also an
excellent time for bird watching.
If you plan to spend most of your time in the
countryside, you could stay with my cousin who has a
large country house. If this sounds suitable, please
write back and I'll arrange it.
With best wishes,
Aviva

UNIT *14*

Reading p.104

1 Item 5 is not mentioned.

2 1 C   2 D   3 D   4 C   5 B   6 C   7 A   8A

4 a) being sought   b) weed out   c) mixed bunch
d) venture   e) mounds   f) hauled   g) setting off
h) jeopardising

Vocabulary 1 p.105

1 1 score   2 have   3 meet   4 fulfil   5 have
6 Take   7 hit   8 achieve

2 1 up   2 up   3 on   4 with   5 across   6 up
7 through/over   8 in   9 up   10 off

3 1 He <u>never gave up</u> hope of meeting another girl
like Sophie.   2 Unexpected problems can <u>come
up</u> even if you are well-prepared.   3 He found it
difficult to <u>face up to</u> his own limitations.
4 Susan always knows how to <u>deal with</u> a difficult
situation.   5 We <u>came across</u> a very cheap and
pleasant hotel completely by chance.   6 It's a
good idea to <u>talk through</u> your ideas with
someone older.

Listening p.106

1 Speaker 1 F   Speaker 2 A   Speaker 3 B
Speaker 4 C   Speaker 5 D

Tapescript

Speaker 1
As far as I'm concerned, the perspective you have on
a city as a tourist is always unreal. You see galleries
and monuments, you follow a guidebook, but there

are all sorts of things you miss that the people who live in the city experience. That's why I really enjoyed my last visit to Barcelona. I went to do a course there and so I had to get up in the morning and go to the university on the metro just like everyone else. We ate lunch in places full of office workers and students. I think you really get to know a city when you do something like that because you see how it is for the people who live there.

Speaker 2

When I was young, everyone was doing it. We left home and either hitchhiked or bought an old van and drove ... often as far as India or even to Australia. Most of us didn't really have enough money and a lot of the time it was terribly uncomfortable or even dangerous, but we really experienced the places we visited. There were no *Lonely Planet* or *Rough Guides* in those days, so information about where to stay and what to eat passed by word of mouth. As far as I'm concerned, those really were the good old days. Nowadays even young people are often on package holidays where so much is organised for you: flight, accommodation, visits. It's just not travelling if you ask me.

Speaker 3

I did a lot of travelling when I was younger, much of it because of my job. I've visited every continent and most of the major capital cities. I loved it of course but now I really can't be bothered. Let's face it, travelling involves enormous expense, anxiety and physical effort. No matter how carefully you plan, you end up carrying your luggage up and down stairs in airports and railway stations and at my age it's just too much. And then there are the hours and hours you spend in the airport. The last time I went away we were delayed and it took me 18 hours to get to where I was going. From now on, I've decided I'm staying put.

Speaker 4

We had a copy of a guidebook called *Rough and Ready Travel* and it really was a bit too rough for us. In the entry for one of the places we visited they recommended two guesthouses and said they were both cheap and clean although a bit basic. Honestly, we couldn't have possibly stayed in either of them. Maybe we're getting soft in our old age but I really don't enjoy travelling unless I can stay somewhere quiet with a decent bathroom and, in hot countries like Thailand, air conditioning. If I can't sleep at night, I'm tired the next day and that can really ruin a holiday for me. Anyway we stayed in a four-star hotel and it really wasn't very expensive.

Speaker 5

A lot of my friends spent half their time in Internet cafés downloading information about where to stay in the next place they were visiting or trying to find out about the cheapest places to eat. But we spent our time actually seeing the cities we were visiting and we had all sorts of historical and cultural information at our fingertips as well. It was a bit heavy to carry around so we would tear out the sections that referred to the places we'd already visited and post them home. By the end of the trip, it was only about fifty pages long! It really was invaluable though. I'd always make sure I had one with me wherever I was.

Vocabulary 2 p.107

1 1 B 2 B 3 B 4 C 5 B 6 A 7 C 8 C
9 C

2 1 holiday 2 backpackers 3 expedition
4 guide 5 package holiday 6 trekking
7 luggage 8 cruise 9 difference 10 hand

Tapescript

Both these photographs show groups of people on holiday. In the first photograph there is a group of backpackers about to set out on an expedition. I'm not sure exactly where they are but it could be a country like Nepal or India. Something that this photograph has in common with the other photograph is that there is a guide leading the group. The tourists in the second picture are on a package holiday and they will be travelling around by coach whereas the first group of tourists will be trekking. They will probably have to carry their own luggage but the people on the cruise ship have all their luggage on board and don't have to worry about carrying it from place to place. Another difference is that in the first photograph it is obviously very cold – everyone is wearing anoraks and big boots. In the second photograph, on the other hand, it seems to be either spring or summer as the people are wearing light clothing like T-shirts and sleeveless dresses. Personally, I would prefer to be with the people in the first photograph. I think that is real travelling.

3 1 A 2 C 3 D 4 A 5 B 6 A 7 D
8 C 9 D 10 C 11 A 12 D

Grammar p.108

1 1 It's advisable ~~applying~~ *to apply*
2 You should also ~~to sleep~~ 3 make sure to ~~telling~~ *tell* people 4 you ought *to* try to learn
5 ✓ 6 The tour guide advised *us* that
7 He recommended ~~to~~ *that we should* go out
8 Don't attempt ~~seeing~~ *to see* 9 ✓
10 I would ~~wearing~~ *wear* a money belt

2 1 up 2 on 3 much 4 all 5 few 6 the
7 them 8 as / because / since 9 so
10 most 11 for 12 so

4 1 definitely take 2 they're really essential
3 we could take 4 would be a pity 5 a bit worried about 6 wouldn't go 7 should we
8 The trouble is 9 not necessary
10 anything at all 11 leave room for
12 we definitely have

Tapescript

D=Daniella   L=Loukas

D: I think we should definitely take a mobile phone. If we have an accident or get lost, we can always call and tell someone we are in trouble.

L: Yes, I agree. They're quite light anyway and they're really essential in that kind of situation. I think the camera would be a bit too heavy, don't you?

D: It depends. A lot of the new digital cameras are tiny. Perhaps we could take one of those mobile phones that is also a camera.

L: That's a good idea. It would be a pity to go on a trip like that and not be able to take any photos, but I'm a bit worried about the weight – we don't want to carry too much – and if we're going to carry a torch …

D: Are we going to take the torch?

L: I wouldn't go on a camping trip without a torch. It can be very dark in the mountains at night, and we could also use it to attract attention if we get lost.

D: Well, I'm sure you don't think that taking a laptop computer is a good idea then.

L: Why should we take a laptop computer with us?

D: Well, it's a long camping trip so we might want to write letters or keep a diary or something. The trouble is we wouldn't be able to recharge the battery up there in the mountains. Some binoculars would be good though. We could use them to watch birds and animals.

L: In my opinion they're not necessary and they're too heavy to carry.

D: OK we'll leave the binoculars behind, but I want to bring my personal CD player. It hardly weighs anything at all and I love music.

L: I think we should leave room for more important things like sunscreen, but if you really want to take it, then that's up to you.

D: So we want to take the mobile phone, the torch, the sunscreen and what about the chocolate?

L: I love chocolate so we definitely have to take that!

Writing p.110

1 a) 5   b) 3   c) 2   d) 1

2 Travelling is fun and you can have lots of adventures.   ☺

It can be difficult to settle down when you come back.   ☹

You can get to know other cultures.   ☺

You can make friends with people from all over the world.   ☺

You can feel homesick.   ☹

Travelling can be exhausting and even dangerous.   ☹

3 1 travelling is fun and you can have lots of adventures.   2 you can get to know other cultures   3 you can make friends with people from all over the world   4 travelling can be exhausting and even dangerous 5 you can feel homesick   6 it can be difficult to settle down when you come back

4 Conclusion A is more suitable

5 ~~belief~~ *believe*
~~propper~~ *proper*
~~other~~ *another*
~~proffit~~ *profit*
~~is~~ *does* not agree
don't like *it*
~~travel~~ *travelling*
~~experiment~~ *experience*
relaxing~~,~~ ~~ob~~viously relaxing. *Obviously*
~~unnusual~~ *unusual*
~~ballance~~ *balance*
~~In addition,~~ *On the other hand,*

6 Model answer:

The Pros and Cons of Technology

Many people believe that technological developments such as the Internet and mobile phones stop us communicating with one another. It is certainly true that these developments have brought about major changes in communication but these are both positive and negative.

On the positive side, we have the fact that people can communicate much more easily and quickly. Instead of waiting days, weeks or months to receive a reply to a letter, with text messages and email we sometimes get an answer in a few minutes. We can also send and receive messages at any time of the day or night. Furthermore, it doesn't matter where we are as long as we have access to a computer or mobile phone network.

It is not all positive, however. Firstly, because people are so fascinated by electronic media, they probably spend less time actually talking to their friends and family. Secondly, the speed of communication means we sometimes say things in email or text messages that we later regret.

On balance, however, I believe that these innovations have benefited humanity. It is now important to make sure everyone has access to them.

Practice Exam

Paper 1 Reading

PART 1 1 D   2 B   3 C   4 D   5 B   6 B   7 D   8 C

PART 2 9 G   10 D   11 B   12 H   13 E   14 C   15 A

PART 3 16 E   17 C   18 C   19 B   20 A   21 B
22 D   23 E   24 E   25 D   26 D   27 A
28 B   29 C   30 B

Paper 3 Use of English

PART 1 1 B   2 D   3 C   4 C   5 A   6 B   7 A
8 B   9 A   10 A   11 C   12 D

PART 2 13 it   14 in   15 be   16 how   17 as
18 what   19 All   20 them   21 been
22 have   23 Although   24 over

PART 3 25 friendship   26 evidence   27 suggestion
28 unhappiness   29 unexpectedly
30 strength   31 connection   32 behaviour
33 emotional   34 completely

PART 4 35 It's the <u>first time I have</u> seen such an exciting
film.   36 Pete wanted to <u>know where Sue
worked</u> now.   37 It's very easy to <u>stay/keep in
touch</u> with friends nowadays.   38 I wouldn't
live in New York <u>if it was/were not</u> a very exciting
place.   39 If <u>only I had bought</u> a better car.
40 The game <u>was called off</u> because of the rain.
41 I would <u>love to be able to</u> speak Italian.
42 It's <u>up to you whether you</u> accept the job.

Paper 4 Listening

PART 1 1 C   2 A   3 B   4 B   5 C   6 A   7 C   8 A

Tapescript

*Hello, I'm going to give you the instructions for this test.
I'll introduce each part of the test and give you time to
look at the questions. At the start of each piece you'll
hear this sound (bleep). You will hear each piece twice.
Now look at Part 1.*

*You will hear people talking in eight different situations.
For questions 1–8, choose the best answer A, B or C.*

Extract 1

A: Can I help you?

B: I hope so! You see, I've got these tickets for tomorrow
evening – but I've bought four and now one of my
friends isn't coming. I know that you don't give
refunds on tickets but what about if I change the
seats for a different day? We could make Saturday –
preferably the matinee performance.

A: The best I can do is to take the tickets back and try to
sell them again – but you'd have to buy your tickets
for Saturday now.

B: Oh I see – well, I'll talk to my friends and come back

later.

Extract 2

I have talked to a lot of people about this, and it
seems to me that we are not doing enough to look
after our planet generally – I mean that we could all
do a lot more. Recycling, saving energy – all that sort
of thing. I agree that it's not easy – and it seems a lot
to do – but we could all take more responsibility for
our own bit of the world. We can learn so much from
nature and the natural world – and we have certainly
made a lot of mistakes in the past. We have to
conserve what we have now, for the future.

Extract 3

Let's just check the diary before we do anything else –
I've got a meeting at 11 – that should be about an
hour – and then I'm meeting new clients this
afternoon. That means I won't be able to go to the
presentation on the new management structure –
you'll have to arrange for someone to take notes for
me. Oh, and I'll need to have the figures for the
accounts for last year – that's for the meeting this
afternoon. They should make a good impression!
Could you get them from the accounts department
and then make copies for everyone?

Extract 4

We've known each other for such a long time that if
we can't have a disagreement and still remain friends,
then I think it's a shame. I can't say that I think that
what you did is right – in fact, I think you should have
thought about it a lot more before you did it – but
that's in the past and we need to put it behind us.
After all – we can all make mistakes – I know that I
make plenty – but we have to learn from them and
move on.

Extract 5

A: That was really great – the music was just
fantastic!

B: Yes – I can't believe that was their last show. Did
you see that they're going to put out a film of it
later on – that will be something to look out for –
a chance to watch it all again! It's such a shame
that they won't be on stage together any more –
they have so much energy and their performance is
just amazing.

A: It will be on DVD as well I suppose. I'll definitely
buy that when it's released – though it won't be as
good as tonight!

B: Better than nothing, though.

Extract 6

Well – it wasn't easy to decide – there seemed to be so many things to think about. I just knew that I wasn't happy in the work I was doing. I went for another job in the company and that was quite attractive – it was in marketing and so I could have travelled quite a lot – we've got offices on the continent and travelling more is something I've always wanted to do. They were even going to pay for me to do a marketing course one day a week. But then I knew that I regretted not taking the chance to go to university when I turned it down before – so even though I'll miss the money I think I have to go for it now.

Extract 7

A: How did the big presentation go?

B: Oh – it was fine in the end. I managed to make the technology work – that's always a worry when you're using a computer in front of the managers! There were a lot of questions afterwards, and some very good points were raised. It was very interesting.

A: Well – all the work you'd done on it at home in the evenings was obviously worth it.

B: Yes – the family got a bit fed up with it – but now I've only got to write up the report. I'll be distributing that to everyone in the department – probably on Monday.

A: I look forward to reading it!

Extract 8

Here we are in the area known as the play zone. That is because it's intended to be hands-on, unlike the research area we've just walked through – you can touch all the exhibits, watch films and see what life was really like hundreds of years ago. There is a reconstruction of a house as it was in 1860 in the next room – and you can experience how it might have felt to be part of that family at that time. You can have an hour here, before we move away from this part of the town to have lunch and then you will be taken to spend the rest of the afternoon in Waterworld.

That's the end of Part 1. Now look at Part 2.

PART 2   9 serious   10 back up   11 examiners
12 practical   13 popular / more recent   14 influence
15 repeat the year   16 bigger variety   17 edit
18 confidence

Tapescript

You will hear part of an interview with Luke Harding, a young student. For questions 9-18, complete the sentences. Before you start, spend 45 seconds looking through Part 2.

A: And in this week's programme, *Education Today*, we talk to seventeen-year-old Luke Harding, who has chosen to do a two year course in film studies. Tell us, Luke, why did you decide to do this particular course?

B: Well, I wasn't sure what I wanted to do when I went to college, but I've always loved seeing films at the cinema, and this course gives you the chance to watch them at college and get a qualification at the same time. No, but seriously, it's a proper serious course, just like History or English, and you need to be *really* interested in films – you have to have seen lots, and just sitting there watching is not enough, you can't just say 'oh this one's cool and that one's no good' – I mean, you need to have opinions about them, and you've got to be able to back up your theories, too.

A: And who actually chooses the films you watch? Can you do that yourself or is there a syllabus?

B: In the first year it's more or less up to the class to decide … though the teacher does have a say, too. It's not like the second year – although you can choose one or two yourself, then it's the examiners who specify the majority of them. But basically you can do anything that you find interesting in the first year.

A: Really. And what about the other stuff you do on the course … how much of it is practical?

B: About twenty per cent of the course … in the first year, that is. The rest of it is theoretical – and we have to write essays too.

A: What else do you do apart from practical work?

B: Well, you get to understand how films are put together – both old and more recent ones. In fact, one example of a popular film was … last week we were looking at how a Harry Potter film was made. The techniques were amazing – they're very clever.

A: That sounds as if you have a very good time!

B: Well – yes – but of course as I said there are essays and things as well. We have to research people who are important – who can use their influence in what happens – I've just done a study of the director Meera Syal – she's quite famous, and she's made a lot of films about the Asian community in Britain.

A: And is there an exam at all?

B: Sure – and you've got to pass it – it counts for two thirds of the marks, and the coursework for one third. If you fail, they make you repeat the year.

A: And how about the second year. Is that the same sort of work again?

B: Yes, basically. But it's a lot harder because … you don't watch just mainstream English and American stuff – you need to see a bigger variety of films, like foreign language films. And there's a lot more theory. And then on the practical side, you have to apply what you've learned by making a short film yourself – so you script it, actually make it, and then edit it – I'm really looking forward to doing that.

A: So will all this work set you up for a brilliant career?

B: Well, it's really good preparation for a degree in Media Studies, which is what I want to do. And it's already given me lots of confidence … I mean, of course you can't just walk off and become the next big Hollywood director at the end, you've got to be realistic, but it's a great course. And on the plus side it means I've always got an excuse when mum and dad complain I'm watching too many videos!

A: Well – it's been interesting to talk to you – and I now know a lot more about film studies! Luke Harding, thank you for joining us today.

Now you will hear Part 2 again.
(Part 2 repeated)
That's the end of Part 2. Now look at Part 3.

PART 3   19 F   20 B   21 D   22 A   23 C

Tapescript

You will hear five people explaining what they think about crime prevention. For questions 19-23, choose which of the opinions A–F each speaker expresses. Use the letters only once. There is one extra letter you do not need to use.

Speaker 1

I'm not really worried about being mugged – I think I can take care of myself most of the time. Mind you, I do try to be sensible – like I don't keep all my money in one place – not all in one purse – and I certainly don't take it out of my purse in public unless I'm actually in a shop buying something. And I do look after my mobile phone. But I think we can get all this out of proportion – I've actually never met anyone who's been mugged and I do think that we spend too much time thinking about it. I have more important things to think about!

Speaker 2

It seems to me that the police should do more than they are doing to protect us on the streets – after all, that's what we pay our taxes for, isn't it? I don't think it's up to us to tell them what to do, though – they should know. They have to follow the orders of their bosses – and they are influenced by politicians – but I think they spend too much time on other things – you know, handing out parking tickets, or speeding fines – minor things like that – instead of doing the really important things like catching criminals and preventing crime like mugging.

Speaker 3

I went on a course – it wasn't only about crime but was also driving safely, first aid – all that kind of thing. I wasn't really worried about crime, but I wanted to

find out more and I knew that I wanted to learn about self-defence – and there was a part of the course on that – but it was all really interesting and useful. It was quite high-tech, too. I feel more confident now that I can take care of myself – and be a better driver as well. And I think I have a better understanding of some of the problems that police have to deal with nowadays, which many people don't seem to realise.

Speaker 4

I accept that some of it comes down to me – but I don't think the police have enough real back-up – I mean on the technical side – I know they have mobile phones and CCTV cameras – but do they really have enough computer back-up? I don't know enough about the background to that. With all the resources they could use now they should be able to stop a crime before it is committed. Or is that too unrealistic? Maybe we expect too much from them nowadays – but maybe there are options that are not being taken up.

Speaker 5

It can actually make people feel better if they know something about how to defend themselves. I'm certainly not suggesting that people should confront a thief directly, but it gives people confidence if they know some basic self defence. I run basic courses and I teach a range of people of all ages and backgrounds. It does give people a lot more confidence, and if you look confident, that means you're less likely to be the victim of a crime in the first place. Sounds easy, but it's true – and it is always better to prevent a crime than deal with it once it's happened!

Now you'll hear Part 3 again. (Part 3 repeated)
That's the end of Part 3. Now look at Part 4

PART 4   24 B   25 A   26 C   27 B   28 A   29 A
30 C

Tapescript

You will hear an interview with an expert on different senses. For questions 24–30, choose the best answer A, B or C.

A: So we're here for the third programme in our series 'It Makes Sense' – when we investigate the five senses of hearing, seeing, touching, tasting and smelling – this week the sense we're going to be talking about is smell. I have with me Jane Stone, who has just published a series of articles on how our senses affect our daily lives – Jane, welcome to the programme.

B: Thanks – nice to be here.

A: Jane, how did you become an expert on smell?

B: Well – I didn't intend to specialise in it, and of course I do write about all the senses, but when I was at university studying them – there was a module on the course – the other senses seem to be more concrete somehow, easier to be precise about, but smell is so personal. I found it fascinating.

A: You said in one of your articles that smell is actually the sense we rarely use now – at least for anything important. Is that right?

B: It certainly is – it used to be rather more vital to us than it is now. You see, smell is linked to survival and it's actually quite useful in that way – more than you might think. After all – if food smells bad then that tells you that food has gone off – or is dangerous – we can instantly recognise a poisonous food. And of course it tells us when it's nice to eat too! That's a really vital use of the sense in the animal world, but not so much for people in the modern world. We can trust our food manufacturers, I hope!

A: Let's hope so! But it's more complicated than that, surely.

B: Of course it is. Our sense of smell is still actually very important – but not so much for identifying danger as for social reasons. You see, we respond to smells sensitively – with our feelings, not with logic or even with common sense – but we don't all respond to the same smell in the same way. How we respond depends on the emotional associations we have with that particular scent.

A: What do you mean by that?

B: For instance, the smells of autumn may create happy memories for one person, but the same smell could make another person unhappy. This could be if it makes them think of cold, dark winter days, or something bad that happened to them in winter once.

A: They're all natural smells – what about artificial ones?

B: It's not really very different. Perfumes can bring back both good and bad memories – and they can be very emotional memories, too. The perfume manufacturers are well aware of this – they have very good marketing techniques which they use all the time. They know all about associations people have with smells – we've all got a favourite perfume, because it reminds us of something nice, or just because it makes us feel good – and they use that. Of course they are selling an image as well – one that's tied up with the lifestyle the particular brand of perfume suggests.

A: And they are expensive too! Maybe that's part of the marketing. But do you have any other interesting information to give us about smells? Or anything different about the sense of smell.

B: Well – let's see – did you know that it's harder to forget smells than to forget facts? Or, putting it another way, we remember smells longer? There have been experiments where people could pick out a particular smell thirty days after smelling it for the first time.

A: That's interesting! So smells bring back more memories than – say – music?

B: That seems to be the case.

A: But then what happens if you lose your sense of smell – when you have a cold, for instance?

B: Well, smell is actually linked to taste – we smell the food at the same time as we taste it and this is how we get the flavour of food. When we eat, our mouths and noses work together – and that's why when you have a cold, you lose your sense of taste as well. People who lose their sense of smell permanently as a result of an injury or illness feel that life doesn't have many pleasures – after all, we all enjoy eating!

A: So, what's your favourite smell?

B: Oh, I have lots of different ones – the smell of the sea reminds me of happy family holidays, and the smell of roses makes me think of my friend's house. Strangely enough, I like the smell of aircraft fuel at airports – then I know I'm going to fly somewhere exciting! But it's the general smell of my garden in the rain that I really like the most – that means I'm at home where I should be. I enjoy smelling different things and I think I'd be very unhappy without my sense of smell.

A: Jane, thank you for talking to us. Next week we'll talk about sight. But now we move on to…

Now you'll hear Part 4 again.
(Part 4 repeated)
That's the end of Part 4.

Paper 5 Speaking

PART 1

Tapescript

First of all, we'd like to know something about you, so I'm going to ask you some questions about yourselves.
Where are you from? (*bleep*)
Which town do you live in now? (*bleep*)
Have you always lived there? (*bleep*)
What do you like or dislike about living there? (*bleep*)
Can you tell us something about your family? (*bleep*)
What do you enjoy doing at the weekends? (*bleep*)
Can you speak any other languages apart from English? (*bleep*)
Do you enjoy learning English? (*bleep*)
What kind of transport do you prefer to use when you travel? (*bleep*)
What kind of films or television programmes do you enjoy watching? (*bleep*)
Do you play any sports? (*bleep*)
What kind of magazines do you enjoy reading? (*bleep*)

PART 2

Tapescript

Now, I'd like each of you to talk on your own for about a minute. I'm going to give each of you two different photographs and I'd like you to talk about them.

Candidate A, here are your two photographs. They show people who have been successful. Please let Candidate B see them. Candidate B, I'll give you your photographs in a minute.

Candidate A, I'd like you to compare these photographs and say which person you think has had to work harder to be successful. Remember, you only have about a minute for this, so don't worry if I interrupt you. All right?

(*bleep*) (*bleep*)

Thank you. Candidate B, what do you think has been your greatest success?

(*bleep*)

Candidate B, here are your two photographs. They show people eating out. Please let Candidate A have a look at them.

I'd like you to compare these photographs and say what you think are the advantages and disadvantages of each place. You have about a minute for this, so don't worry if I interrupt you. All right?

(*bleep*) (*bleep*)

Thank you. Candidate A, which place would you prefer to eat in?

(*bleep*)

Thank you

PART 3

Tapescript

Now I'd like you to talk about something together for about three minutes. I'm just going to listen.

I'd like you to imagine that your friend wants to go on holiday with their extended family which includes grandparents and young children and they have asked for your advice. Here are some holidays they are considering.

First, talk to each other about the advantages and disadvantages of these ideas. Then say which one would be the best to recommend to your friend for their holiday.

You have only about three minutes for this, so, once again, don't worry if I stop you.

Please speak so we can hear you. All right? (*bleep*)

Thank you.

PART 4

Tapescript

Would you prefer to go on holiday with your family, or with friends? (*bleep*)

How do you prefer to travel when you are on holiday? (*bleep*)

How have holidays changed since your grandparents were young? (*bleep*)

What areas of your country are popular with tourists? Why? (*bleep*)

What benefits or problems can tourists bring to a country? (*bleep*)

Would you like to live in another country for a short time? Which one? Why? (*bleep*)

Pearson Education Limited
Edinburgh Gate
Harlow
Essex CM20 2JE
England
and Associated Companies throughout the world.

www.longman.com

First published by Longman Group Ltd 1996.
This edition published 2008.
Fifth impression 2010.

ISBN 978-1-405-87679-7 FCE Gold Plus Maximiser and CD (with key) Pack

ISBN 978-1-405-84871-8 FCE Gold Plus Maximiser (with key) for Pack

ISBN 978-1-405-84870-1 FCE Gold Plus Maximiser CD 1-2 for Pa ck

Set in 10/12pt Frutiger 45 Light

Printed in Malaysia (CTP - KHL)

Acknowledgements
The authors and publisher would like to express special thanks to Jacky Newbrook for her expert advice on the exam tasks and strategies and to Katherine Stannett for her superb editorial assistance.

We are grateful to the following for permission to reproduce copyright material:

A Bit O Blarney Inc for an extract adapted from 'Irish Genealogy' as published on www.abitoblarney.com; Susan Aldridge for an extract adapted from 'What makes someone intelligent' published in *Focus Magazine* November 2001; Atlanta Journal and Constitution for an article adapted from es 'Insincerely Yours: In addition to wasting time, e-mailed hoax and chain letters can harm people and reputations' by Anne th Meyers published in *The Atlanta Journal and Constitution* 12 December 1999; Leslie Whittaker from the Press Office of Manolo Blahnik for the text of an interview with Manolo Blahnik; The Christian Science Monitor for an article adapted from 'Fast Times at Sushi U' by Nicole Gaouette published in *The Christian Science Monitor* 12th May 1999 © 1999 The Christian Science Monitor, www.csmonitor.com All rights reserved; The Economist Newspaper Limited for an extract adapted from 'From zoo cage to modern ark' published in *The Economist* 11th July 1998; The Independent for extracts adapted from 'Living Dangerously' by Rupert Isaacson published in *The Independent on Sunday* and 'Interview with Ellen MacArthur: Life change follows the sea change' by Andrew Longmore published in *The Independent on Sunday*

12th September 2001; Mirrorpix for an extract adapted from 'I walked out of one of the world's top art galleries with a masterpiece under my arm; Remembered.. Paul's daring raid to claim back Irish Collection' by Nicola Tallant published in *The Sunday Mirror* 15th December 2003; The Observer for an extract adapted from 'Rows out as parents and teens bury the hatchet' by Ben Summerskill published in *The Observer* 6th October 2002 © The Observer; Origin Publishing for extracts adapted from 'The World of the Commercial Diver' by Sally Palmer published in *Focus Magazine* November 2001 and 'Exploring the Volcano' by Sally Palmer published in *Focus Magazine* November 2002 © Focus www.focusmag.co.uk; The Press Association for an extract adapted from 'Clothes style: Beware what you wear' by Hannah Stephenson published in *The Birmingham Post* 13th August 2003; Rough Guides Ltd for an extract adapted from 'Snorkelling and Diving' published in *The Rough Guide to Thailand*; Miss Rachel Smith for an extract adapted from 'Women at the North Pole' published on www.aiglon.ch 30th September 2000; The Telegraph Group Limited for an extract adapted from 'Prosperity comes to posterity as the fashion for burying a selection of artefacts to amaze future generations takes off' by Andy Goldberg published in *The Daily Telegraph* 15th April 1999; TV Land for an article adapted from *Gunsmoke* published on www.tvland.com; University Times, University of Pittsburgh for an extract adapted from 'Fire-Walking' by Mike Sanja published in *University Times* 21st November 1996.

In some instances we have been unable to trace the owners of copyright material and we would appreciate any information that would enable us to do so.

We are grateful to the following for permission to reproduce photographs:

A1Pix pages 34, 45 bottom, 93 bottom; Art Directors & TRIP/R J Winstanley page 45 top; Sally Burgess pages 74 bottom, 80 top, 98; Camera Press/Jonathan Player page 74 top; Cartoonstock.com page 83; ©Jean Guichard/Corbis page 25; Tom Craig page 127 top right; James Davis Worldwide page 107 left; Greg Evans International page 107 right; Sally & Richard Greenhill page 127 top left; The Image Bank/Flip Chalfont page 80 bottom; Erik Lindkvist page 17; ©Roy Morsch/Corbis page 66 left; Neighbours, Grundy Television Pty Ltd/Fremantle Media 2003 page 10; PA Photos/EPA page 21; Pearson Education page 40; Photofusion page 49 top; Popperfoto.com page 94; Punchstock pages 26 bottom, 49 bottom; Barry Raynel Photography page 93 top; Rex Features pages 66 right, 70, 127 bottom left & right; Ronald Grant Archive: Liffey Films 30; Stone/Thatcher/Kaluzny page 60; Topham Picturepoint page 26 top; Universal/The Kobal Collection page 9; David Willey page 78. All other images @ Pearson Education

Picture Research by Louise Edgeworth and Sally Cole.

Illustrations by Patrick Williams and Katherine Charlesworth (*Pennant Inc*).

Designed by Venita Kidwai (*Wave Digital Design Development Ltd*) and Oxford Designers & Illustrators Ltd.